Responding to the Call for Educational Justice

Transformative Catholic-Led Initiatives in Urban Education

A Volume in Research in
Contemporary Perspectives on Access, Equity, and Achievement

Series Editor

Chance W. Lewis
University of North Carolina at Charlotte

Contemporary Perspectives on Access, Equity, and Achievement

Chance W. Lewis, Editor

(List continues on next page)

Responding to the Call for Educational Justice

Transformative Catholic-Led Initiatives in Urban Education

Editors

L. Mickey Fenzel
Loyola University Maryland

Melodie Wyttenbach
University of Notre Dame

INFORMATION AGE PUBLISHING, INC.
Charlotte, NC • www.infoagepub.com

Library of Congress Cataloging-in-Publication Data

CIP record for this book is available from the Library of Congress
http://www.loc.gov

ISBNs: 978-1-64113-429-3 (Paperback)

   978-1-64113-430-9 (Hardcover)

   978-1-64113-431-6 (ebook)

Printed in the United States of America

CONTENTS

FOREWORD

As a kid growing up in one of the toughest neighborhoods in Detroit, I was forced to stare down my own mortality at an early age and survive a shooting in my neighborhood while being emotionally incarcerated during my father's physical incarceration. There were moments of doubt. There were moments of anger. There were moments of outrage. Through it all, my mother and grandmother stood with me. They stood against the rampant drug dealing in my neighborhood. They stood with the countless other families in my neighborhood equally committed to protecting their children while providing them with life changing opportunities.

Perhaps the most significant life changing opportunity took place in 1988 when my mother put me on the public bus at Wyoming and Tireman for my first day at my urban high school—University of Detroit Jesuit High School and Academy. As I rode past two public high schools that many of my friends were going to, I quickly realized that my journey was going to be very different from theirs. Walking into my first Catholic school as a 14-year-old, I was challenged to consider my positionality in the world as a Black man amidst White privilege, a Eurocentric curriculum, and other Black students who had economic privileges that I had never known.

As many of my White classmates left school every day to travel back to their comfortable suburban homes, and some of my Black classmates did the same to two of the most historically wealthy neighborhoods in Detroit, Sherwood Forest and University District, my grandmother would pick me up every day or I stood outside the school and took two buses to get home a few miles from the epicenter of the 1967 social uprising at 12th and

Responding to the Call for Educational Justice:
Transformative Catholic-Led Initiatives in Urban Education, pp. ix–x
Copyright © 2019 by Information Age Publishing
All rights of reproduction in any form reserved.

Claremont in Detroit; a home in a neighborhood struggling amidst the crack cocaine epidemic, but a home full of love from a caring mother and grandmother—my warriors for justice; my warriors to protect me. During my high school journey, I would almost get kicked out because of academics and behavior. Yet, something in me kept pushing me. Was it after school detention, the love and patience of my mother and grandmother, or God's will? Certainly, I would lean on all of these as factors that helped me get through my Catholic school experience. But one element is missing—the passion of the staff. From Mr. Knight elevating a discussion on the Rodney King assault at the hands of the LAPD, Mrs. Rowe's constant encouragement, Mr. Tenbusch's support of the Black Awareness Society for Education; without them, I would probably be in a different place in my life.

As this book focuses on *responding to the call for educational justice* at the intersection of urban education and Catholic education, I stand as a witness to the power of Catholic education in an urban community. This power is not simply because of the academic rigor or the college acceptance rates of alumni from my Jesuit high school; nor is it directly connected to the amazing opportunities that have opened up as a result of attending my high school. The power resides in the numerous opportunities I was given to critique power structures, elevate the plight of Black people in America, and still fully participate in an imperfect community no different from any other. It's the balance between *responding to the call for educational justice* deeply embedded in the Catholic education ethos and its imperfections that makes this text so meaningful. Whether using critical race theory as a lens through which we can examine the imperfections or elevating the amazing impact Homeboy Industries has on returning citizens, *Responding to the Call for Educational Justice: Transformative Catholic-Led Initiatives in Urban Education* tells a compelling story and elevates the role of Catholic education in the milieu of urban education.

Robert W. Simmons III, EdD

CEO, See Forever Foundation and Maya Angelou Schools

PREFACE

Growing up in Baltimore and attending Catholic schools there in the 1950s and 1960s contributed meaningfully to my awakening to social, economic, and educational injustice. My senior year religion teacher, a De La Sale Christian brother, challenged us students to delve deeply into social issues of race, war, and poverty and the nature of God and God's presence and participation in the world. At the large secular university I attended in the Northeast, this awakening continued as I witnessed the African American students demanding greater educational equity and marched in Washington against the Vietnam War, influenced in part by the example of the University's Catholic chaplain. Fast forward a couple of decades when, as a faculty member at Loyola University Maryland (then Loyola College in Maryland) I developed service-learning courses and accompanied my students to underserved urban communities and Catholic schools and challenged them as my high school religion teacher had challenged me. Since I first started to examine the effectiveness of urban Nativity schools in Baltimore in the mid-1990s, I have involved myself in a number of community- and Catholic-led initiatives aimed at addressing issues of urban poverty, violence, and educational injustice. Most memorable about these encounters have been the Catholic religious and lay women and men who commit to the painstaking work of breaking the cycle of poverty through education in important and heroic Christ-like ways.

In this volume, we proudly illustrate a number of urban initiatives that have responded to the call to work to eradicate all forms of injustice and advance the cause of human freedom and dignity that has characterized

Responding to the Call for Educational Justice:
Transformative Catholic-Led Initiatives in Urban Education, pp. xi–xiv
Copyright © 2019 by Information Age Publishing
All rights of reproduction in any form reserved.

much of the Catholic Church's formal teachings, especially in the years since Vatican II. The authors of chapters in this collection of reports on high quality initiatives in urban education have put the call of the Church's teachings on educational and economic justice into practice to change the educational experiences and life trajectories of tens of thousands of children, adolescents, and adults historically underserved, marginalized, and unwelcomed. While most of the initiatives addressed here center on educational enterprises in various parts of the United States and those that address education through secondary school, others examine education and job training for adults, as well as initiatives in other countries where the Church's calls for economic and educational justice have spurred many communities into action. The life-changing service and educational immersion excursions I have taken with Loyola students to high poverty communities in Central America and the Caribbean showed me how vital it is to also examine educational efforts beyond the U.S. that have brought the tenets of liberation theology alive.

In Chapter 1, we provide some context for the continued need to improve access to quality education and other services for children and families of color for whom pathways out of economic poverty have been blocked. This chapter includes an introduction to principles of Catholic Social Teaching and the Church's focus on the *preferential option for the poor* that have contributed to its commitment to act in support of those kept at the margins. Following this introduction, we present four chapters that address specific Catholic initiatives in P–12 education. The first two initiatives are NativityMiguel (Chapter 2) and Cristo Rey (Chapter 3) schools that have grown into substantial national networks that support a number of schools following a particular educational model designed to propel students placed at risk toward positive futures. These initiatives were begun by the Jesuits, first in New York City with Nativity Mission Center middle school, and later in Chicago with the first Cristo Rey high school, that introduced a unique model of Catholic high school education that combines a college-preparatory curriculum with a corporate work study program. A number of other communities of Catholic religious men and women have joined in these particular efforts. We also examine the development and success of the independent St. Benedict's Preparatory School in Newark, New Jersey (Chapter 4) and the Catalyst schools (Chapter 5), charter schools in Chicago founded by the De La Salle Christian Brothers who had been operating, and continue to operate, a number of NativityMiguel middle schools. In Chapter 6, we discuss the Graduate Support function of NativityMiguel Schools, which is a unique and important aspect of the educational model that underscores the importance of providing continuing support for young people historically underserved and placed at risk as they negotiate the challenges of high school and college.

In the remaining chapters, we widen the lens with which we explore a number of Catholic-led organizations that provide structures and leadership to help meet the educational needs of children, adolescents, and adults placed at risk both in the United States and other countries. Chapter 7 highlights the work of the NativityMiguel Coalition which supports the development and success of NativityMiguel schools in the United States and Canada. In Chapter 8, we explore the efforts of Notre Dame Mission Volunteer AmeriCorps (NDMVA), an initiative of the Sisters of Notre Dame de Namur, which trains and provides tutors for urban public and Catholic diocesan and independent schools, including NativityMiguel Schools.

In Chapter 9, we venture outside of the U.S. to examine aspects of the work of Fe y Alegría in Latin America, a faith-filled movement initiated by a Jesuit priest over 60 years ago to provide a quality education to children in Caracas, Venezuela and which has grown to serve over a million children, adolescents, and adults in marginalized communities in 21 countries. Finally, in Chapter 10, we document some of the work of Homeboy Industries that provides employment, training, and education, including degrees and certifications, for youth placed at risk and former gang members in the Los Angeles area who seek to lead productive and meaningful lives amidst the dangers of gang violence.

Together, these initiatives portray some of the effective Catholic-led efforts that respond to the preferential option for the poor and marginalized through the frameworks of Catholic social teaching and liberation theology. The reader will find that these initiatives are not those that are designed to "save" but rather those that build on love, respect, and the mandate to restore to those who have been systematically denied fair and just access—something that simply belongs to them as daughters and sons of God. The reader will find that central to the Catholic approach to effective urban education are relationships and the kind of life-affirming and restorative love that Jesus exemplified. This love is readily apparent when one walks into a Cristo Rey or NativityMiguel school or meets Fr. Gregory Boyle, Society of Jesus, fondly called G-dog by his homies whom he has served and loved at Homeboy Industries.

This work is important because history has clearly shown that, left to politicians and those whose wealth and position provide them with excessive legislative influence, true educational reform is washed away in the torrent of counterproductive and often harmful policies and practices that undermine the real work of educating. The initiatives examined here represent a few of the many effective, high quality ones from which educators, politicians, researchers, and potential funders can find applications to ensure the common good and build a more productive and just society in the process. We believe that readers will find seeds among these chapters that can be sowed in more public and independent educational contexts and that can yield a rich harvest of increased numbers of young people from marginalized communities who are realizing their promise.

These life-changing efforts reflect the kind of work envisioned by Robert F. Kennedy in his "Ripple of Hope" speech delivered at the University of Cape Town, South Africa on June 6, 1966, in which he said:

> Few will have the greatness to bend history itself, but each of us can work to change a small portion of events, and in the total of all those acts will be written the history of this generation. Thousands of Peace Corps volunteers are making a difference in isolated villages and city slums in dozens of countries. Thousands of unknown men and women in Europe resisted the occupation of the Nazis and many died, but all added to the ultimate strength and freedom of their countries. It is from numberless diverse acts of courage and belief that human history is shaped. Each time a man stands up for an ideal, or acts to improve the lot of others, or strikes out against injustice, he sends forth a tiny ripple of hope, and crossing each other from a million different centers of energy and daring those ripples build a current which can sweep down the mightiest walls of oppression and resistance. (Robert F. Kennedy Human Rights, 1966)

L. Mickey Fenzel, PhD

Loyola University Maryland

REFERENCE

Robert F. Kennedy Human Rights. (1966). Robert F. Kenney, a brief biography. Retrieved from http://www.usccb.org/about/public-affairs/backgrounders/history-catholic-church-united-states.cfm

ACKNOWLEDGMENTS

This project would not have been possible, first, without the vision and commitment of the many educators and leaders who have put into practice the Church's teachings on economic and social justice in the many educational programs featured in this volume. Without their passion and dedication to historically marginalized families and communities, the stories that unfold in the following chapters would not exist. We are grateful to those who dedicate their lives to Catholic education and to Christ who makes all things possible.

We also acknowledge the support of our respective universities, Loyola University Maryland and the University of Notre Dame, as well as that of our colleagues both at Loyola and the Alliance for Catholic Education who have helped us make contact with many of the authors of these chapters. Loyola's Pastoral Counseling Department provided funds to support translating and editing functions. In addition, the Catholic Education SIG of the American Educational Research Association (AERA) has brought together a number of these authors at annual meetings of AERA. We are grateful for the leadership that gathers these practitioners and scholars together to further dialogue and exchange ideas to make our Catholic educational initiatives for children placed at risk stronger.

We want to also thank those who assisted in the completion of the various chapters. Nate Radomski and Erika Meyer of Friends of Fe y Alegría in the United States were instrumental in helping us secure the author of the chapter on the Fe y Alegría educational programs and serve as the communication conduit. Fr. Jack Podsiadlo, Society of Jesus, has continued

Responding to the Call for Educational Justice:
Transformative Catholic-Led Initiatives in Urban Education, pp. xv–xvi
Copyright © 2019 by Information Age Publishing

to encourage this work over the past several years and faculty members at Loyola University Maryland led us to translators, in particular Heidi Schneider, a Loyola instructor, of the work submitted in Spanish. In addition, Loyola faculty members and doctoral students, including Janet Preis, Timothy Hanna, Cynthia Canner, and Kathy Richardson, provided feedback and research support, and Stephanie Durnford edited the chapters for clarity and APA manuscript style. Tom McCabe assisted with the chapter on St. Benedict's Preparatory School, Bill Muller, Society of Jesus, executive director of the Jesuit Schools Network, helped to connect us with Fe y Alegría.

Finally, we thank our children and spouses for their patience, understanding, and continued support of all our endeavors, and Robert Simmons introduced the topic of this book to Information Age.

CHAPTER 1

INTRODUCTION

L. Mickey Fenzel and Robert Helfenbein
Loyola University Maryland

Determined to fix the failures and broken promises of No Child Left Behind and provide the necessary resources to do so, President Barack Obama proclaimed a message of hope and optimism in the early years of his presidency. He sought to convince the American people that the educational establishment could provide a high-quality education for all students, regardless of economic status, race, sex, or ability, enabling more young people to take control of their futures and prepare them for the demanding careers of the future. As the final days of his presidency approached, he noted some successes such as improving high school graduation and college attendance rates and increasing the number of children enrolled in preschool education. He also recognized that there was much more to be done to bring the hope of equal access to quality education for all to fruition (The White House, 2016).

The calls to improve educational access and quality for historically underserved children and adolescents in the U.S. have dominated much of the discourse on urban education for decades now. These calls have contributed to some progress and narrowing of differences in standardized test scores and high school graduation rates between racial/ethnic, socioeconomic, and gender groups, but widespread social inequities and discriminatory practices in medical care, family supports, law enforcement, employment, and education have crippled the hope and promise of greater gains for children of color living in urban contexts. The ecology of

Responding to the Call for Educational Justice:
Transformative Catholic-Led Initiatives in Urban Education, pp. 1–14
Copyright © 2019 by Information Age Publishing

influences on children's development in underserved urban neighborhoods have been identified as Persistent Traumatic Stress Environments (PTSEs) because of the effects that exposure to physical and structural violence has on children's mental and spiritual health and well-being and their efficacy and agency self-perceptions (Ginwright, 2016). In addition, a growing body of research is showing how exposure to local violence and other urban stressors adversely affects children's cognitive performance and brain development (Ginwright, 2016; McCoy, Raver, & Sharkey, 2015; Sharkey, 2010).

As Ginwright (2016) eloquently pointed out, change that improves living conditions and access to quality health care, housing, employment, and education, and brings genuine hope to poorly served urban neighborhoods cannot rest on narrowly-focused federal education policy alone or attempts to improve individuals' social-emotional competencies. Effective and lasting change requires a multipronged approach that addresses educational practice along community development and the involvement of multiple partnerships that can help support schools and communities (Noguera, 2011).

A number of public and independent initiatives, including those organized and funded by religious communities, have provided much reason to hope for breaking the cycle of poverty that continues to devastate urban communities and pave the road referred to as the school to prison pipeline. Among these initiatives is the Broader, Bolder Approach (BBA) in Newark, New Jersey that focuses on expanding learning opportunities, enhancing the curriculum, and building community partnerships (Noguera, 2011). Although not without controversy, initiatives such as the Harlem Children's Zone (HCZ) and KIPP (Knowledge Is Power Program) schools show promise in changing significant numbers of lives through high quality education and community involvement. In addition, endeavors emerging from President Obama's *My Brother's Keeper* initiative, introduced in 2014, are guided by efforts to provide resources to educators that can make a difference for boys and men of color (Harper & Wood, 2016).

Catholic religious communities and dioceses have been at work for several decades now to provide educational programs and opportunities for underserved children, adults, and families that seek to break the cycle of poverty and help individuals live meaningful lives of promise. A number of Catholic educators and groups involved in effective and successful urban initiatives show from the programs examined in this volume that there continues to be much reason to hope that educational programs can make a big difference in the lives of the children, adolescents, and adults historically marginalized and denied equal access. We examine these initiatives within the context of our perspective on what we mean by urban education.

The Context of Urban Education

> Urban education is different because it is the emergent American culture, a complex, urban, multidimensional culture.... How we invent the next phases of American urban schooling is how we invent the nation. (Anderson & Summerfield, 2004, p. 282)

Certainly, the term urban is often used in the U.S. context as code for the presence of Black and Brown people, Black culture, and, most troubling, in education discourse as denoting failing schools, incompetent teachers and administration, as well as a host of racist and classist suppositions. While our project is rooted in the effort to reject these deficit perspectives, our hope is to present work that both recognizes the assets that those who attend and work in urban schools bring with them but also to do so in a way that acknowledges the historical and persistent structural inequity that marks the realities of urban education (see Dixson, Royal, & Henry, 2013).

For most geographers, the term urban simply denotes population and infrastructure density; for those studying urban education, it remains important to understand the characteristics of urban schooling as socially constructed and sedimented in a history of racial and class dynamics. Kincheloe (2004) listed 12 characteristics that mark an urban experience in education: (a) high population density; (b) big schools, big school populations; (c) profound economic disparity; (d) high rates of ethnic and racial diversity; (e) factionalized struggles over resources; (f) ineffective business administration; (g) increased student health problems; (h) higher student and educator mobility; (i) higher immigrant populations; (j) linguistic diversity; (k) unique transportation problems; and (l) teacher/community separation (pp. 5–8). In the 2013 *Handbook of Urban Education*, Miller and Lomotey (2013) established three criteria for defining and conceptualizing urban schools:

1. The size of the city in which schools are located: dense, large, metropolitan areas;
2. The students in the schools: a wide range of student diversity, including racial, ethnic, religious, language, and socioeconomic; and
3. The resources: the amount and number of resources available in a school, such as technology and financial structures through federal programs, as well as property taxes. (p. xv)

While certainly recognizable to urban educators, the contemporary moment is marked by demographic changes that follow economic and political shifts. Given this, it seems reasonable to suggest that schools, like other components of the urban context (i.e., housing, voter registration, transportation, etc.) are in a process of restructuring. Further, it should be noted that nonurban schools are seeing increasing rates of economic, linguistic, and cultural diversity, immigrant populations, and income disparity. The old models of studying urban education no longer hold.

What must be maintained however—even within a context of changing dynamics—is the central place of race in the study of urban schools. As Murrell (2007) noted, "there is an increasing, not a decreasing, impact of race in school practices and policy" (p. 6) and, furthermore, that "cultural racism inheres in those practices and policies that outwardly intend to deal with issues of equity and difference, but end up maintaining or increasing the disadvantage of the cultural group" (p. 7). The shift from explicit to institutional or systemic racism allows for a more nuanced analysis of urban school practice and policy that privileges the lives and experiences of students, teachers, and communities of color. But, of course, this type of work proves difficult and challenging to both researchers and practitioners alike in that it exposes the ways we may be complicit with systems of marginalization and inequity.

As we have moved into our contemporary moment, "the urban" as a concept has become a popular item for both public and scholarly attention. The restructuring of urban spaces provides an interesting example of how thinking about our current, globalized moment might affect education. Downtown gentrification—seen quite visibly in the city where these authors reside, Baltimore—fundamentally changes the realities of urban schools. The processes at work in this reorganization include a renewed interest in privatizing schools, a continued assault on the public schools as "broken" and not worth the money, and impassioned efforts at "tax reform" aimed at gutting the funding for public education. These political efforts operate at the same time as the rhetoric of making urban areas attractive to the global marketplace and continually echo in media outlets and statements from political leaders. Some areas of the urban core, or "inner city" as some might call it, have become attractive again, resulting in escalating property values and taxes and economic incentives to move the people who reside there out. However, instead of what is seen in historical urban geographic analysis, the extending out into the next urban layer toward the suburbs, small pockets of either poverty or wealth scattered about the city become the only option.

As many scholars suggest, major cities in the United States have been reorganized around the economic principles of neoliberalism. Harvey (2007) described how New York City underwent a major metamorphosis in the 1970s that has resulted in an entirely new urban formation—in particular, that of the cordoning off of Manhattan for a global elite. The revitalization of Manhattan, in Harvey's analysis, came at the cost of other parts of the city and importantly signaled a shift in the city's priorities from benefitting the population as a whole to creating a "good business climate" (pp. 9–10). One the effects of this restructuring of urban spaces relevant for thinking through how these changes might affect communities revolves around the change in cost of living around specific areas. Kozol (1992), in one of his several critiques of the shame of public education, documented the effects of these efforts on children and teachers in the public schools and communities of the South Bronx. Populations at middle- or lower-class levels have found themselves priced out of formally or historically occupied neighborhoods and banished to underresourced, largely ineffective urban schools.

Gentrification of urban areas has not only become more intensified but is increasingly being noted as a concern by organized communities and social advocacy movements (see Lipman, 2011). Urban "revitalization" or "renewal" now integrates residential development with commercial and recreational enterprises, in effect making downtown areas a destination again. Ultimately (albeit not immediately), schools and youth enter into the equation of defining what these new urban spaces look like and, conversely, what they do not look like. In this sense, urban revitalization is as much about moving people out as it is about moving people in—certain things cannot, at least visibly, coexist. To be clear, much of this urban restructuring falls neatly onto lines of historic and sedimented racist policy—it is primarily communities of color being displaced and it is important to continue to note how capitalism is rooted in racism. Here the contradictions of massive influx of funding to the development of urban core areas and simultaneous de-funding of urban school districts points us to taking these racial and spatial dynamics seriously (see Anyon, 1997, 2005; Helfenbein, 2011).

FUTURE OF URBAN EDUCATION REFORM

The research on "what works" in urban education reform is fairly clear on a few key characteristics: (a) effective leadership at the school and district levels; (b) community-parent-school connections and supports; (c) strong professional development; (d) a learning environment marked by student-centered instruction and policies; and (e) clear and shared understandings of the curriculum and reform efforts (Payne, 2010). Several academic studies of contemporary education reform efforts in Boston, Chicago, and New York City have all emphasized these general attributes (see Boyd, Kerchner, & Blyth, 2008). Translating this research into public policy has often proved difficult, however, and the road to reform remains contentious due to differing political views.

Conservative and liberal reformers often approach education policy from two different perspectives. Conservative thinkers tend to believe that institutional change lies solely in the creation of incentives, both positive and negative. Pay-for-performance measures for teachers and the public "grading" of schools and school districts, for example, embody both financial and public opinion incentives to raise student achievement. Many conservatives also believe that making it easier for districts to fire teachers and administrators, along with threatening school closure, state takeover, and increased competition from charter or voucher-supported private schools, can improve performance. More liberal reformers tend to support teacher unions and professional development for teachers and school leaders but increasingly also support accountability measures. The politics of education reform has certainly always been complex but tracing how policy and its implementation flows from ideological positions to impact at the school level has only become more difficult (Lipman, 2011).

High-stakes accountability measures also appear to be a consistent aspect of future reform in education. The term "high-stakes," once only referring to the consequences that were increasing for students as standardized tests were becoming a part of final course grades and/or graduation requirements, increasingly connotes an evaluation of effectiveness at both the school and individual teacher levels. Many of its proponents seek to tie student test scores to both incentive based compensation and potential firing or probation mechanisms for teachers. Known as "performance pay," this type of education reform is clearly influenced by business community logic pointing to the need for public services to follow the principles of the private market. Critics of performance pay are concerned about how well such measures will take into consideration the vastly different populations whom teachers teach as well as the negative effects of competitive forces within school buildings. There is an additional concern that the best teachers will leave the schools, communities, and students with the most need in order to preserve their careers.

The future of education reform in the United States almost certainly contains new conceptions of the types of training teachers need. Traditionally, teachers have been trained in Schools of Education housed in universities and held to a certification process managed by the states. Increasingly, education reformers have advocated new ways of certifying teachers as an answer to increasing student achievement. Several programs have emerged encouraging second-career professionals to join the teaching ranks (specifically in science, math, and technology). Critics of these reform efforts point to the lack of research on the effectiveness of "alternative certification" programs and suggest that obstacles to high-quality teaching lie within the school structures themselves rather than traditional Schools of Education.

A different approach to contemporary urban education reform is the formation of the "full-service community school." Based on a philosophical approach that the school ensures student access to the multifaceted conditions necessary for learning, community and university partners work together to provide an array of onsite support services for urban students (see Murrell, 2001; Hollis & Goings, 2017). Such services may include mentoring, tutoring, after-school activities, physical and mental health programs, youth leadership initiatives, parent enrichment efforts such as adult English as a Second Language instruction, academic remediation, cultural competency, college preparation, community service, civic engagement, public recreation, and conflict resolution/violence-prevention programs. With the shared mission of reaching school-wide, high academic goals that encourage high school graduation and postsecondary enrollment, the community school serves as the hub for varied, needs-based services. Proponents of urban charter schools see the increased flexibility afforded them as an ideal structure for a community school model; others see the greater financial and community support of the approach as the answer to the persistent challenges faced by large bureaucratic urban school districts. Regardless of the structure within in which the model is embraced, many reformers contend that this is the best hope for urban school reform.

While the question of reforming urban public education is a complex one, certain aspects appear to be critical. High expectations for all students must accompany sensitivity to cultural difference. Teachers must be effectively trained to teach diverse learners through quality professional development and the creation of school cultures of support and ownership (see Emdin, 2016; Milner, 2010). Community partners need to be involved in the development and support of urban schools as students and educators all benefit from connection to the contexts in which they work. The question of education has always been political in the United States, but the future only points to increased ideological struggle about the role of schools in society. While "education reform" is a contested term, almost everyone believes it critical that it be pursued vigorously.

While we recognize that many of the reform efforts in the public arena have been successful in providing students and communities with improved access to good quality education, the push to privatization and profit has undermined widespread reform and improvement and has even contributed to a reduction of access to students most in need in some cases. Catholic and other religious groups that have been in the business of providing a high-quality alternative to public education have not stood idly by; rather they have sought to contribute to the realization of the goal of providing a high-quality education for all children.

Catholic Social Teaching and Urban Education

Among the earlier documents that paved the way to a fuller Catholic commitment to ensure the dignity of all human persons was outlined by

Pope Leo XIII in his 1891 encyclical, *Rerum Novarum*, and reinforced by the U.S. Catholic bishops and other Catholic groups since that time. Among the seven principles that form the foundation of Catholic social doctrine are, first and foremost, the respect for the dignity of every human person, created in God's image and endowed with the respect for and love of all persons as God loves (Kirylo, 2006; Lanari, 2011). The principles of participation and solidarity outlined in *Rerum*, echoed some 7 decades later by the Second Vatican Council, and also evidenced in the Church's teaching on the *preferential option for the poor*, challenge all Catholics to participate in the building of a just society—one in which the "stranger" is welcomed as one of our own and those at the margins are provided with the basic necessities and tools to live in peaceful community and contribute to the common good.

Vatican II has served as a turning point for the renewed commitment of the Catholic Church to enacting the preferential option for the poor and marginalized in education, a call that has been underscored in a number of formal and informal Church documents since that time (e.g., Oldenski, 1997; United States Conference of Catholic Bishops [USCCB], 2005, 2015). The USCCB, for example, has continued to insist on access to quality education for all, as it states in its recent publication approved at the 2015 meeting of the Bishops:

> All persons have a right to receive a quality education. Young people, including those who are poor and those with disabilities, need to have the opportunity to develop intellectually, morally, spiritually, and physically, allowing them to become good citizens who make socially and morally responsible decisions. This requires parental choice in education. It also requires educational institutions to have orderly, just, respectful, and non-violent environments where adequate professional and material resources are available. The USCCB strongly supports adequate funding, including scholarships, tax credits, and other means, to educate all persons no matter what their personal condition or what school they attend—public, private, or religious. (Article 83)

In this document, we see the Bishops' support for public funding to ensure quality education for all persons.

Popes also in recent years have sounded the call to work for justice. For example, in his apostolic exhortation, *Evangelii Gaudium*, on proclaiming the gospel in contemporary society, Pope Francis (2013) communicated the mandate to commit to the gospel message of caring for underserved persons and communities as follows:

> Every individual Christian and every community is called to be an instru-
> ment of God for the liberation and promotion of the poor, and for en-

abling them to be fully part of society. This demands that we be docile and attentive to the cry of the poor and come to their aid. (Article 187, p. 61)

Pope Francis also elaborated on the meaning of solidarity as actions to "restore to the poor what belongs to them" (Article 189, p. 61).

In education, a number of religious communities, including those represented in this book, have carried the banner of the preferential option into high poverty urban and rural communities where far too many young people continue to be denied access to high quality education and opportunities for personal and community development. Essential to actualizing the preferential option in urban schools is for educators to enter into relationship with historically underserved students and families and provide students with a level of compassionate teaching and outreach that will enable them to learn and succeed (Kirylo, 2006). In this work, teachers committed to the preferential option set high standards for students while they engage students with patience and provide developmentally appropriate instruction (Kirylo, 2006).

HISTORICAL PERSPECTIVES OF
URBAN CATHOLIC SCHOOLS

Catholic schools in U.S. cities have long been a part of the educational landscape with the first Catholic school having been established in the early 17th century in Florida by the Franciscans. These schools would be followed throughout the colonies by those constructed by the Jesuits, Franciscans, Ursuline Sisters, and others. Spurred on in part by the Catholic bishops' concerns about the quality of, and the Protestant influence in, the nation's public or "common" school, along with a new influx of Catholic immigrants, the construction of Catholic schools took off in earnest in the mid-19th century (Hamilton, 2008; USCCB, 2017). In addition to the numerous parish-controlled schools were high schools operated by the diocese or religious orders of men or women.

Enrollment in Catholic elementary and secondary schools peaked in the mid-1960s with approximately 4.5 million elementary and one million secondary school students, only to have it decline to half that number shortly after the turn of the century (Hamilton, 2008; USCCB, 2017). The decade of the 1960s was significant also in that the movement of more affluent white Catholic families from the cities to the suburbs was accompanied by a new wave of immigrants from Latin America, the Caribbean, and Asia who settled in the cities seeking a better life for themselves and their families, as the immigrants from European countries had decades before (Louie & Holdaway, 2009). Also seeking a place in the urban Catholic schools for their children during that time were African American families, some Catholic and some non-Catholic, who also were moving into the spaces abandoned by Whites and with whom the Church had an inconsistent history due to the Church's one-time involvement in slavery and continued racist attitudes among many White Catholics (Green, 2011). With the changing demographic and declining wealth in urban Catholic parishes and schools, these schools began suffering economic challenges that eventually led to the closure of many of them and the accompanying loss of students. Other forces at work included the declining birth rates that followed the post-War baby boom, the decline in the numbers of vowed religious women and men available to teach in the schools, and the decline in the number of Catholics who attended mass and supported the schools.

While urban Catholic parish schools were closing, efforts by members of vowed religious orders, in particular the Society of Jesus, or Jesuits, began to take hold in response to the call to care for the poor and disenfranchised. An early initiative came into being in Manhattan that led to the creation of the Jesuits' first middle school in the United States, which sought to meet the educational needs of the economically poor families and their sons who had come to the Lower East Side from Puerto Rico and the Dominican Republic. The Nativity Mission Center Middle School opened in 1971 with a year-round and extended-day program in a narrow row house that had been the site of a mission serving area families and that grew into a tutoring program (see Chapter 2). It was not until 1990 that a similar school opened in Jamaica Plains in Boston to educate boys from the area who were placed at risk; other schools were soon to follow which eventually grew to a network of schools that followed the same basic approach to educating boys and girls with academic promise but poor preparation in city public schools. At this point, a number of religious congregations and lay leaders became involved to build similar schools and participate in the growing network where ideas, research findings, and best practices could be shared.

The Jesuits also led the way to the formation of urban Catholic high schools that became known as Cristo Rey schools and provided a college prep curriculum and program that included corporate internships that paid most of the students' tuition costs (see Chapter 3). The Benedictines reopened St. Benedict's Prep in Newark, New Jersey in 1973 to respond to the need to educate more of the underserved African American and Latino students in the area using a unique and successful approach that invests considerable control of the enterprise to the students themselves (see Chapter 4). Catholic educators have also become involved in establishing charter schools, such as the Catalyst schools that opened in response to the need for a better-quality education for children in high poverty communities in Chicago (see Chapter 5). These are just a few of the Catholic-led initiatives that are addressed in this volume that have responded

to the call to justice in education and the preferential option for the poor
that has become a sounding call for educational justice.

While most of these initiatives have flourished, some have not, leaving
behind lessons for Catholic and other educational leaders to learn about
ensuring the long-term viability and quality of their efforts. Networks
of schools have supported the efforts of NativityMiguel and Cristo Rey
schools to deliver high quality programs that honor their mission and
ensure student success. Also, Catholic colleges and universities have provided support for urban Catholic schools through teacher education and
other programs and Catholic-led community initiatives have helped turn
around countless lives of children, adolescents, and adults through volunteer tutoring programs and educational offerings, including job training,
in the United States and other countries. We feature a few of these programs in the collection of chapters that follow.

Responding to the Church's Call

The authors of chapters in this collection of reports on high quality initiatives in urban education have put the call of the Church's teachings on
educational and economic justice into practice to change the educational
experiences and life trajectories of tens of thousands of children, adolescents, and adults historically underserved, marginalized, and unwelcomed.
While most of the initiatives addressed here center on educational enterprises in various parts of the United States and those that address education
through secondary school, others address education and job training for
adults, as well as initiatives in other countries where the calls for economic
and educational justice have spurred many communities into action.

These initiatives, and others like them, respond to the redemptive
message of the Gospel in areas where communities have been uplifted due
to the message of love and hope that has shone through darkness of oppression and hopelessness. They show that more than redesigned curriculums
and measures of academic performance are needed to ensure that young
people of color in high poverty communities develop the technical skills
to succeed in education and career, but also the commitment to servant
leadership and spreading the love and hope that propelled them toward
successful and meaningful lives. Nowhere is this more emphatically shown
than in the numerous initiatives sponsored and led by Fe y Alegría, which
is responsible for the education of over 1.5 million historically underserved
children, adolescents, and adults in 21 countries (see Chapter 9).

The educators who serve the students in these educational enterprises
are disciples of Christ who bring healing and hope to their students, as well
as the students' families and communities. The work is not easy, as these

educators will attest, because long-term and ever-present structural elements of poverty and racism continue to erect roadblocks to social change and promising futures. Though the workers may be few, the harvest promises to be abundant as more and more young people emerge from these experiences with the skills, confidence, and the sense of urgency to work for social change and a more equitable society.

REFERENCES

Anderson, P. M., & Summerfield, J. P. (2004). Why is urban education different from suburban and rural education? In S. R. Steinberg & J. L. Kincheloe (Eds.), *19 urban questions: Teaching in the city* (pp. 29–40). New York, NY: Peter Lang.

Anyon, J. (1997). *Ghetto schooling: A political economy of urban educational reform.* New York, NY: Teachers College Press.

Anyon, J. (2005). *Radical possibilities: Public policy, urban education, and a new social movement.* New York, NY: Routledge.

Boyd, W., Kerchner, C., & Blyth, M. (Eds.). (2008). *The transformation of great American school districts: How big cities are reshaping public education.* Cambridge, MA: Harvard Education Press.

Dixson, A., Royal, C., & Henry, K. (2013). School reform and school choice. In R. Milner & K. Lomotey (Eds.), *Handbook of urban education* (pp. 474–503). New York, NY: Routledge.

Emdin, C. (2016). *For white folks who teach in the hood ... and the rest of ya'll too: Reality pedagogy and urban education.* Boston, MA: Beacon Press.

Francis, Pope. (2013, November). *Evangelii gaudium.* Retrieved from http://w2.vatican.va/content/francesco/en/apost_exhortations/documents/papa-francesco_esortazione-ap_20131124_evangelii-gaudium.html

Ginwright, S. (2016). *Hope and healing in urban education: How urban activists and teachers are reclaiming matters of the heart.* New York, NY: Routledge.

Green, P. (2011). African Americans in urban Catholic schools: Faith, leadership and persistence in pursuit of educational opportunity. *Urban Review, 43,* 436–464. doi:10.1007/s11256-010-0171-9

Hamilton, S. W. (2008, April 10). Introduction. In S. W. Hamilton (Ed.), *Who will save America's urban Catholic schools?* Washington, DC: Thomas B. Fordham Institute. Retrieved from https://edexcellence.net/publications/who-will-save-americas-urban.html

Harper, S. R., & Wood, J. L. (2016). *Advancing Black male success from preschool through Ph.D.* Sterling, VA: Stylus.

Harvey, D. (2007). Neoliberalism and the city. *Studies in Social Justice, 1*(1), 2–13.

Helfenbein, R. (2011). The urbanization of everything: Thoughts on globalization and education. In S. Tozer, B. Gallegos, & A. Henry (Eds.), *Handbook of research in social foundations of education* (pp. 319–326). New York, NY: Routledge.

Hollis, T., & Goings, R. (2017). Keeping the dream through the CARE model: Examining strategies to bridge the gaps in education among urban youth.

In W. T. Pink & G. W. Noblit (Eds.), *Second international handbook of urban education* (pp. 887–905). Switzerland: Spring International Publishing.

Kincheloe, J. (2004). Why a book on urban education? In S. R. Steinberg & J. L. Kincheloe (Eds.), *19 urban questions: Teaching in the city* (pp. 1–28). New York, NY: Peter Lang.

Kirylo, J. D. (2006). Preferential option for the poor: Making a pedagogical choice. *Childhood Education, 82*, 266–270. doi:10.1080/00094056.2006.10522839

Kozol, J. (1992). *Savage inequalities: Children in America's schools*. New York, NY: Harper Perennial.

Lanari, B. (2011, May). *"Rerum novarum" and seven principles of Catholic social doctrine*. Retrieved from http://www.ignatiusinsight.com/features2011/print2011/blanari_rerumnovarum_may2011.html

Lipman, P. (2011). *The new political economy of urban education: Neoliberalism, race, and the right to the city*. New York, NY: Routledge.

Louie, V., & Holdaway, J. (2009). Catholic schools and immigrant students: A new generation. *Teachers College Record, 111*, 783–816.

McCoy, D. C., Raver, C. C., & Sharkey, P. (2015). Children's cognitive performance and selective attention following recent community violence. *Journal of Health and Social Behavior, 56*, 19–36. doi:10.1177/0022146514567576

Milner, R. (2010). *Start where you are but don't stay there: Understanding diversity, opportunity gaps, and teaching in today's classrooms*. Cambridge, MA: Harvard University Press.

Milner, R., & Lomotey K. (Eds.). (2013). *Handbook of urban education*. New York, NY: Routledge.

Murrell, P. (2001). *The community teacher: A new framework for effective urban teaching*. New York, NY: Teachers College Press.

Murrell, P. (2007). *Race, culture, and schooling: Identities of achievement in multicultural urban schools*. New York, NY: Lawrence Erlbaum.

Noguera, P. A. (2011). A broader and bolder approach uses education to break the cycle of poverty. *Phi Delta Kappan, 93*(3), 8–14. doi:10.1177/003172171109300303

Oldenski, T. (1997). *Liberation theology and critical pedagogy in today's Catholic schools: Social justice in action*. New York, NY: Garland.

Payne, C. (2010). *So much reform, so little change: The persistence of failure in urban schools*. Cambridge, MA: Harvard Education Press.

Sharkey, P. (2010). The acute effect of local homicides on children's cognitive performance. *Proceedings of the National Academy of Sciences of the United States of America, 107*, 11733–11738. doi:10.1073/pnas.1000690107

United States Conference of Catholic Bishops. (2005). *Seven themes of Catholic social teaching*. Washington, DC: Author. Retrieved from http://www.usccb.org/beliefs-and-teachings/what-we-believe/catholic-social-teaching/seven-themes-of-catholic-social-teaching.cfm

United States Conference of Catholic Bishops. (2015). *Forming consciences for faithful citizenship: A call to political responsibility from the Catholic bishops of the United States*. Washington, DC: Author. Retrieved from http://www.usccb.org/issues-and-action/faithful-citizenship/upload/forming-consciences-for-faithful-citizenship.pdf

United States Conference of Catholic Bishops. (2017). *History of the Catholic Church in the United States*. Retrieved from http://www.usccb.org/about/public-affairs/backgrounders/history-catholic-church-united-states.cfm

White House, The. (2016, October 17). *Remarks by the president on education*. Retrieved from https://obamawhitehouse.archives.gov/the-press-office/2016/10/17/remarks-president-education

CHAPTER 2

EARLY INITIATIVES

Nativity and NativityMiguel Schools

L. Mickey Fenzel
Loyola University Maryland

Urban Catholic K–12 schools in the U.S. continued to face declining enrollments during the 1960s as descendants of European immigrants moved to the suburbs and made room for a new group of immigrant and African American families seeking work in urban centers. During this time, which coincided with Second Vatican Council (1962–1965), the Society of Jesus (SJ) was responding to the call of its new Superior General, Pedro Arrupe, SJ, to commit to a faith that seeks justice and focus more on the needs of the economically poor and oppressed members of society (Kirylo, 2006; Whitehead, 2007). This call to justice was to be addressed in the various ministries of the Society, including education. It was during this time that, on the Lower East Side of Manhattan, the Jesuits were providing academic tutoring for economically poor Puerto Rican children and young adolescents at the Nativity Mission Center (NMC) to help prepare them for success in New York's Catholic high schools (Fenzel & Podsiadlo, 2009).

As support for the Nativity Mission Center program grew with volunteer tutors from Fordham University and area Catholic high schools, the tutoring program added a residential summer camp experience in the 1960s near Lake Placid in New York State. Soon the decision was made to open

Responding to the Call for Educational Justice:
Transformative Catholic-Led Initiatives in Urban Education, pp. 15–38
Copyright © 2019 by Information Age Publishing
All rights of reproduction in any form reserved.

a middle school at the site of the Mission for area boys from high poverty families. In the fall of 1971 the Nativity Mission Center School opened its doors to its first students (Fenzel & Podsiadlo, 2009).

Strong and devoted leadership and a program that made use of the best practices of educating underserved urban boys were instrumental in the success of NMC during its early development (Fenzel & Podsiadlo, 2009). Because families, which could not afford the tuition of regular Catholic schools, paid a small monthly tuition, effective fundraising and business management practices were established, as support was sought from private and corporate donors and foundations. In addition, the school aligned its curriculum to state and archdiocesan standards and adopted a teacher support program that ensured that the young teachers who came to the school developed into highly effective instructors. As the number of graduates grew and continued to require academic and social support while in high school, where they found themselves in the minority, the school started a graduate support program that helped counsel students while in high school and prepare them for college application and admission (Fenzel & Podsiadlo, 2009).

Development and Growth of the Nativity School Model

During the next 2 decades, the Nativity Mission Center Middle School provided a unique program for Latino boys placed at risk because of economic poverty. The program included small classes for instruction, tutoring and mentoring during an extended day and week, a summer program of academic enrichment and leadership development, and a focus on Christian values and caring for one another (Fenzel, 2009; Podsiadlo & Philliber, 2003). The first middle school operated by the Jesuits in the United States, it demonstrated its commitment to making use of a strong educational program to tackle poverty by accelerating the academic skill development of its students and preparing them to succeed in schools that catered mostly to the more privileged members of society. Although not every student from the first classes at NMC succeeded in the challenging high schools and college, the students overall out performed New York City students from similar backgrounds on standardized tests of basic academic skills and graduated from high school and matriculated into college at significantly higher rates (Podsiadlo & Philliber, 2003).

As the Nativity Mission Center Middle School developed and solidified its curriculum, financial and fund-raising processes, and teacher development program, and was exhibiting impressive success, it began to attract notice from other urban centers. The second school of its kind, Nativity Preparatory School, opened in Boston in 1990 led by the efforts of a former

Nativity Mission teacher and sponsored by the New England Province of the Society of Jesus. The third Nativity model program, the Gonzaga program for middle school boys, opened the following year at St. Aloysius School in Harlem. As the Jesuits continued to open more Nativity model schools in the 1990s, other Catholic religious communities joined what was becoming a movement to provide a high-quality middle school experience for underserved boys and girls of color in cities such as Boston, New York, Baltimore, and Milwaukee in the mid-1990s. At this time, the De La Salle Christian Brothers also opened the first San Miguel middle school program in Providence, Rhode Island.

Having hired a research firm to conduct a thorough evaluation of the success of the NMC graduates, Fr. Jack Podsiadlo, SJ, and a principal of the firm coauthored a 2003 article that appeared in the *Journal of Education for Students Placed at Risk* that outlined the nature of the school's program and indicators of the high levels of success of its graduates (Podsiadlo & Philliber, 2003). Fr. Jack moved to Baltimore in 2001 to found the Nativity Educational Centers Network to help support the 27 schools at the time that followed the Nativity model, as well as religious and other groups interested in studying the feasibility of opening new Nativity-model schools. In 2002, Fr. Jack and I began to collect standardized test score and other data on the success of the member schools and, during the 2003–04 school year, I began an investigation of how the Nativity model was implemented in 12 Nativity schools that had been in operation long enough to have sent at least a few classes on to high school. Through classroom visits, the collection of standardized test score data, and questionnaires administered to, and interviews conducted with administrators, teachers, and students, I was able to provide the first large scale examination and evaluation of the Nativity model of middle-level education (Fenzel, 2009; Fenzel & Domingues, 2009; Fenzel & Monteith, 2008).

Building a Network

Having opened the first Lasallian San Miguel middle school in Providence, Rhode Island in 1993 that was similar to the original Nativity School model, the De LaSalle Christian Brothers developed a parallel network, the Lasallian Association of Miguel Schools (LAMS), to support their middle schools. In 2006, LAMS and the Nativity Network joined together to form the NativityMiguel Network of Schools with over 60 member schools. Supported in large part by foundation funding, the network sponsored national gatherings that enabled teachers and administrators to share best practices and engage in professional development, supported feasibility studies for the founding of new schools, provided a central data gathering operation, and monitored the fidelity of school programs to the model. This national organization was short-lived, unfortunately, as it abruptly ceased operations in the spring of 2012 due to a loss of funding and a structure that was not entirely compatible with the independent identities of the member schools (Fenzel, 2009; see also Chapter 7 of this volume).

Fortunately, leaders of the NativityMiguel Network and others soon formed a new organization, the NativityMiguel Coalition, that has continued the schools' emphasis on a rigorous academic program that is faith-based and focused on advancing the success of children from high-poverty backgrounds (NativityMiguel Coalition, n.d.). With 46 schools in the United States and Canada (there are two Canadian schools in the Coalition), the new international organization continues to carry out the original mission of the Nativity, San Miguel, and NativityMiguel networks. In addition, 17 schools operated by the Society of Jesus, 9 of which also belong to the Coalition, have been included in the Jesuit Schools Network, formerly the Jesuit Secondary Education Association (www.jesuitschoolsnetwork. org). In the Jesuit Schools Network (JSN), the member middle schools are referred to simply as Nativity schools, after the name of the first school of its type founded by the Jesuits on the Lower East Side of Manhattan and the name that identified all of the schools in the Nativity Educational Centers Network prior to the formation of the NativityMiguel Network in 2006. Both the NativityMiguel Coalition and JSN continue to provide school personnel with the tools and support needed to offer a high-quality faith-based education for historically underserved children and families consistent with the original Nativity model.

The 2010 Annual Report of the NativityMiguel Network of Schools (2011) indicated that a large majority of its 64 member schools at that time were operated by 22 different Catholic religious communities that included 14 by the Society of Jesus, 13 by the Christian Brothers, and four by the School Sisters of Notre Dame (SSND). Although nearly all of the 27 schools founded by the Jesuits or Christian Brothers are operated solely by these communities, several NativityMiguel schools have been operated by a partnership of two or more Catholic orders. Examples of these are Mother Seton Academy and the Sisters Academy in Baltimore which are led by six and four Catholic communities, respectively; both involve the School Sisters of Notre Dame.

A recent annual data report from the NativityMiguel Coalition (2015) showed that approximately 14% of the 35-member schools in the Coalition at that time were operated by Episcopal groups and 14% were nondenominational, interfaith schools. Two Florida schools, the Academy Prep Centers of St. Petersburg and Tampa, previous members of the Nativity and NativityMiguel Networks that were not associated with any religious group, continue to base their educational model on the Nativity and NativityMiguel schools but do not participate in the national coalition (Academy Prep Center of St. Petersburg, n.d.; see also Chapter 7 of this volume).

Researching the Structures and Successes of NativityMiguel[1] Schools

Since I began my work with Fr. Jack in 2002, I have had the opportunity to conduct two large-scale studies of the success of the NativityMiguel schools, present at and attend several regional and national meetings of the Network and Coalition, and serve as a consultant and Board member for one of the schools. Prior to this time, in the mid-90s, I had the opportunity to explore educational outcomes and classroom processes of five middle schools in Baltimore City, two of which had been recently opened Nativity schools, two were public middle schools, and one was a more traditional K–8 Catholic archdiocesan school. In this earlier work (Fenzel, Peyrot, & Premoshis, 1997), we saw that students benefitted academically and socially by the more intimate and supportive environment, small classes, and extended day program of the NativityMiguel model schools.

In 2002, Fr. Jack and I sought information of student standardized test scores from schools in the newly formed Nativity Educational Centers Network and received data from seven schools that had been in operation for at least 5 years (Fenzel, 2003). Results showed standardized test score gains in reading and math for six of the seven schools to be the equivalent of an increase of at least one grade level equivalent (GLE) per year from sixth to eighth grade.

During the 2003–04 academic year, I included the seven schools that participated in this 2002 pilot study in a study of 12 schools in the Network. During that time, I visited the schools for at least one full day, interviewing faculty, administration, and students and attending classes (Fenzel, 2009). I also collected data on student enrollment, standardized test scores, staffing, fund raising, and the like at each school and administered surveys to students and faculty. One of these schools, a pre-K–8 school in Philadelphia included a middle school program that did not quite fit the Nativity model and was not included in subsequent analyses. The middle schools for this investigation included eight single-sex schools for boys (5) or girls (3) and three that educated both boys and girls located in seven different cities from St. Petersburg, Florida, to Milwaukee, Wisconsin. Seven of the schools educated students in grades 5 through 8 and four in grades 6 through 8, and the two largest schools were schools for both girls and boys and included a fifth-grade class. The mean number of students per grade level in the schools was 18.2 at that time and total school enrollments ranged from 52 (single-sex school for girls) to 96 (Fenzel, 2009). The NativityMiguel Coalition, in a 2015 report, reported a mean school enrollment of 79, with 21 students per grade level. Over the past several years, a few schools have expanded by adding either a fourth or fifth grade as they moved into larger school buildings; others are adding even younger grades.

Focusing on long-term benefits of a NativityMiguel education and the graduate support process, I conducted another interview and online survey study in 2012–13 for which I interviewed graduates of seven schools, five of which were included in the 2003–04 study. Some of the findings from this study are presented in Chapter 6.

School Characteristics

Students and Teachers

My research on 11 Nativity schools in 2003–04 (Fenzel, 2009) showed that 49% of the 516 students self-identified as African American or Black, 35% as Hispanic or Latina/o, and 11% as biracial or multiracial, with most of those having African American or Black as one aspect of racial identity; 94% of the students qualified for the federal free or reduced-price meal program. The NativityMiguel Coalition (n.d.) website reported very similar percentages with 88% qualifying for free and reduced price meals.

Students are recruited largely from urban public schools where teachers and other school personnel may recommend students for consideration. Parents or guardians must file an application and provide evidence of income in order to qualify. Nearly all of the schools employ a screening process of qualifying applicants to assess whether students and parents/guardians will commit to the school's mission and structure, including the long school day. Part of the screening includes a consideration of whether students' educational needs are beyond the capability of school resources. (Epiphany School in Massachusetts, as well as other Episcopal schools in the Coalition, are noteworthy exceptions where most students are chosen by lottery among those who apply and special needs are not assessed.) Contrary to the concerns raised by some educational observers, I have found that the admissions process does not typically involve *cherry-picking* the most academically gifted students, as some students who show considerable academic ability are often encouraged to take advantage of strong public school programs rather than be accepted to a NativityMiguel school. Most schools appear to want to set aside the small number of student slots for those who are likely to benefit most by attending the school and not those who can be better served in a more suitable educational environment or who do not meet the family income requirement. Siblings of current students or graduates tend to be readily accepted by most schools, even if the family's financial situation has changed. Admissions decisions are guided by the mission of the school to provide a high quality education for historically underserved students from high poverty contexts.

Mission and Vision

The mission statement of the NativityMiguel Coalition (n.d.) emphasizes "breaking the cycle of poverty through faith-based education," consistent with the stated mission of the former Nativity Educational Centers Network (n.d.). The mission of individual NativityMiguel schools has been phrased in a number of ways with central themes reflecting transforming lives, reducing poverty, and developing leaders with an orientation towards service and improving society. Providing an education anchored in faith has been a *sine qua non* of the model since its initial development in the early 1970s.

The Catholic charisms of the Society of Jesus, the Brothers of the Christian Schools, the School Sisters of Notre Dame, as well as those of other religious communities of men and women, are reflected in all of the schools that have adopted NativityMiguel educational mission and model. These charisms reflect a mission to serve those who have been marginalized and left behind in contemporary society, especially with respect to public education, and to provide a holistic educational program that, in the words published by De Marillac Academy (n.d.) in San Francisco, "liberates students and graduates to lead lives of choice, meaning and purpose" ("Mission & Vision"). The mission of the initial San Miguel School of Providence, Rhode Island (2015) is reflected in the following: "Inspired by the pillars of faith, service, and community, each 'Miguel Man' is encouraged to learn, to serve, and to grow to reach his full potential" ("Mission & History"). The Cornelia Connelly Center in New York (2017), founded by the Society of the Holy Child Jesus, "champions girls at risk, empowering them to realize their full potential from middle school through college and beyond" ("Mission").

NativityMiguel schools purport to realize their mission by implementing practices and structures that support the formation and achievement of its students and graduates in a faith-based environment through regional and national conferences and other information sharing mechanisms, including web-based communications. By studying and sharing best practices, the Coalition works to support individual schools with respect to instruction, governance, administration, advancement, and operations (NativityMiguel Coalition, n.d.). Similarly, the Jesuit Schools Network (2016) "initiates programs and provides services that enable its member schools to sustain their Ignatian vision and Jesuit mission of educational excellence in the formation of young men and women of competence, conscience, and compassion" ("About us").

My research clearly has showed that the schools do live up to their mission and charisms of the religious communities of men and women that support them. Christian values of service and justice are reinforced through prayer and other religious services and the staff, in the spirit of St. Francis of Assisi, "preach" the gospel through both words and deeds. I have never met more committed, talented, and caring teachers and administrators, who personify these gospel values, than I have at the nineteen schools I have visited that are committed to the NativityMiguel educational model. The leaders of these schools are people who see an opportunity to provide a high quality, values-based education to urban children who have truly been left behind in public schools that were not serving them well. Every year some 4,000 young girls and boys are provided the tools to live productive, responsible, and caring lives and respond to the call to help others do so as well.

Outcomes and Successes

The research studies I have been involved with (e.g., Fenzel, 2009; Fenzel & Domingues, 2009; Fenzel & Monteith, 2008; Fenzel & Richardson, 2017; Fenzel & Wyttenbach, 2013) have shown consistently that students attending NativityMiguel schools accelerate their academic skill development at a level greater than that of students from similar backgrounds who attend public and parochial schools. These gains are evident in the increases in standardized test scores in reading and mathematics during middle school, from being below grade level upon entry (most students are one or more grade levels behind) to scoring at or above grade level at graduation. Admission to and success at good quality independent and high performing public high schools, as well as the high rates of college attendance and completion, also speak to the academic gains the students make during middle school, as well as to the personal qualities that they develop to enable them to persist.

With respect to standardized test score performance, our study (Fenzel, 2009; Fenzel & Monteith, 2008) of seven schools in the Nativity Educational Centers Network and two comparison parochial schools for which standardized test score data were available showed that NativityMiguel school students were achieving at a significantly higher level in reading (61% vs. 28% at or above grade level) and math (57% vs. 23% at or above grade level) in seventh grade. Mean reading and math percentiles (29%

and 27%, respectively) of six public middle schools in the same urban center where two NativityMiguel schools were located showed that students were achieving at levels much lower than at the NativityMiguel schools. The findings from these investigations also showed that Nativity school students' test scores were increasing at higher rates in reading and math achievement compared to the two comparison parochial schools.

High school graduation rates among NativityMiguel school graduates are substantially higher than they are for public school students from comparable economic and racial backgrounds (Fenzel, 2009; NativityMiguel Coalition, 2015; NativityMiguel Network of Schools, 2010; Podisadlo & Philliber, 2003), where 4-year high school graduation rates have consistently been in excess of 80% for Nativity middle school graduates. The most recent data provided by the NativityMiguel Coalition (2015) showed a 90% 4-year high school graduation rate for students who completed eighth grade in 2010.

In addition to the statistical indicators, interviews showed that graduates in high performing high schools have gained much from the discipline and study skills they developed that brought them high levels of performance in their subsequent studies (Fenzel, 2009; Fenzel & Richardson, 2017). Many of them took pride in how they developed into confident public speakers in higher education and their professional careers. In addition, having had many opportunities to meet and interact with people of influence in their cities, the graduates saw the fruits of firm handshakes and exuding confidence, which afforded them a measure of social capital.

Contributions to School Success

Structures: School Size and Learning Time

There are several reasons for the success students experience in NativityMiguel middle schools. The small school and class size, with accompanying low student-teacher ratios, ensures that the progress of every child can be monitored closely. Truly individualized instruction and universal design strategies can be adopted to ensure substantial gains in student academic skill development and achievement The extended day format, in which students are engaged in learning for 8 to 10 hours a day, as well as the summer camp experiences that extend learning over the summer months, provide a much more engaged educational experience for the students than are realized in public and parochial middle school programs. The significant educational needs of many of the students have also necessitated a low student-teacher ratio, which averaged 5.8-to-1 in my 2003–04 study (Fenzel, 2009).

Local high school and college students and adults from church and other communities also provide tutoring and homework completion support that reinforces learning and helps students understand the material at a deeper level. This kind of support also affords teachers the opportunity to engage students in more higher-order and critical thinking. The small school size and the use of intern teachers to oversee and staff activities such as clubs, sports, and tutoring sessions also enables teachers to plan and execute coordinated interdisciplinary lessons rather than use a more compart-mentalized approach to teaching and learning that is seen in most middle schools. In addition, the summer programs are structured to reinforce and extend students' quantitative and language literacy skills and provide opportunities to learn through group projects and in ways that set them apart from parochial and public school programs that serve urban students placed at risk (Fenzel, 2009).

Instructional Quality

Numerous classroom observations, in addition to several discussions with NativityMiguel teachers, students, administrators, and graduates, which I conducted over the past 20 years, have revealed a good bit of variety in the quality of teaching and several approaches to hiring and developing teachers (Fenzel, 2009; Fenzel, Dean, & Darden, 2014). Dictated in part by the amount of funding available, the original Nativity Mission Center school depended on some classroom instruction being delivered by recent college graduates without a teaching credential, including some hired through AmeriCorps, Jesuit Volunteer Corps, and similar agencies; they committed to teach at the school for 2 or 3 years. During my 2003–04 visits to 11 Nativity middle schools, I found that the percentage of full-time equivalent teachers who fell into this noncertified, nonpermanent category ranged from a low of 13% in one school to a high of 71% in another (Fenzel, 2009). During a subsequent round of visits to many of these schools, I found that those with a high percentage of inexperienced and noncertified teachers had made changes to reduce this number and put processes in place to better prepare first-year teachers for the challenges of providing high quality instruction and managing classroom dynamics. Some of the schools that were able to hire a high percentage of certified, experienced teachers had the financial ability to do so, or they were able to make use of Catholic religious men and women supported by their communities. This particular situation has changed somewhat in recent years with the decline in vocations to religious life (Fenzel, 2009; Fenzel et al., 2014).

Being able to employ staff members who received some AmeriCorps funding has been beneficial financially, but without considerable preparation and supervision, several of the first-year intern teachers I observed lacked the skills to manage a classroom well or monitor student learning effectively during a lesson. In recent years, some schools in the Northeast seem to have found a formula that has ensured high quality instruction while employing intern teachers who study for a master's in education through a partnership with a local university while they develop their skills. In this program, first-year interns coteach in core subject areas with a more experienced teacher while also having primary responsibility for other classes or school activities. These intern teachers also receive considerable supervision and feedback that support their development. At a number of schools, I observed second-year intern teachers engage students quite well in learning with well-organized lessons that made use of excellent transitions and clear and caring communications (see Fenzel, 2009; Fenzel et al., 2014). The workshops provided by the national networks, which have included well-informed educational leaders, researchers, and practitioners, have contributed to the development of a strong teaching force in the schools. In my research, I also spoke with several master teachers who were drawn to the NativityMiguel schools because of their mission and provided a strong and expert presence and support for the less experienced faculty.

Curricula and Accreditation

The presence of highly qualified educational leaders with urban teaching experience has helped the schools develop curricula that have propelled students toward exceptionally high academic gains in mathematics and language arts. Most schools have placed high importance on reading which is reinforced throughout the school day as well as during the summer programs. These curricula have been developed to provide students with the skills to succeed in high performing high schools and colleges and qualify the schools for accreditation. The NativityMiguel Coalition (2015) has reported that 66% of their member schools are accredited with 31% in preparation to secure accreditation. The pursuit and maintenance of accreditation has led schools to conduct a thorough self-study and engage in ongoing curriculum reviews to stay current and prepare students for success as they continue their education.

In order to prepare students to succeed in selective high schools and 4-year colleges, the schools have placed a strong emphasis on the development and use of technology skills and have pursued grant funding to fully equip the schools with computers and wireless computer networks to support student learning. They have also invested in hiring specialists in technology education, as well as in reading, art, music, and physical education in order to provide a broad, holistic education. This investment in technology has been an important focus of the Sisters Academy of Baltimore, where I served as a Board member for 6 years and continue to be involved.

An important part of the curriculum in the schools is the approach taken to ensure that students and staff interact in a mutually supportive and conflict-free environment. Teachers who have not had much experience with the kinds of stressors and issues that urban students placed at risk bring with them to school require expert training that will help them engage and respond to students in culturally sensitive and consistent ways; students in the older grades often take leadership roles in socializing the newer ones to the expectations and processes of the school. The first summer program for new students helps them understand the school culture and the academic demands of the curriculum so that they can assimilate easily when they join the full student body in the fall. Regional and national meetings led by the Coalition help teachers receive the level of training in cultural awareness and responsiveness that individual schools may find difficult to sponsor.

Leadership, Character Development, and Service

The small size of the original Nativity Mission Center School was dictated in large part by the size of the four-story narrow row house on Forsythe Street on the Lower East Side where the Mission was located. When I asked one school leader at a different school why Nativity model schools did not educate larger classes of students, he replied that the schools could clearly educate more students who would be academically successful in high school and beyond but that the small size was required for the development of character and leadership that was an equally important part of the mission of the schools. In addition, the level of emotional support that many of the students and families required as a result of their lack of financial resources and the stressful and often violent neighborhoods in which they lived could only be provided in the intimate school context that became a consistent and important characteristic of the NativityMiguel model schools. The small size has helped create the kind of family environment that a number of graduates have referenced as important in our studies (Fenzel, 2009; Fenzel & Richardson, 2017).

The summer camp experience was another important aspect of the NativityMiguel model that supported the development of students' leadership, character, and commitment toward service, in addition to their academic skills and community belongingness. The 2014–15 data report from the NativityMiguel Coalition (2015) identified 91% of its member schools as supporting summer school, summer camp, or both. School leaders noted how the benefits of the summer camp experience, which has served as the beginning of the school program for new students, helped to integrate them into the ethos of mutual respect and caring of the school community, learn from the example and leadership of the veteran students, internalize the behavioral expectations of the school, and situate them on the path of positive social development. Although not all of the schools have been able to operate a residential camp of several weeks duration, the various summer experiences have enabled students to continue their academic skill development in language arts and mathematics and engage in learning away from the school in museums, the campuses of high schools and colleges where they would almost certainly not have visited otherwise, or on scientific excursions in area waterways. Students in many of the camps are also introduced to canoeing, hiking, and other outdoor activities that challenge them physically and help them develop as leaders, strengthening relationships among one another and with staff. The camp experience also contributes to students' spiritual development through prayer and religious services (see Fenzel, 2009).

Spiritual and religious development is addressed throughout the school day and the opening assembly sets the tone for the day through prayer, which may take the form of reciting the Ignatian prayer for generosity, the singing of "Let Every Voice Sing," or the offering of personal prayer requests from students and staff. Some schools hold weekly chapel services which are often led by students and regular liturgical celebrations in which students have a role in preparing and providing leadership (Fenzel, 2009).

Community service experiences at the schools vary and, in my most recent interviews with graduates of some of the schools, we (Fenzel & Richardson, 2017) learned that their commitment to service continued in the years following middle school graduation and on into adulthood. The long-term effects of the emphasis on service during the middle school years were evident among graduates of two NativityMiguel schools for boys who found lasting lessons from their middle school service experiences. For example, several graduates of a school in the Midwest that served Latino students mentioned how they viewed their current service with the elderly or young Latinos in their communities as an aspect of their identities as adults that was formed as young adolescents. Other graduates of this school had committed to serving as mentors of current eighth-grade students and will meet with their mentees on a regular basis to serve in a role similar to the one they benefitted from years before.

Other interviews of graduates from other NativityMiguel schools showed how so many of them have engaged in service occupations that included community organizing, teaching, college and high school advising, and K–12 school administration. One graduate of the flagship, Nativity Mission Center, who serves in a big way as a math educator, blogger, author, and activist, wrote how his Nativity Mission education has been about "paying service forward" (Vilson, 2014, p. 32). One way that several graduates have realized their commitment to serving those at the margins has been to return to their NativityMiguel school to teach. This was the case for three graduates of Nativity Mission Center whom I interviewed during the 2003–04 study. They all strongly felt the call to realize through teaching and other service to the school an unofficial mission statement that I heard from many Nativity Mission graduates and students: "An opportunity is Nativity's gift to you. What you do with it is your gift to Nativity." They and other graduates often served as counselors at the summer camps where they helped the younger boys, as they had been helped, develop into caring, service-oriented leaders who reflected deeply on their roles in an often unjust and difficult world.

A graduate of one of the East Coast coeducational schools serves as an illustrative case study of the transformation of a servant leader. I first encountered Francisco (not his actual name) when I was conducting research for the 2003–04 study and was able to follow his career through college and into professional life, interviewing him again in 2013. As a fifth grader, Francisco was not accepted at the first NativityMiguel school where he applied but his mother persisted, and he was accepted for entry into the seventh grade at his eventual middle school. He was supported through Catholic high school and a Catholic college where he excelled as a leader. Returning to his home town to pursue a law degree, he has served on the Board of Directors at his NativityMiguel school, has provided financial support for the school, and still actively mentors a number of students and graduates. He also has served the school and its students by challenging the administration to understand their students better and turn that knowledge into a program of study that expects more of the students than they had of him when he was a student.

Young women graduates have distinguished themselves in leadership and service as well, as two examples from schools for girls that first opened in 1993 show. The website of the Cornelia Connelly Center in New York (2017) profiled an alumna of the first graduating class (1995) who became a tax accountant and in 2012 joined the Board of Trustees. Another graduate of the same class, a New York City teacher for a number of years, was also featured as she joined the school staff as Director of Graduate Support. The Mother Caroline Academy and Education Center (n.d.) in Dorchester, Massachusetts, lists three of its successful graduates on its Board. The website of Notre Dame School of Milwaukee (n.d.), a single-sex school for girls, features a member of its class of 2003 who, after receiving both a bachelor's and master's degree from local universities and serving an internship at one of the Smithsonian museums in Washington, DC, is employed as the Youth Programs Director at the Casa Romero Renewal Center in her home town.

Relationships and Community

So much of the value of a NativityMiguel education lies with the quality of the relationships students have with teachers, administrators, graduates, and school mates. In the numerous individual and group interviews I have conducted with students and graduates, I have seen how fondly they talk about supportive teachers and administrators who go the extra mile to help them succeed and find their way in the world. Among Nativity Mission Center graduates, for instance, Fr. Jack Podsiadlo has often been cited as such a supportive friend and mentor. He spent many years at the school, first as a teacher and later as an administrator. Fr. Jack speaks proudly of the successes of the NMC graduates and beams at the career choices and many ways that graduates have contributed to young people placed at risk.

The director of graduate support has been cited often in these interviews as one of the school staff members who have had a profound influence on graduates' social, emotional, and academic development and success. For example, graduates of a coeducational NativityMiguel school on the West Coast spoke about a teacher who also served as the graduate support director and continued to provide guidance for graduates several years after they graduated. She was the kind of teacher that students enjoyed seeking out when they would return to their NativityMiguel school to check in and interact with current students. Several young women who had graduated from this school noted that they relished how this teacher persisted patiently to support them through times of self-doubt and credited her commitment to them as a big factor in their social development and educational success.

Graduates of a school for boys in the Midwest spoke fondly of a graduate support director and teacher who worked hard to maintain a relationship with the graduates throughout their high school years and beyond. The level of respect that graduates had for this middle-age man was remarkable; they articulated how he would both challenge and encourage them to do well in their studies and give serious consideration to pursuing college after high school. Some graduates expressed how important this support and challenge was for them since they realized that they could easily get to the point of wanting to give up and withdraw from high school like so many Latino adolescents they knew from their neighborhoods. They knew that the challenge brought to them was accompanied by genuine caring and concern for their welfare and the graduates appreciated it (see Fenzel, 2009; Fenzel & Richardson, 2017).

Two terms that were frequently echoed in these interviews were *family* and *genuine*. It was the graduates' perception of their middle school as a family, in which relationships were genuine, that led them to return to their school to connect with teachers they had and seek ways to give something back to the current students. Graduates noted the small size of their NativityMiguel school and the long tenure of many of the teachers and administrators as important contributing factors to this sense of family. In comparing the support provided by graduate support directors and their college counselors in high school, graduates remarked how much more personal and individualized the graduate support directors' assistance was. This shows in how well they make use of their knowledge of the graduates' strengths and family situations to guide them in certain directions for postsecondary education.

Part of the family experience in school shows up in the graduates' continuing connections with one another. Graduates have expressed how the challenging academic experience of middle school contributed to an ethos of cooperation and mutual support shown in the continuing desire to see one another succeed in life, in whatever form that success takes. I found that a sense of *brotherhood* was particularly strong in the single-sex schools for boys, as well as a sense of *sisterhood* among the graduates of the schools for girls; many graduates of these schools used these terms readily to express the closeness and genuine concern they have for one another. They recognize that they can approach any classmate, graduate of a different class, teacher, or administrator for support, advice, and direction. Their connection to their NM school continues in their visits to the school for an alumni flag football game, to speak with the current students, or even return to the school to teach for a period of time or serve in a formal or informal mentoring role for students and younger graduates. This sense of community and connection with one another is reinforced in summer camp activities where students share cabins and activities for 2 to 7 weeks away from the city and spend evening time together in discussions. For many graduates, the summer camp provided a unique and special opportunity to mature, to experience the value of working together for a common purpose, and to develop leadership skills. Several graduates continue to return to the camps to work as counselors.

Research has shown how important emotionally nurturing support, along with appropriate academic challenge, is to the development of resilience in the face of living in challenging and stressful urban environments (Rivera-McCutchen, 2012). This kind of support was a common theme expressed by graduates of the schools with whom I spoke during both large-scale studies of NativityMiguel schools (Fenzel, 2009; Fenzel & Richardson, 2017). For some graduates, this kind of support and mentoring has been extremely influential in turning some of their lives around from ones that resolved disputes through reactive fighting to ones that incorporated more adaptive ways of problem solving and learning to understand another's perspective. My experiences of conducting research in these schools and workshops for teachers have shown me that the kind of genuine and persistent relationship building evident among NativityMiguel teachers and administrators is an essential factor in the outstanding success of the schools in developing graduates for leadership, service, and subsequent academic and career success.

School Leadership

A typical administrative structure in NativityMiguel schools consists of a president or executive director, a principal, headmaster or headmistress, a Director of Graduate Support and possibly a half- or full-time assistant director, and a Director of Development. Some schools also employ a Director of Admissions or other specialized program, such as mentoring. All schools have a Board of Directors or Trustees and, at Catholic schools supported by more than one religious community, a corporate Board comprised of the representatives of the supporting religious communities (see Fenzel, 2009).

The school president or executive director tends to serve as the face of the school in the community, with the responsibility of overseeing budgets, strategic planning, determining school personnel needs and processes outside of the curriculum, recruiting Board members and serving as a liaison between the school and the Board, and leading the fund raising efforts. I observed one president, a Jesuit priest who exuded passion for his students and a strong commitment to the mission of the school, teach a weekly seminar on family life for eighth graders. At the same time, he was a master fund raiser with strong ties to other Catholic institutions in the Midwest and to the larger community. Among the eleven schools included in my 2003–04 study, seven presidents were members of a sponsoring religious community and one was a former Catholic religious (Fenzel, 2009), a number which, according to the executive director of the NativityMiguel Coalition, continues to decline among member schools. All presidents have at least some ongoing contact with students, often through school assemblies and other school events, but rarely have the time to teach a class. In a few cases, the president or executive director oversees the operation of a consortium of two or three schools (as has been the case in Florida and New York City) or a larger unit that includes the school itself in addition to an adult education center or other program.

As operational costs increase, many schools have committed to building an endowment fund to support these expenses and ensure a sound financial future. At the same time, the chief executive and the Board are charged with raising the funds necessary to meet expenses, which includes recruiting involved and supportive Board members with many skills and community connections to assist with this challenge. A look at the annual reports posted on the websites of individual schools that follow the educational model show a considerable range in the annual operating costs and cost per student in their budgets. Recruiting students, conducted in part by visiting area public elementary schools, is overseen by the president even if it is the primary responsibility of another school administrator.

School principals, headmasters, or headmistresses serve as curriculum leaders who recruit, train, and supervise faculty and lead the effort to establish and maintain the mission and ethos of the school, as well as address the many challenges that arise during the school day. Many of the academic leaders in the schools I visited had been teachers who understood well the mission of the school, as well as the students and their families. One important task of the academic leader is to communicate the school mission and vision to teachers, parents, and students, help teachers, especially those who lack experience with urban children, understand the needs of the students of color, and help convince the students themselves that they possess the skills to succeed and develop as leaders. Although many of these school leaders have been White women and men, some schools have been fortunate to hire school leaders of color and even one of their graduates.

Graduate support is also an intrinsic part of the school structure and school personnel communicate to students and parents early on that the school program extends through high school with academic, social-emotional, and, often, financial support. Schools employ between one and two full-time graduate support administrators to carry out this important aspect of the school program. (We discuss this aspect of the school program in greater length in Chapter 6.)

The fourth position in the administrative structure of NativityMiguel schools is the development director who works closely with the president or executive director. Since the schools charge little or no tuition, considerable funds must be raised annually to ensure continuous operation of the school. This task has become more challenging in recent years with the decline in the number of vowed religious available to assume administrative, teaching, and other supportive roles for the schools and the need to hire lay personnel which increases operational costs. At the school where I served as a member of the Board, we faced the need to hire a lay principal to replace a religious sister, as well as a director of development with the experience to take our development program to a higher level. Fortunately, with the help of the school president, a School Sister of Notre Dame, we began to develop succession plans for replacing her and the principal when the time came and saw the need to step up our fundraising efforts in order to establish an endowment fund to better address budget pressures.

I found that NativityMiguel schools differed in their effectiveness in establishing connections with influential and generous donors and partners and securing a sound financial future. At least two of the schools in the Nativity Educational Centers Network, including the flagship Nativity Mission Center School, were forced to close because of a failure to adequately plan for the possibility of events that took place and from which they were not able to recover.

Effective school boards have become an essential aspect of the success of NativityMiguel schools and wise school presidents and sponsoring religious communities seek to recruit board members who can contribute meaningfully to strategic planning, financial analyses, physical plant maintenance, and fund raising, as well as to student academic and social development. In Baltimore, the three NativityMiguel schools have established effective Boards whose members are committed to the schools' goal of providing a high quality, faith-based education to underserved urban children who will have a chance to complete college and engage in a meaningful career—an opportunity that they would likely not have had otherwise. Some schools have sought to include graduates, parents, and former parents on their Boards, which I feel contributes to the board members' improved understanding of the kinds of challenges that the school faces in providing an effective education for urban children placed at risk. I have also found in my Board experience that educating Board members who lack experience in urban educational or health and safety issues is needed to contribute to their understanding of the students and families served by the school and the urban communities in which they live.

Challenges

School Closings

While the first part of the 21st century has seen the founding of new schools, it has also seen the closing of others. In the case of two schools that have closed since the new millennium began, major events, Hurricane Katrina in one case and the loss of property in another, contributed mightily to the closings. With respect to Bishop Perry Middle School in New Orleans, which educated economically poor African American boys since 1994, Hurricane Katrina drove away many of its students and donors (Troeh, 2006). In the case of the Nativity Mission Center, which closed its doors in 2012, having discontinued accepting new students after 2009, many of its students were no longer a part of the Lower East Side community due to gentrification and the school lost its identification with the area (Gonzalez, 2010; Rearick, 2012). The financial downturn of 2007–08 also cost the school much of its donor base, adding to the difficulties faced by the school. Although it hoped to relocate the school by the time it was to close, this never materialized. At Bishop Perry, the school reopened in 2013 as a center that provides educational, medical, and job preparation services to underserved persons in the area (Stroup, 2014), while the Nativity Mission Center building has been replaced by condominiums that sell for over $3 million each (Litvak, 2015).

Financial Challenges

The cost of providing what amounts to a private school education to underserved middle school students can run from $10,000 to more than $20,000 per student per year, depending on the size of the teaching and administrative staffs and the kinds of services provided. The annual operation budgets for most schools range from $1 million to over $3 million. Of the schools I have studied, the one with the highest annual operating cost is Epiphany School in Dorchester, Massachusetts, that provides medical, dental, and psychological services to students and families and accepts a number of students enrolled with the Department of Children and Families, who have suffered abuse or neglect (Epiphany, n.d.).

As a member of the Board of Directors for a NativityMiguel school for girls, the Sisters Academy of Baltimore, I was directly engaged in addressing many of the challenges the school, and others like it, faced in a challenging fiscal environment. The Board and school administration experienced the challenges of rising costs of providing a high quality education, raising adequate funds to meet the needs of the budget, and addressing the decline of available members of religious communities to take on teaching and administrative roles.

Some schools, such as those in Milwaukee, New Orleans, and two cities in Florida, have made good use of voucher program funds to meet their budget demands and operate with a much more sustainable model. Although somewhat controversial, the Milwaukee Parent Choice Program (MPCP) has shown positive outcomes for religious-affiliated schools in the city (Cowen, Fleming, Witte, Wolf, & Kisida, 2013) and has enabled the two Milwaukee Nativity model schools to thrive and to extend the education they provide to children in younger grades as well.

The Future of NativityMiguel Schools

There is little doubt that NativityMiguel schools have been shown to be important and effective in providing thousands of students placed at risk because of urban poverty and neighborhood dysfunction an education that propels them forward on a pathway to higher educational attainment, worthy careers, and a life of leadership and service. Its model has also influenced other educational initiatives, such as the KIPP (Knowledge is Power Program) charter schools in several U.S. urban centers.

As some of the schools have developed a strong financial footing, they have looked to extend their programs into earlier grades, with some Grade 6-through-8 and 5-through-8 schools adding a fifth or fourth grade and others embarking on plans to develop an associated elementary school program. These efforts are undertaken to strengthen students' academic skill development and leadership preparation beyond what the middle school program alone can provide, especially for the countless students who are being inadequately prepared in many urban public schools.

Voucher programs that support student choice from high poverty families, such as MPCP, have made it possible for schools to recruit more students and provide a more financially sustainable model. Many schools that have established a strong pattern of annual support and multiyear commitments from donors to provide substantial support have also worked to establish and grow an endowment fund to further secure their financial futures. Although somewhat controversial, researchers (Cowen et al., 2013) have found positive outcomes for religious-affiliated schools in the city.

Alumna and alumni involvement can and does help support the educational programs of the schools as graduates have served as mentors and tutors to current and recently graduated students, returning to their schools to inspire and encourage the middle school students to excel and anticipate a successful future. Graduates can also provide a service to faculty and other staff of the schools, the vast majority of whom continue to be White from middle and upper class backgrounds, by helping them to understand better the needs of their students and develop a more nuanced understanding of racial justice as well as their privileged status and the social justice issues that accompany it (Allen & Rosatto, 2009). We (Fenzel & Wyttenbach, 2013) found that school leaders were effective for the most part in helping their faculty view their students from an asset perspective and learn about the cultural strengths of the families of the children they serve. In some situations, the intern teachers live together in community within the neighborhoods of their students. In other cases, however, terms such as a "culture of poverty" that has appeared in some of the work on multicultural education have guided some of the preparation of NativityMiguel teachers. As Gorski (2008) and others have pointed out, this kind of orientation can undermine an understanding of sociopolitical conditions that maintain the cycle of poverty and reinforce negative stereotypes of persons of color. The Coalition would be wise to maintain a strong educational program that encourages ongoing reflection on teachers' attitudes and classroom practices.

Hiring former students as teachers and other support personnel can have particularly beneficial effects on students, most of whose teachers are not likely familiar with the kinds of struggles their students face when they leave the school grounds at the end of the day. In addition, encouraging many of the graduates to serve as principals, presidents, Board members, and in other roles can contribute meaningfully to future success of the schools. One teacher who graduated from his single-sex school provided a particularly important and valuable understanding of what someone like he can offer students who live in neighborhoods similar to the one he did. Knowing how difficult it was for him to assimilate into a highly selective and competitive independent high school, he, and other graduates who return to their schools to teach, are in a unique position to prepare students for the challenges that lie ahead in a world of the privileged class that really does not want them to be a part of it and who erect obstacles to their success.

As I remarked in my 2009 publication, three aspects of the NativityMiguel programs that distinguish them from other less effective ones are parent involvement, graduate support, and educating for character development, leadership, and service. Increasing the size of each class would undermine the schools' effectiveness in providing a holistic, individualized, and family-oriented program. Undergirding these program characteristics are the relationships that administrators and teachers seek to build with each child who joins the school community and the mission to educate for social change. The schools will continue to thrive with effective leadership and planning and continued commitment to the mission and the value of each NativityMiguel student. Public school educators and consultants would be wise to take a page from the playbook of the faith- and values-based education provided by NativityMiguel schools to improve the educational opportunities and attainment of more historically underserved urban young people.

NOTE

1. For the remainder of this chapter, schools that had been associated with the Nativity, San Miguel, or NativityMiguel Networks and, currently, the NativityMiguel Coalition or Jesuit Schools Network will be referred to as NativityMiguel Schools, except where greater clarity is gained by another term.

REFERENCES

Academy Prep Center of St. Petersburg. (n.d.). *About*. Retrieved from http://academyprep.org/stpete/about/

Allen, R., & Rossatto, C. (2009). Does critical pedagogy work with privileged students? *Teacher Education Quarterly, 36*(1), 163–180.

Cornelia Connelly Center. (2017). *Mission*. Retrieved from http://www.connellycenter. org/our-center/mission

Cowen, J. M., Fleming, D. J., Witte, J. F., Wolf, P. J., & Kisida, B. (2013). School vouchers and student attainment: Evidence from a state-mandated study of Milwaukee's Parental Choice Program. *The Policy Studies Journal, 41*, 147–169. doi:10.1111/psj.12006

De Marillac Academy. (n.d.). *Mission & vision*. Retrieved from https://demarillac.org

Epiphany. (n.d.). *Mission statement and overview*. Retrieved from http:// epiphanyschool.com/mission-statement-overview-2/

Fenzel, L. M. (2003, June). *Report on an evaluation of selected Nativity schools*. Unpublished manuscript.

Fenzel, L. M. (2009). *Improving urban middle schools: Lessons from the Nativity schools*. Albany, NY: State University of New York Press.

Fenzel, L. M., Dean, R. J., & Darden, G. (2014). Effective learning environments and the use of teaching fellows in alternative urban middle schools. *Journal of Education for Students Placed At Risk, 19*, 20–35. doi:10.1080/10824669.20 14.924320

Fenzel, L. M., & Domingues, J. (2009). Educating urban African American children placed at risk: A comparison of two types of parochial middle schools, *Catholic Education: A Journal of Inquiry and Practice, 13*, 30–52

Fenzel, L. M., & Monteith, R. H. (2008). Successful alternative middle schools for urban minority children: A study of Nativity schools. *Journal of Education for Students Placed At Risk, 13*, 381–401. doi:10.1080/10824660802427686

Fenzel, L. M., Peyrot, M. F., & Premoshis, K. (1997, March). *Alternative model for urban middle level schooling: An evaluation study*. Paper presented at the annual meeting of the American Educational Research Association. Chicago, IL. ERIC Document No. ED 409387.

Fenzel, L. M., & Podsiadlo, J. J. (2009). The Nativity school model. In L. M. Fenzel. *Improving urban middle schools: Lessons from the Nativity schools*. Albany, NY: State University of New York Press.

Fenzel, L. M., & Richardson, K. D. (2017, April). *Supporting continued academic success, resilience, and agency of urban boys in Catholic alternative middle schools*. Paper presented at the annual meeting of the American Educational Research Association, San Antonio, TX.

Fenzel, L. M., & Wyttenbach, M. (2013). Preparing NativityMiguel teachers to work with children of color from high poverty environments. In S. Grineski, J. Landsman, & R. Simmons (Eds.), *Talking about race: Alleviating the fear* (pp. 260–266). Sterling, VA: Stylus.

Gonzalez, D. (2010, August 10). Lower east side has less to offer Jesuits who teach the poor. *New York Times*. Retrieved from http://www.nytimes.com/2010/08/11/ nyregion/11mission.html

Gorski, P. (2008). Beyond the "culture of poverty": Resources on economic justice. *Multicultural Perspectives, 10*, 27–29. doi:10.1080/15210960701869488

Jesuit Schools Network. (2016). *About us*. Retrieved from https://www. jesuitschoolsnetwork.org

Kirylo, J. D. (2006). Preferential option for the poor: Making a pedagogical choice. *Childhood Education, 82*, 266–270.

Litvak, E. (2015, May 1). Condos at 204 Forsyth St. hit the market for $3 million and up. *The Lo-down*. Retrieved from http://www.thelodownny.com/leslog/2015/05/condos-at-204-forsyth-st-hit-the-market-for-3-million-and-up.html

Mother Caroline Academy and Education Center. (n.d.). *Leadership & staff.* Retrieved from http://www.mcaec.org/about-mcaec/board-members/

NativityMiguel Coalition. (n.d.). *Our mission.* Retrieved from http://nativitymiguel.org

NativityMiguel Coalition. (2015). *NativityMiguel Coalition: National data executive summary report, 2014–15*. Retrieved from: http://nativitymiguel.org

NativityMiguel Network of Schools. (2011, February). *Executive summary report of national data 2010*. Washington, DC: Author.

Nativity Network. (n.d.). *About the Nativity Educational Centers Network.* Retrieved from http://nativitynetwork.org/about/index.html

Notre Dame School of Milwaukee. (n.d.). *Alumnae.* Retrieved from http://notredamemke.org/en/alumnae-stories/

Podsiadlo, J. J., & Philliber, W. W. (2003). The Nativity Mission Center: A successful approach to the education of Latino boys. *Journal of Education for Students Placed At Risk, 8*, 419-428. doi:10.1207/S15327671ESPR0804_3

Rearick, J. (2012, May 1). A closer look: Why Nativity Mission Center School closed. *The Lo-Down*. Retrieved from http://www.thelodownny.com/leslog/2012/07/a-closer-look-why-nativity-mission-school-closed.html

Rivera-McCutchen, R. L. (2012). Caring in a small urban high school: A complicated success. *Urban Education, 47*, 653–680. doi:10.1177/0042085911433522

San Miguel School of Providence. (2015). *Mission & history.* Retrieve from: http://sanmiguelprov.org/about-us/mission-history

Stroup, S. (2014, July 12). Bishop Perry Center brings help and hope to downtown neighborhoods in New Orleans. *The Times-Picayune*. Retrieved from: http://www.nola.com/religion/index.ssf/2014/07/bishop_perry_center_brings_hel.html

Troeh, E. (2006, July 21). Lack of students, donors closes New Orleans school. Retrieved from http://www.npr.org/templates/story/story.php?storyId=5572807

Vilson, J. L. (2014). *This is not a test: A new narrative on race, class, and education*. Chicago, IL: Haymarket Books.

Whitehead, M. (2007). "To provide for the edifice of learning": Researching 450 years of Jesuit educational and cultural history, with particular reference to the British Jesuits. *History of Education, 36*, 109–143.

CHAPTER 3

A CRITICAL RACE THEORETICAL EXAMINATION OF THE CRISTO REY NETWORK

Ursula S. Aldana
University of San Francisco

Sajit U. Kabadi
Metropolitan State University

The Cristo Rey Network (CRN) is an association of 32 secondary schools that implement a college preparatory curriculum and Catholic education alongside its corporate work-study program. Supporters of the model laud the CRN because it specifically serves low-income families and ensures students have access to a Catholic education. An unintended consequence of the model is the CRN schools primarily serve Latino and African American students (97% of CRN students)—a demographic that is uncommon, but not unique, to Catholic education. This chapter will examine the Cristo Rey Network of schools utilizing critical race theory, which centers on the experiences of people of color and is an important vehicle for racial justice. More specifically, the study uses Derrick Bell's (1980) interest convergence theory and Kimberle Crenshaw's (1988) theory of intersectionality to understand how interests of the CRN and students of color converged and how this

Responding to the Call for Educational Justice:
Transformative Catholic-Led Initiatives in Urban Education, pp. 39–57
Copyright © 2019 by Information Age Publishing

might or might not be beneficial for both groups (Bell, 1989). Data from two CRN schools and interviews with their school leaders, students, and alumni were analyzed using this framework detailing the short- and long-term outcomes as they pertain to the CRN schools and students.

INTRODUCTION

Historically, Catholic schools have served working class and immigrant communities in urban centers throughout the United States (Hunt & Walch, 2010), in part due to Catholic social teaching that emphasizes a call to action against injustice and a collective effort to remedy the issues that plague the marginalized. Research has suggested that Catholic schools, especially in urban areas, provide a better education to students from underserved and historically marginalized communities than public schools. For students of color, attending Catholic school has positive influences on academic achievement (Coleman & Hoffer, 1987; Coleman, Hoffer, & Kilgore, 1982; Greeley, 1982; Morgan, 2001; Sander & Krautmann, 1995) as well as high school completion and college matriculation rates (Evans & Schwab, 1995; Martin, 2009; Neal, 1997). In particular, Murnane, Newstead, and Olsen (1985) found positive effects on achievement for Latino students, and Figlio and Stone (1999) found religious schools to have a positive effect on achievement for Black and Latino students. Similarly, Altonji, Elder, and Taber (2005) and Neal (1997) found a positive effect on educational attainment for urban minority students. Additionally, the dropout rates for minority and low-income students have been consistently lower in Catholic schools (Coleman & Hoffer, 1987; Lee & Burkam, 2003). Bryk and colleagues (1993) found that the achievement opportunity between White and minority students decreased from sophomore to senior year in Catholic schools while achievement opportunities widened in public schools. Together, this research provides strong evidence that Catholic schools have a positive impact on academic achievement for students of color, particularly those in urban contexts.

Urban Catholic schools then face the tremendous challenge to work alongside underserved minority communities to disrupt the cycle of poverty by offering youth the resources to prepare for, apply to, and hopefully attend college. Despite the positive effect Catholic education can have on students of color and particularly those in urban and underserved communities, only 17% of the 1.3 million students attending Catholic schools nationwide are Hispanic, with just over 20% identifying as students of color overall (McDonald & Schultz, 2017). Over the last 40 years, the percentage of total Catholic schools located in urban areas has dropped from 47% to 40%, while the percentage of total Catholic schools located in the suburban areas increased from 25% to 39%. Simply put, the influence of Catholic education in the urban parts of America is decreasing. Much of this is due to costs with the average annual tuition ($4,400 for elementary, $9.800 for secondary education) and overall school costs for a Catholic education continuing to rise (McDonald & Schultz, 2017). We focus on the Cristo Rey Network of Catholic schools precisely because of their commitment to serve students from urban communities and working-class homes. For researchers and educators interested in equity and social justice, the Cristo Rey Network of schools provides an important case study in the field of Catholic education.

In this chapter, we begin with a summary of the broad impact of the Cristo Rey Network and emerging research on its schools. We provide a background to critical race theory, its impact on the field of education and explicate the need for a framework centered on race to examine the Cristo Rey Network model. We share data from two research projects on Cristo Rey schools to further interrogate how the CRN segregates and racializes youth of color and their Catholic school experience. We explore the successes and tensions of the CRN as voiced by teachers, leaders, and alumni. Drawing on the Church's tenets of Catholic social teaching and the "preferential option for the poor," we aim to highlight the complex and important ways in which Cristo Rey schools have maintained and changed the Catholic educational experience, especially for students of color and students from low-income backgrounds, with particular attention to segregation and its impact on Cristo Rey schools. The chapter concludes with a summary of the schools' institutional responses to racism and implication for other schools working with similar demographic contexts.

THE CRISTO REY NETWORK

The Cristo Rey model has been a successful Catholic urban school model in countering declining enrollment in American Catholic education. The original Cristo Rey school was created in Chicago in the predominantly Hispanic neighborhood of Pilsen in 1996. This innovative school created an economically sustainable model by having students work one full day a week at one of the Fortune 500 companies located in downtown Chicago to earn money to cover their tuition costs. Consequently, the annual tuition for any Cristo Rey school is kept comparatively low (can range from $300 to $500 per school year) which makes the school affordable and accessible to more students (Cristo Rey Network, n.d.; Thielman, 2012). The corporate work study program provided financial sustainability for the school while exposing many of these students to an experience that proved valuable for them in terms of their future college and career plans. Many of the Cristo Rey students would be the first generation of their families to complete high school and, with determination, to graduate from college. With the assistance of venture capitalist B. J. Cassin of the Cassin Foundation, The Cristo Rey Network was founded in the early 2000s and has contributed to the expansion of the Cristo Rey model into a network of 32 high schools across the United States. In 2000, the Cristo Rey Network was formed to oversee the creation and sustainability of these schools. In April of 2012, the network signed a formal agreement with the Walton Foundation to build 25 more Cristo Rey schools over the next decade (Cristo Rey Network, 2016).

CRN schools can range from newly established schools but also include a few number of redesigned Catholic schools that were once at risk of closing. The high schools are comprised of both single sex and coed high schools and pride themselves in offering students a rigorous academic experience and social skills via a work program that prepares them for postsecondary and career success. To date, more than 11,000 students (97% students of color) have attended a Cristo Rey school and 90% of Cristo Rey graduates are currently enrolling in college at a higher rate than low-income high school graduates overall (61%). Even more impressive, 35% of Cristo Rey graduates are completing bachelor's degrees which is more than twice the rate of high school graduates from low-income families (16%) nationwide (McDonald & Schultz, 2017).

The research on the Cristo Rey Network is scant but emerging. Thielman (2012) demonstrated how the Cristo Rey model was used as a mechanism for school turnaround and to improve the quality of education for students in Boston. In a study of two urban Catholic high schools, findings point to the prevalence of a college-going culture in a Cristo Rey school facilitated by a college-going discourse utilized by staff, corporate work partners, and students alike (Aldana, 2014). A Boston College research study (Crea, Reynolds, & Degnan, 2015) examined parent engagement at a Cristo Rey school and used survey data to determine the differences between immigrant and U.S. born parents. Other studies have examined the corporate work study model and its influence and impact on Catholic social teaching and mission of the school. Lopez's (2003) dissertation used a Freirean analysis to document the turnaround of an urban Catholic high school into a Cristo Rey Network school and reveal the tension between corporate interests and the urban community surrounding the CRN school. Kabadi (2015) provided a philosophical examination of Catholic social teachings and their role in a Cristo Rey Network Jesuit high school exploring the links and differences between the more traditional Catholic Jesuit high school and the Jesuit-sponsored Cristo Rey high schools. The traditional Jesuit High School educates a predominantly White, wealthy population and the Cristo Rey Jesuit high school that educates a more urban, diverse, and economically poorer population he referred to as the Jesuit Social Justice Dialectic (Kabadi, 2015). Aldana's (2015) ethnographic study demonstrated the need for culturally relevant pedagogy in CRN religion classrooms and, more importantly, revealed how the corporate work-study program experience complicates students' understandings of their social class standing within Catholic social teachings.

The CRN schools require students to participate in the corporate work study program provided they come from families whose earnings demonstrate they are low-income. Given this unique requirement, CRN schools segregate students from economically poor and working-class families in hypersegregated Catholic high schools rather than integrate them across other Catholic schools. Economic segregation results in de facto racial segregation for the CRN schools which serve almost all students of color. In doing so, these CRN schools create racially/ethnically and socioeconomically segregated learning environments that should not ignore but rather leverage the cultural and linguistic assets of these students and their families (Martinez, Morales, & Aldana, 2017). As Catholic educators and researchers interested in racial justice as a matter of Catholic social teaching, we seek to understand how race is constructed and treated in CRN schools and how model has reinforced racial hierarchies in Catholic educational contexts.

THEORETICAL FRAMEWORK

Critical Race Theory

Critical race theory (CRT) is study of the role of race as an instrument of power and how it has been historically used to justify racial oppression by the American legal system (Calmore, 1992). It consists of theoretical frameworks and social discourses that reject positivist natures of knowledge that preserve the status quo regarding issues of race. CRT dialectics of thought deconstruct societally accepted historical, cultural, and economic analyses that are often systemically institutionalized (Crenshaw, Gotanda, Peller, & Thomas, 1995).

CRT is a field of study that originated in the American law profession to examine the social construct of race with American governance and law; it challenges the false notions of universality regarding the experience of race. These notions of universality come about using primarily the experiences of white people to create the standard mainstream understanding of race that often excludes the people of color who are under examination themselves. CRT concludes that this American status quo endeavors to regulate, control, and censure the conditions of proper thought, expression, presentation, and behavior in society essential in moving towards greater racial justice (Crenshaw et al., 1995). In this context, CRT challenges the dominant discourses of race as they relate to law, but also in other fields such as education (Ladson-Billings, 1998). CRT centers the experience of racism experienced by people of color as legitimate, appropriate, and most importantly, relevant in analyzing the legal, cultural, and political systems for procedures, laws, norms, and hegemonies that fuel racial subordination at all levels of the American ethos (Calmore, 1992).

Researchers Gloria Ladson-Billings and William Tate (1995) brought forth the need for a CRT of education to examine issues of equity in schools in a larger context of White supremacy within the United States. They point to the connection between race and property in the United States as a mechanism of systemic oppression against working class people of color and reinforced by the educational system. Central to CRT is the warrant that race/ethnicity continues to be a central factor that can predict inequality in U.S. schools and society. Yosso and colleagues (2009) found that Latino college students experienced racial microagressions at their universities, which had negative impacts on their educational experience. Likewise, studies of Catholic schools point to issues of racism affecting African American and Latino students in Catholic schools (Aldana, 2016; Simmons, 2012) and class issues impeding Latino families from participating in parish life (Suhy, 2012). Theologian, Bryan Massingale (2010) wrote about the racism inherent in the Catholic Church and encourages Catholics to consider Catholic social teachings and our religious responsibility to combat racism. To that end, we employ a CRT analysis to the study of Cristo Rey Network schools.

Interest Convergence Theory and Intersectionality

The CRT frameworks that are used to analyze the Cristo Rey model here are Derrick Bell's (1980) interest convergence and Kimberle Crenshaw's (1988) Intersectionality. Both CRT frameworks look at issues of race from political and economic perspectives that pertain to the Cristo Rey model.

Interest convergence (Bell, 1979) occurs when the needs of the people of color, often in a marginalized position, converge with the needs of the White people, often in a position of privilege. Interest convergence is a mechanism that ensures that particular efforts towards racial justice be accepted by White Americans, that is, when it serves their own self-interest. Bell (1980) used the *Brown vs. Board of Education* ruling as an example of this principle as serving White and Black citizens in seeking the desegregation of schools in part because America was engaged in the Cold War with the Soviet Union at the time (Bell, 1979). During this Cold War, it served the United States to adhere to certain aspects of racial justice to appease and attract people of color from other parts of the world serving its own hegemony (Dudziak, 1988).

Kimberle Crenshaw (1988) created the discourse of intersectionality to address a propensity by many constituents to use various cultural aspects such as race or gender in isolation or at odds with each other rather than in complementarity, thus diminishing one of them from historical, political, economic, and sociological perspectives. Intersectionality intentionally interweaves issues of racial justice with other justice frameworks, such as gender or economic class justice and fully acknowledges the complexity, as opposed to the compartmentalization of certain issues of culture that contribute to ideas of universality which can be problematic (Crenshaw et al., 1995). These cultural issues are not mutually exclusive or separate but are often linked. Intersectionality calls for discourse that addresses simultaneously multiple systems of oppression. Crenshaw pointed to three constructs of intersectionality:

1. *Structural intersectionality* which looks at the systemic structures of society that perpetuate domination.
2. *Political intersectionality* which looks at the politics utilized to hegemonize and ideologically perpetuate the domination of women of color.
3. *Representational intersectionality* which looks at how certain images of race and gender together create or contribute to certain false, stereotypical, oppressive narrative of women of color (Crenshaw, 1997; Crenshaw et al., 1995).

Methodology

We employed a qualitative data methodology focused on capturing how Cristo Rey Network schools address race and/or experiences of youth of color. Interview data from two distinct case studies on Cristo Rey high schools was examined with a CRT analysis. In this section, we provide historical context for each school site as well as background information on the larger research study from which the data originated.

School Site One

After experiencing serious financial debt and low student enrollment throughout the late 1990s, St. Peter High School[1] was faced with closing its doors. St. Peter, located in a severely economically depressed neighborhood, served a predominately Latino and African American community. However, in 2000, the Society of Jesus, more commonly referred to as the Jesuits, studied St. Peter's financial problems and determined the school could never exist under a tuition-funded model as most other schools in the Archdiocese have done. Instead, the new Jesuit school administration took over the school, replaced the Society of the Divine Word, and adopted the Cristo Rey model in 2003, which established a work study program for its male student body. As a result, the school now had a unique financial and work requirement of its young men of color and their families. The data from this study were collected as part of a larger, year-long research project, a comparative ethnography of two urban, all male, Catholic high schools, including St. Peter High School's corporate work study program. For this study, interview data from eight alumni and eight staff members were coded for theories and constructs relevant to critical race theory.

School Site Two

St. Ignatius High School is one of the more established Cristo Rey Jesuit high schools in the network. Jesuit sponsored, it is located in close proximity to a Jesuit university and retains a close partnership so that many of their graduates consider it as their college of choice. There is also a traditional Jesuit high school located on the other side of town whose clientele is predominantly wealthier and located in the suburbs. St. Ignatius was created and supported by constituents, mainly from the traditional Jesuit high school, who sought to provide a Catholic Jesuit education for a more diverse, working class population. The data from this study were collected over a 4-month span as part of a larger research project that consisted of a historiography of the Jesuits and their social justice mission based on the vision of the late Jesuit Superior General, Pedro Arrupe. This historiography included the origins and history of the Cristo Rey school model and its influence on Catholic urban education. The case study data from the Cristo Rey school used in this study came from this larger research project. For this study, interview data from a snowball sample of over 30 interviews was coded for theories and constructs relevant to critical race theory.

Data Collection

The interviews collected come from both school sites were conducted with staff and alumni who attended and graduated from St. Peter and former staff, trustees, and donors formerly affiliated St. Ignatius. The sample was utilized with the key criteria for participants to be included who had graduated and were now alumni of St. Peter High School and/ or had a direct affiliation—current or past—with St. Peter or St. Ignatius.

Both sets of interviews were conducted either in person or via phone or Skype with each participant. Each case study interview consisted of general thematic talking points presented to each interviewee for their response and subsequent follow up. Themes explored included:

- Reflections on the Cristo Rey high school experience, in particular, the Corporate Work Study Program and their views of it;
- Their past or current connection or relationship to the school and what previously drew them to the school;
- Their personal worldviews on Catholic Social Teaching and/or social justice in connection to their experience with Cristo Rey;
- Challenges and strengths of the Cristo Rey school model.

Interview talking points were intentionally vague so that there was ample opportunity for the participant to answer the question in a variety of ways. Many participants asked for further clarification of the talking points and subsequent follow-up in a dialogical way. Both researchers reassured them that they could answer how they saw fit. The result was often that the participant would answer the question while providing additional information, which was the goal of the data gathering process.

Data Analysis

Transcriptions from interviews were coded for analysis at two levels. Initially, each set of interviews was coded based on general themes that emerged from the data. These initial findings were discussed by both researchers which subsequently led to another more focused review of the data. We developed a list of codes based on CRT literature such as interest convergence, racial microaggressions, cultural deficit, racial hegemony, and intersectionality. The authors engaged in conversations to explicate our understanding of each theme/code using examples from the interview data. In the next section, we present the findings from the study.

Findings

Interest Convergence: The Link Between the Cristo Rey School and Traditional Catholic Schools

A review of the data pointed to a common understanding between research participants that the Cristo Rey network was a way for Catholic education to remain viable in urban areas. In other words, it was generally understood that the Cristo Rey Catholic school experience was reliant on the concessions and philanthropy of wealthy Catholics and corporate partners. Chris, an alumnus of St. Peter explained,

> Yeah, a lot of teachers bring that up and also saying that—they would say "Oh, do you know how much the [St. Peter] is education is worth?" And a lot of students didn't know. "They would say "Oh, it's worth like $14,000, and you only pay $2700 or whatever it was at the time." And so they were saying, "You're getting a great education for a good price and because of the Corporate Work Study Program or other donations that the school receives."

For the alumni in particular, many shared how attending the local Cristo Rey Network school was the better option when compared to the public high school in their community. But for these families, the local CRN school was not a bargain as sometimes was suggested by staff. For these former students, the CR school was the only Catholic school option they could afford while staff often reiterated the generosity of others that made this possible. And yet, the establishment of CRN schools maintains the status quo where "traditional" and elite Catholic schools continue to serve affluent students while CRN schools serve economically marginalized families. Danny, an alumnus from St. Peter, explained how people referred to St. Peter as the "[elite Jesuit school] of the ghetto" when asked how people perceived the Cristo Rey school. He further shared how staff would use negative stereotypes about life in the ghetto as a necessary part of philanthropy.

> He would use a few students to come to orientation to show them what the firm produces. He would say, "And a lot of students there are from impoverished communities"—like myself, a lot of my friends. And it was just important for us to recognize it, I think, that we came from those backgrounds, whether we wanted to talk about it or not—the staff, other students, specifically us.

Danny helped us understand how confusing and frustrating it could be for students to hear issues of poverty being talked about as a tool for philanthropy but not dealt with in other spaces that might be beneficial for students.

The CRN can also be seen as a pragmatic way to address issues of economic and cultural diversity within the context of Catholic Jesuit schools. St. Ignatius emerged as a result of a traditional model Catholic high school, located in the same metropolitan area but in the wealthy suburb, having a challenging time working with poor, marginalized students due to its elevating tuition costs and location. Yet, it was the wealth and resources of this traditional school's constituency that helped create and support St. Ignatius as summarized by the following donor.

> St. Ignatius was created due to political and financial support from a small group of donors that originated from the local traditional Catholic Jesuit high school. These donors represent the demographics and worldviews of the traditional school. They were people who had succeeded financially and politically who either grew dissatisfied with the traditional Catholic model because of their leaving the working class behind and amid concerns of the growing lack of diversity at these schools.

Interviews from the St. Ignatius study pointed to the failure of the other Catholic school to deal with a lack of diversity on its campus. For many elite Catholic schools, the struggle to integrate and serve students from working class homes or students of color is a constant issue of mission.

> I had a heavy involvement with [the local traditional Jesuit high school] and recognized and was frustrated by the fact that there's just not nearly enough emphasis there on diversity. They're renting more of a traditional, I don't want to use the term suburban, white kid school. I'm not trying to be over simplistic, but you know what I mean. I just feel that—that's the way most really successful Jesuit schools are.

Rather than deal with the issue of "diversity" or the "limited resources" families, the development of CRN schools assuages white Catholic guilt as the number of students of color remains extremely low and urban Catholic schools continue to close down. These Catholic schools maintain their superiority and status quo while those that want to serve students of color and the marginalized can do so without disrupting the privilege of those elite Catholic schools.

Cultural Deficit and Mismatch

Both St. Peter High School and St. Ignatius maintained a mostly White staff comprised of outsiders to the local communities and to ways of being in working class communities. St. Peter served a working class and immigrant Latino and African American community in an economically depressed region of the city. St. Ignatius served a predominantly working-class, Catholic, Hispanic, Spanish-speaking student body, many whose parents did not attend college. Interviews revealed the people who spearheaded the creation and leadership of these CRN schools did not have much in common with the communities they were seeking to serve. Danny, an alumnus from St. Peter explained,

> Our teachers were mostly Caucasian and our administrators and staff were
> mostly Caucasian…. We had a hard time trying to adapt to what they were
> saying in the classroom to discipline us. And sometimes, we feel kind of
> bad because you see the students kind of intimidating the staff members.

This cultural disconnect was made more problematic because the leaders,
founders, and donors were collectively convinced that the issue was purely
about socioeconomic status and had nothing to do with culture or race.
This cultural knowledge gap was reinforced by the lack of structural diversity within the institution itself. The leaders, faculty, and staff of St. Peter
and St. Ignatius came primarily from a traditional Jesuit high school educational background and lived far from the school. This cultural gap and
lack of representation was a concern articulated by this participant affiliated with St. Ignatius:

> There's a level in which it's a valid critique. There's no doubt that we are
> strong—but it doesn't change the fact that I think we would do well to be
> sensitive—to reflect more of the community that we're working with. If we
> could have 70% of our active [staff] Latino, 10% be at meetings, I mean
> that reflection academically, that would be clearly the ideal, but we're just
> not there yet.

The educational culture at St. Ignatius and St. Peter sought to expose
students to a blend of notions of American success—college, career, and
ultimately, economic mobility—along with aspects of the Jesuit mission:
justice, service, Catholic spirituality, and forming people of character. The
school staff sought to create a school culture of capitalist and spiritual
success, but they alienated the local community by not including them,
causing a social rift between the school and the neighborhood. This cultural disconnect was evident to students, so much so that alumni from the
school pointed to a need for faculty and staff that represented the community. Chris, an alumnus from St. Peter, referred to some racial incidents
occurring at his corporate work study site but did not feel like he could
speak to most staff about it.

> The majority of the staff is not people of color. But I think it shouldn't hap-
> pen with those people, the white people or the white staff. I think it should
> happen with the small percentage of people of color that are there already.
> Like they should plant like those seeds of cultural awareness, I guess you
> could say because nobody knows that. Nobody knows it better than our
> people, your people in common with the local community.

Chris clarifies the need for faculty and staff that are representative of the
students' community in a school environment that is majority youth of

color. In the sample CRN schools, the faculty and school staff generally lacked an understanding of students' racial and ethnic identity. The failure to address how their racial and ethnic identity impacted students' academic and social experience in high school or college revealed a cultural mismatch between white teachers from middle class backgrounds and students of color living in low-income households.

Microaggressions and Race in Corporate Work Study

The issue of human dignity and privilege arise when Cristo Rey students are immersed in a world that is racially and economically homogenous, which is what the corporate work study program can represent. In this setting, many students are exposed to a world of privilege where they may feel they have to sacrifice their cultural identity and background to assimilate to the white, wealthy, male world of "success." In working these jobs, they have to assimilate or conform in the appropriate way or else be asked to leave the school. Alumni in particular shared how they certainly had to change to be able to work in a corporate setting but not in the ways the Cristo Rey staff articulated. Corporate culture was often understood and essentialized as something poor kids of color had to learn. This person, an important benefactor of St. Ignatius, summarized this view.

> It gives them those soft skills which they would not have learned before: how to shake someone's hand, how to answer the phone. In Mexican culture for a young person to look at an adult in the eye is considered disrespectful. When you shake someone's hand or you meet someone that is older than you, the polite thing is to avert your gaze. And, so all of a sudden this kid doesn't know how to shake hands, because they're afraid to look someone in the eye. So, we spend a lot of time on that telling them why that is important, and teaching them how to shake someone's hand.

Alumni often explained that the change they made had more to do with ways of speaking or acting more adult-like but did not see these cultural markers even though their school staff reified cultural stereotypes and White privilege. Instead of helping students understand and challenge these cultural stereotypes, the CRN schools encouraged students to accept this status quo and work at these corporate work-study jobs to cover their education costs and to contribute to the financial sustainability of the school.

The exposure to corporate America certainly offered students social capital in the forms of mentors at work, but it also came with tension for students of color. Like other research participants, Nestor, an alumnus from St. Peter, shared the frustration he felt the first time he realized how much money people in corporate American make in contrast with members of his own family. In line with his Catholic faith, Nestor questioned if these people really were deserving or in need of this much money when he knew others, like himself, could do so much with so little. Over time, Nestor would come to understand that these class divides were also racialized. He explained,

> I mean, at the end, like after you worked there for a few years and you start moving away from your naiveness, we're like "Okay, you know, they put me in the mail room with all the Latinos, but—or in the IT department with the African Americans or whatever," but we didn't really talk about it. It is what it is, so that's why I'm going to college.

The corporate work study sites often manifested the cultural and racial tensions already existing in society. Alumni explained how this was indeed something they noticed as students but did not feel like the school knew how to address institutional racism, let alone critique it. Instead, alumni like Nestor learned to accept "it is what it is" when confronted with racial hierarchies.

Institutional Responses

St. Peter High School. In the case of St. Peter, the teachers struggled to identify and discuss issues of racial justice. When I asked Ms. Roberts about race and culture she offered,

> I think, they're really interested like we talk about people like Cesar Chavez or Gandhi or like when we like study this figure, there is additional buy in from them, because they're leaders in their community. But I don't think we talk about [race] as much as we can or should. I would say that maybe it's across the board. Yeah, faculty. I wonder why we don't do it. I wonder if it's like teachers who are not in the minority—I'm not Latino or African-American, if they feel like it's not their place to have that conversation. I mean, you are intimidated, even amongst your peers or faculty member. If I say something and it's taken the wrong way. I don't know.

Ms. Roberts' made obvious the difficulty she and other White faculty might have when dealing issues of race and culture. She further pointed to how the school staff failed to prepare the students at St. Peter for the injustices and racism that they may face in the future. And yet, despite her uneasiness to take on the work around racial justice and engage in culturally relevant pedagogy, Ms. Roberts recognized how much students stood to gain from engaging in critical discussions about racism and power in the classroom, school, and work.

Eventually, leadership at St. Peter would focus on the recruitment and retention of faculty of color as an important consideration when hiring. Additionally, an elective would be redeveloped to include critical concepts such as cultural stereotypes, implicit bias, and racial microaggressions to help students make sense of what they encountered in the workplace.

St. Ignatius High School. Over the last few years, St. Ignatius has proceeded on specific strategic initiatives to promote community engagement with the community of students being served. A Jesuit priest was specifically bought into the school to oversee a committee of staff to intentionally work on community engagement efforts with neighborhood members, particularly the parents and families of the students. This committee started slowly but has now expanded into several outreach efforts led by different representatives of the school engaging the community at several different levels, including parent, current student, and alumni. Examples of these community engagement efforts include a regular social event spearheaded by the Jesuits or members of the staff, held either at the school or somewhere in the community, to which parents are invited. There is food provided and mass is often celebrated at these events. These parent gatherings take place periodically throughout the year and not just during the school year. Staff members have been tasked to intentionally connect with alumni and their families, cataloging their current information post high school in terms of their career plans, finances, and the like. Efforts to reach out to the community through the celebration of Catholic mass and Jesuits administering the Catholic sacraments to those in the community have been enhanced. These efforts are noteworthy and open the school constituents to a view of the community that broadens the perceptions of everyone. It also animates the mission for the St. Ignatius staff as this staff member articulated with humility.

> Just making sure that we're spending time building relationships that ground us in the community we're serving. Part of it is that I think it's part of our own weaknesses, and when you are not used to interacting with kids or kids coming from communities that you're not fairly familiar with.

As mentioned, there is legitimate value in who these students are, where they come from, and what they bring to the classroom at St. Ignatius. Only through relationships within the community on their terms and on their turf, as well at the school, could legitimate engagement happen. Everyone sought to negate the deficit perspective driving school culture with a more balanced perspective of the benefits these students bring from their personal experiences into the classroom. By engaging deeper within the community, the Cristo Rey School can do more than simply serve its families—but rather reimagine itself as a hub within the community where all stakeholders can participate without scrutiny or exclusion.

CONCLUSION

Over the last 2 decades, Cristo Rey has proven to have been an enormously successful, innovative model of Catholic urban education. It has proven to be effectively scalable, expanding into a network of schools nationwide with more on the way. The model combines the faith-filled, mission-centered values of Catholic education with a rational, pragmatic approach, the corporate work study program, for economic sustainability. This chapter sought to go into greater depth to glean insights into the dialectic complexity of Cristo Rey's mission, particularly as it pertains to the role of race since the majority of students come from underrepresented populations in Catholic education.

Based on the findings from the two case study schools, the concept of race within this model requires greater awareness, ongoing dialogue, and communal celebrations within the institutions and in the surrounding communities. Cristo Rey schools are blessed with tremendous racial and economic diversity, but there are also areas of growth for both schools. This process begins with a genuine openness towards having ongoing dialogues on race in pursuit of greater communal engagement and growth. CRT provides frameworks such as interest convergence and intersectionality that can foster this growth. Interest convergence exposes areas of common ground and common interests between communities as one possible way to frame the dialogue. In both case studies, the common interest was the desire for the Cristo Rey model. This was an interest shared by wealthy, influential, and mission-centered traditional Catholic school constituents who wanted to serve and the diverse, underserved, population who would be served by it. Both groups, integral in the creation and sustainability of the model, need to be more engaged and collaborative with each other. Both case studies concluded the importance of both the Cristo Rey school and the neighborhood or community working in collaboration to assist students attending these schools to successfully persist on to college.

Intersectionality seeks a dialogue that interweaves complex aspects of race, economics, gender, and the like together in an integrated way rather than focusing solely on one aspect. This study demonstrated the importance of examining the Cristo Rey model not solely through an economic lens, but through a racial lens as well. Along with race, other aspects of culture will also need to be included in any dialogue on institutional diversity, inclusion, and community engagement. These dialogues on race can lead to a greater institutional awareness and sensitivity on the very real role that race plays in the day-to-day lives of the students, the staff, and the community at large. Cristo Rey, with its diverse population working with the predominantly White male corporate sponsors in the work study experience, provides a unique firsthand experience on the role race can play in overt and subtle ways. It is important that Cristo Rey schools incorporate the work experience as part of their mission within their learning environment. Traditional Catholic High schools are challenged by issues of diversity and simply lack it at every level of their institutions. Cristo Rey schools are blessed via their location and mission to have a very diverse population and have a tremendous opportunity to invest in this part of the mission and Catholic social teaching.

At the conclusion of this study, both schools took significant institutional action steps in addressing racial justice within their institutions in various ways. Our study serves to show how CRN schools could look at the structural racial diversity within their own schools in comparison to the communities they serve. Leaders in CRN schools should look closely at the diversity of the voices of influence in the visioning of each institution and how these voices are being incorporated within each institution. Finally, interweaving the students' personal experience with the corporate work study site within a curriculum of racial justice in line with Catholic social teaching is essential. Some educators in both schools indicated a sincere willingness to engage these issues of racial justice with community engagement efforts, ongoing dialogue, and action steps. Time will tell the results of this process for both case study schools and the effects on Catholic urban education overall.

NOTE

1. All names of schools and individuals are pseudonyms.

REFERENCES

Aldana, U. S. (2014). Moving beyond the college-preparatory high school model to a college-going culture in urban Catholic high schools. *Journal of Catholic Education, 17*(2), 131–153. http://dx.doi.org/10.15365/joce.1702092014

Aldana, U. S. (2015). "Does Jesus want us to be poor?" Student perspectives of the religious program at a Cristo Rey Network School. *Journal of Catholic Education, 19*(1), 201–222. http://dx.doi.org/10.15365/joce.1901102015

Aldana, U. S. (2016). Brotherhood, social justice and persistent deficit ideologies: Latino students' experiences in an all-male Catholic high school. In A. Darder & L. Fraga (Eds.), Special Issue: Latinos and the Catholic Church.

Journal of Catholic Education, 19(2), 175–200. http://dx.doi.org/10.15365/joce.1902092016

Altonji, J., Elder, T. E., & Taber, C. R. (2005). Selection on observed and unobserved variables: Assessing the effectiveness of Catholic schools. *Journal of Political Economy, 113*(1), 151–184.

Bell, D. A. (1979). *Bakke, minority admissions, and the usual price of racial remedies.* Berkeley, CA: California Law Review.

Bell, D. (1980). Brown v. Board of Education and the interest convergence dilemma. *Harvard Law Review 93*, 518–533.

Bell, D. A. (1989). *And we are not saved: The elusive quest for racial justice.* New York City, NY: Basic Books.

Bryk, A. S., Lee, V., & Holland, P. B. (1993). *Catholic schools and the common good.* Cambridge, MA: Harvard University Press.

Calmore, J. O. (1992). *Critical race theory, Archie Shepp, and fire music: Securing an authentic intellectual life in a multicultural world.* Los Angeles, CA: University of Southern California.

Coleman, J. S., & Hoffer, T. (1987). *Public and private schools: The impact of communities.* New York, NY: Basic.

Coleman, J. S., Hoffer, T., & Kilgore, S. (1982). *High school achievement.* New York, NY: Basic Books.

Crea, T. M., Reynolds, A. D., & Degnan, E. (2015). Parent engagement at a Cristo Rey High school: Building home-school partnerships in a multicultural immigrant community. *Journal of Catholic Education, 19*(1), 223–242. http://dx.doi.org/10.15365/joce.1901112015

Crenshaw, K. W. (1988). Race, reform, and retrenchment: Transformation and legitimation in antidiscrimination law. *Harvard Law Review, 101*(7), 1331–1387.

Crenshaw, K. (1997, January 1). Beyond racism and misogyny: Black feminism and 2 Live Crew. In D. Tietjens Meyers (Ed.), *Feminist social thought: A reader.* Abingdon, England: Routledge.

Crenshaw, K., Gotanda, N., Peller, G., & Thomas, K. (Eds.). (1995). *Critical race theory: The key writings that formed the movement.* New York, NY: The New Press.

Cristo Rey Network. (n.d.). Cristo Rey Network. Retrieved from http://www.cristoreynetwork.org/page.cfm?p=1

Cristo Rey Network. (2016, July). Cristo Rey Network announces $2.4 million gift from Wilson Sheehan Foundation. Retrieved from https://www.cristoreynetwork.org/cf_news/view.cfm?newsid=200

Dudziak, M. L. (1988). Desegregation as a cold war imperative. *Stanford Law Review, 41*, 61–120.

Evans, W. N., & Schwab, R. M. (1995). Finishing high school and starting college: Do Catholic schools make a difference? *The Quarterly Journal of Economics, 110*(4), 941–974.

Figlio, D. N., & Stone, J. A. (2000), Are private schools really better? *Research in Labor Economic, 18,* 115–140

Greeley, A. M. (1982). *Catholic High schools and minority students.* New Brunswick, NJ: Transaction.

Hunt, T. C., & Walch, T. (Eds.). (2010). *Urban Catholic education: Tales of twelve American cities.* Notre Dame, IN: Alliance for Catholic Education Press at the University of Notre Dame.

Kabadi, S. U. (2015). The Jesuit social justice dialectic within the Cristo Rey school model. *Journal of Catholic Education, 19*(1), 183–200. doi:10.15365/joce.1901092015

Ladson-Billings, G. (1998). Just what is critical race theory and what's it doing in a nice field like education. *International Journal of Qualitative Studies in Education, 11*(1), 7–24.

Ladson-Billings, G., & Tate, W. F., IV (1995). Toward a critical race theory of education. *Teachers College Record, 97*(1), 47–68.

Lee, V., & Burkam, D. (2003). Dropping out of high school: The role of school organization and structure. *American Educational Research Journal, 40*(2), 353–393.

Lopez, E. F. (2003). *Oasis or mirage? Catholic education in the context of a changing economy* (Unpublished dissertation). Claremont, CA: Claremont Graduate University.

Martin, S. P. (2009). Catholic schools as models of inspiration and innovation. *Momentum, 40*(3), 4.

Martinez, D., Morales, P., & Aldana, U.S. (2017). Leveraging communicative repertoires using classroom discourse analysis as a tool for equitable learning. *Review of Research in Education, 41,* 477–499.

Massingale, B. N. (2010). *Racial justice and the Catholic Church.* Maryknoll, NY: Orbis Books.

McDonald, D., & Schultz, M. M. (2017). The United States Catholic elementary and secondary schools 2016–17. The annual statistical report on schools, enrollment and staffing. *NCEA.* Retrieved from http://www.ncea.org/NCEA/Proclaim/Catholic_School_Data/Catholic_School_Data.aspx

Morgan, S. L. (2001). Counterfactuals, causal effect heterogeneity, and the Catholic school effect on learning. *Sociology of Education, 74*(4), 341–374.

Murnane, R. J., Newstead, S., & Olsen, R. J. (1985). Comparing public and private schools: The puzzling role of selectivity bias. *Journal of Economics and Business Statistics, 3,* 23–35.

Neal, D. (1997). The effects of Catholic secondary schooling on educational achievement. *Journal of Labor Economics, 15*(1), 98–123.

Sander, W., & Krautmann, A. C. (1995). Catholic schools, dropout rates and educational attainment. *Economic Inquiry, 33*(2), 217–233.

Simmons, R. (2012). Exploring how African American males from an urban community navigate the interacial and intraracial dimensions of their experiences at an urban Jesuit high school. *Journal of Urban Learning, Teaching, & Research, 8,* 4–12.

Suhy, T. (2012). Sustaining the heart: Attracting Latino families to inner-city catholic schools. *Catholic Education: A Journal of Inquiry and Practice, 15*(2), 270–294.

Thielman, J. (2012). School turnaround: Cristo Rey Boston High School case study. *Journal of Catholic Education, 16*(1), 115–147.

Yosso, T. J., & Smith, W., & Ceja, M., & Solorzano, D. G. (2009). Critical race theory, racial microaggressions, and campus racial climate for Latina/o undergraduates. *Harvard Educational Review, 79,* 659–691.

CHAPTER 4

TRANSFORMING THE MISSION OF ST. BENEDICT'S PREP IN NEWARK

The Benedictine Practice of Adaptive Re-Use

Paul E. Thornton
St. Benedict's Prep

Since renewing its commitment to Newark in 1973, St. Benedict's Prep (SBP) has focused its mission on teaching, guiding, and supporting predominantly Black and Latino young men from Newark and urban areas in Essex County and northern New Jersey. In particular, St. Benedict's has adapted its traditions of educating the whole person—body and mind, heart and soul—to addressing the social and emotional needs of its students. Blending the practical wisdom of *The Rule* of St. Benedict in forming strong human communities with the tested guidance of the Boy Scouts in developing boys and young men, the school has enabled new generations

---

A portion of this manuscript coauthored with Louis Laine '12, appeared in *Radius Magazine*, Summer, 2017. Used with permission.

Responding to the Call for Educational Justice:
Transformative Catholic-Led Initiatives in Urban Education, pp. 59–71

of young men to go on to opportunities they may not have imagined, including success in college and adulthood.

Underlying the success that St. Benedict's has enjoyed for more than 40 years is the school's intentional commitment to "expanding (students') hearts," as Fr. Edwin Leahy, OSB, Headmaster at St. Benedict's since 1972, often says. Chosen to lead the school's rebirth at age 27, the perpetually-young Fr. Edwin has kept a relentless focus on putting students first. Often opportunistic and pragmatic, he has seen his role as making sure that the school provides opportunities and choices for students who often enjoy few if any at home or in other contexts with an unerring sense of how to connect with young people, Fr. Edwin's abundant gifts as teacher, coach, and leader have enabled much of the school's success in serving its students (McCabe, 2011). It is an unfortunate reality that, along with school backgrounds that have varied widely in quality, many of the African-heritage and Latino students who come to St. Benedict's have experienced hardships and forms of trauma that can make it difficult for them to reach their full potential. In response to their emotional burdens, St. Benedict's Prep has offered students a unique experience that enables them to learn how to accept themselves, grow in community, and become effective leaders. While its strong academic program prepares students for success in college, the school's focus on this other "silent curriculum" sets it apart. As one of the monk leaders put it early on: "90% of academic problems are non-academic" (Payne, 1994).

When the monks in Newark committed to renew their "vow" to remain and work in Newark, they knew they would need to undertake a massive renovation of the programs that had characterized the school up to 1972. The various factors that had led their larger community to question the school's viability after the 1967 Newark riots, a growing population of African American and Latino students, concern about declining interest from the suburbs, financial stability, and above all, an effective school program for an increasingly diverse and often undereducated student population, all remained daunting challenges (McCabe, 2011). The school's successes over the past forty years are testament to the monks' intrepid capacity to adapt and reuse so much of their own past practices and their deep knowledge of how *The Rule of Benedict* could serve as the foundation for the resurrected St. Benedict's Prep.

To understand the dynamic, renewed life of St. Benedict's, one must start with knowing that the monks who reopened St. Benedict's did so after the school was forced to close in 1972 by a crisis of faith in the school's historic mission within the larger community of monks then at Newark Abbey. Tensions over changes in the surrounding neighborhood, and deep divisions over how the school could or should respond to the needs of a new student population, led the then larger community to decide to close the school. Over half the community left (McCabe, 2011). After this cataclysmic event, for the monks who remained at their Newark monastery, the chance to renew their commitment to one another, to the city, and to young men in Newark and vicinity by reopening the school was daunting, exhilarating, and transforming.

The "new" St. Benedict's would look and feel very different from the old, which had evolved over the century since 1868 into a highly-regarded Catholic prep school for largely middle-class boys from Newark's suburbs by the time the school closed in 1972. The "old" school's alumni, who had distinguished themselves in business and professions, and the school's illustrious athletic tradition, proved tremendous assets that the reborn St. Benedict's could draw upon for public confidence and a potential base of financial support (McCabe, 2011).

From the new beginning, the power of *The Rule of Benedict* to order the life of the school as well as monastery seems undeniable. It is as if the monks' deep individual and community renewal of their vow of stability in 1973 gave them the inspiration to see how the "school of the Lord's service" (Chittister, 2010, p. 21) that Benedict envisioned could be adapted in myriad and innovative ways to rebuild a school to serve boys from more varied backgrounds than ever before.

Implicit in the commitment to renew their service to the young people of Newark, the monks needed to structure a curriculum and overall school program for boys with a broader range of abilities. Many came and still come from schools beset by the woes that afflict so many inner-city and urban schools, lack of adequate resources, high teacher turnover, chronic underachievement, overwhelmed staff, and heavy concentration of poor and low-income students. Students often arrived without a strong enough education to be ready for a college prep program without special supports. Without acknowledging such a design, the monks incorporated the principle of *The Rule* that suggested they arrange the renewed school such that "the strong (would) have something to strive for and the weak have nothing to run from" (Chittister, 2010, p. 178).

All aspects of school have this perspective as an overall focus, from beginning the school year in the summer, within weeks or sometimes days from an eighth grader's public-school graduation, to giving students an extra (fifth) year to complete work, to extra terms to master essential skills in mathematics or critical reading. The concept of school in the summer was originally intended to provide productive activity to urban young men placed at risk who often had few healthy alternatives at that season. The mandatory "summer phase" quickly became the obvious remedy to what has since been almost casually known in school circles as the "summer slide" (Holtz, 2016). Instead of offering formal Advanced Placement classes to such a diverse student body where many struggle to catch up on fundamentals, the school has sought to provide college level work through its relationships with local colleges— Rutgers Newark, New Jersey Institute of Technology (NJIT), and Seton Hall University's "project acceleration," for those students most capable of advanced work. In the 2017–18 academic year, 15 students from the junior and senior classes are enrolled in classes for college credit through these relationships.

From its new beginning in 1973, the school's embrace of "the other" became a guiding insight. The earliest mission statement declared that the school aims to help students overcome the enduring legacies of poverty and racism. While the mission statement has been revised as the school has grown, the focus on serving students of color from low-income backgrounds has been a constant. As the school began to grow slowly with smaller numbers from 1973 to 1980, students from various racial and ethnic groups beyond the African American population nearest the school began to appear. Some alumni families and other suburban White families found the school's new mission a compelling alternative to local public and private schools. Over time, a gradually increasing number of middle class students began to enroll. More surprisingly, a refugee from Bangladesh showed up in early photos, as do Chinese students and a few boys who settled in the Newark area through Catholic migration services helping the "boat people" who arrived after the Vietnam War. The school's population at any given time in recent years has included Muslims from Egypt and the Arabian peninsula, Catholics from Sri Lanka, young men from families who immigrated from many parts of Africa, especially Nigeria and Ghana, and from families who represent most of the religions practiced in the world. So in a rather mysterious, organic way, the monks' desire, expressed in the first mission statement for the "reborn" St. Benedict's to address the ravages of racism and build bridges among people often kept apart in hypersegregated communities, continues to be realized in an increasingly diverse student body (McCabe, 2011). The current enrollment reflects an unusual diversity for this area of greater Newark: African-heritage: 51%; Hispanic: 34%; White: 9%; Other: 6% (St. Benedict's Preparatory School, 2017b, "Facts at a Glance").

The sense of respect for the other shows itself in routine ways as Fr. Edwin frequently reminds the students gathered at convocation just how a student's name should be pronounced. That is one of the many subtle ways that the "silent curriculum" finds a voice in the day to day practice of building a community whose members are meant to care for one another, probably one of the most critical aspects of the school's design.

The Power of Community: The Heart of the School

One of the "designs" in the renewed life of St. Benedict's Prep is the centrality of community. From the earliest days of its resurrection, the Headmaster insisted that the entire school meet every day in a gathering known as convocation. Even the shape of the gathered assembly became a matter of singular importance as Fr. Edwin declared that he had to be able to "see all the faces" every day.[1] Thus a renovated 1921 gymnasium became the site of daily convocation so that all 550 students and 60 adults gathered on the bleachers and the floor of the gym could be readily seen. Within that simple structure all would get to know everyone's name more quickly and those missing on any given day could be readily identified and inquired about. Fr. Edwin never tires of saying that "convocation" (i.e., encountering one another in community) is the "most important thing we do each day." Everyone, monks, lay teachers, as many adults in the community as possible, is expected to be at convocation every morning.

Even the possibly tedious ritual of taking attendance by group and announcing the missing to the assembly is an intentional way of stressing the importance of every member to the community. For students, the practice is meant to drive home every day in this singular way that showing up to work is a value by itself and that their presence is important to the entire community. Individual group leaders can be delegated, as often happens, to search out why a group member is missing after a couple of days absence.

The regular practice of gathering together as a community to begin the day in prayer and reflection is also quite clearly a compressed version of the monks' liturgy of the hours. The gathering begins with the recitation of a psalm with an antiphon response, a prayer of the season, a scriptural reading, and a reflection by a student or adult. No day passes without time made for individual petitions and often individual responses to the scripture reading. This little liturgy is woven into the morning assembly led by students and faculty members with each group in rotation responsible for leading convocation.

Over time, the school aims for each student to develop a sense of genuine community whose members care for one another. That lives out in the simplest acts in the daily life of the school through the motto: "What hurts my brother hurts me" (St. Benedict's Preparatory School, 2017a, "About SBP"). For young men who have had limited, if any, sense that they can trust others, whether family members or neighbors or schoolmates, it can take a lot of exposure to wear down their bred-in-the-bone resistance to very different values and behaviors. The school's culture of trust and cooperation in building a cohesive, caring community is deliberately a counternarrative to a self-seeking, aggressive, violent atmosphere that many students experience prior to and outside of school. This too echoes and reflects the major Benedictine vow, "conversion of life" (Chittister, 2010, pp. 18–21). For many boys coming to St. Benedict's from experiences of "the street" and behaviors that reflect a nihilistic perspective on life's possibilities, St. Benedict's can seem to expect a wholesale conversion. Thus, the daily practice of building a community works slowly over days and years to form young men who can live the school's motto and utter the powerful words of affirmation of their love for one another at convocation. Words that can so astound and move visitors: "I love you. You're worth it. You can be anything you want to be through Christ who strengthens you ..."

The Structure of Leadership: How Students "Run" the School

One hears from adults, beginning with the long-time "founding" Headmaster, Fr. Edwin, that "the students run the school." St. Benedict's approach to educating young men cannot be reduced to a formula. But a set of clear guiding principles has emerged over time. These guidelines stress that working with young men takes a common-sense focus on seeing what they most need: they ought to be provided with meaningful responsibility for their lives as students. At St. Benedict's, this means that students "run the school" in some critical ways, taking responsibility for an atmosphere of learning, appropriate behavior, and respect for each other. One of the monks of Newark Abbey responsible for shaping the resurrected St. Benedict's, Fr. Mark M. Payne, OSB, who died in 2016, brought a unique combination of insight and skills to help develop the school's approach to organizing its work with boys and young men. As a former Boy Scout and scoutmaster, he recognized how many guiding practices in scouting developed leadership and responsibility among boys, and as the prior of Newark Abbey, he was a leader responsible for embodying and teaching the principles of *The Rule of Benedict*.

Fr. Mark designed a school structure wherein all St. Benedict's students would be organized into small and large groups of peers. Each group would require students to be held accountable for much of what they do together. Students are formed into small groups as soon as they enter St. Benedict's for freshman orientation. They are immediately engaged by older student leaders in exercises to learn each other's names, so they can get to know one another and, through continual practice each day, understand how to work together for the good of the group. All students are organized into an assembly of 18 groups with each group a microcosm of the school from youngest to seniors. This approach has shown its impact by enabling students to learn to use positive peer pressure to lead one another in meaningful ways in academic performance, involvement in school activities, and personal growth. The routine responsibilities of these groups include taking and reporting daily attendance, managing the daily schedule of student life, and arranging for peer counseling and tutoring (Holtz, 2016).

The continual practice of the behaviors that build strength in the school community are exhibited in many simple routines. The importance of each member is emphasized through each group's announcing attendance at convocation and all members of a student's group are expected to identify those missing and "track them down" if a pattern of absence or lateness is noticed. Groups meet several times each week to identify those who are struggling and provide tutoring and encouragement.

From their first moments in the school during freshman orientation, a student realizes that his participation will be important, that he will have to learn to work with his "teammates" and come to trust in them and in their selected or appointed leaders. Over time, the opportunities to develop and practice the skills of leadership are extended to every student in the school.

Each group is named after significant leaders in the school's past, teachers, headmasters, or coaches. The logic behind this emphasis on certain historic school figures and traditions probably needs little explanation. Many students come from families that have been fractured, from neighborhoods disrupted by violence or neglect, often from schools where even attendance is a big challenge and learning falls short of meaningful standards; for them to have a sense that they have joined a community that values its members is a powerful revelation. It is deliberately in contrast to the sense of aimlessness and pessimism that can be a constant experience of many students from the most impoverished urban areas or the most distressed families (Holtz, 2016).

All the emphasis on community intends to help these boys and young men come to a deeper sense of what value they have, as individuals and as members of a real community, that they are embraced by the school family and involved in a "cause" or purpose larger than themselves. Many of these lessons are learned through the constant exposure through daily school life. Through peer leadership and the power of example, new students come to grasp what is expected of them as members of the St. Benedict's community. They realize at certain moments that "what we need now is more important that what you want."

When Father Edwin says that "students run the school," he clearly means that students are expected to take charge and be responsible for maintaining a certain atmosphere and managing certain daily operations of the school. This can be a tricky, even risky, proposition for him and the adults in school, akin to a high-wire act without a net. Yet, it quickly becomes clear to these young leaders that he is also suggesting that in "running the school," students need to learn when to ask for help. Senior leaders, especially the Senior Group Leader, have the authority to change the day's schedule; for example, to call a second after-school convocation if attendance is a problem or the morning gathering was poorly organized. This approach can tax the patience of even the most attuned adults, whether in discipline situations or simply adjusting the schedule when the calculus teacher had a test scheduled. The senior leadership corps meets regularly with senior adult leaders, continually debriefing and gaining "on-the-job" training. This system has its obvious pitfalls when relying on teenagers to make the right calls. When they tackle a larger issue, "they better be right," Fr. Edwin says. "No one will come after a seventeen-year-old for a call he got wrong that affects us all" (Holtz, 2016, p. 35).

Over the past 10 years, the St. Benedict's model of student leadership came to the attention of the U.S. Naval Academy. The Academy became intrigued by the idea that involvement with our young men, just slightly younger than their youngest Navy enlistees, might be mutually beneficial. So we have had groups of 15 to 30 midshipmen nearing the end of their Academy training coming each spring and summer to assist our young leaders in learning to be leaders.

Counseling: Attacking the Nonacademic Causes of Academic Problems

One of the most important ways students learn to help one another is in urging those who appear to need it to seek help in our counseling programs. Being able to ask for support is one of the key lessons that students are expected to learn while growing as leaders at St. Benedict's. Thus, it is no surprise that student leaders have often been the ones to suggest directly to a student in his group, or through an adult, that a classmate or friend may benefit from counseling services, or "seeing Dr. Lamourt" in school shorthand. Pointing a group member or fellow student to the counseling center is often one of the most significant ways one student helps another.

The counseling center at St. Benedict's is staffed by two school psychologists, two full-time counselors, and several psychology interns from local universities. To respond to students' emotional needs, the counseling staff adopts a clinical approach while also utilizing the positive peer pressure that is already present among students. Counseling services vary from individual "one-on-one" counseling to group counseling sessions. The school is totally "up front" about them as a regular part of the school program. The group sessions, some with catchy names, focus on key adolescent concerns such as anger management, depression ("Blues Men"), and missing fathers ("Unknown Sons"). Group meetings are advertised each day on the school's electronic calendar. Students have the opportunity to support one another by sharing and listening to each other's stories of struggle with issues that may have been a source of anguish and a heavy emotional burden for years (Holtz, 2016).

Nothing adults can say about the value of counseling has as much power as student testimony. A few years ago, one student riveted a community assembly with his own story, how he overcame his reluctance to seek help and how the counselor he spoke to for many sessions over a year's time changed his life. His long-simmering anger about his father and the constant pain and hardship in his often destitute family periodically boiled over into self-destructive and inappropriate behavior in and out of school. Over time, with steady work with his trained counselor, he learned how to cope with his challenges and began turning his school life around. After St. Benedict's, he went on to graduate from a Catholic college in the Midwest and is now in graduate school. Not all student stories are so dramatic but the positive changes in the 200 or so students (about 40% of grades 9–12 students) who regularly benefit from such support are lasting and life-enhancing. Two students in the past decade received recognition and significant college scholarship help as National Horatio Alger Scholars. Both had overcome extraordinary hardship and achieved great success in school with help in our counseling center.

One of the motives for the school's creation of a student dorm for 60 students in 2000 was the opportunity to help more students with such issues by providing them more structure and more opportunities for informal counseling with caring adults. For students with more challenging problems, there is a special area of the dorm that uses a behavior management approach to help them develop more positive behaviors and cope with their issues and focus more effectively on their academic potential (Holtz, 2016).

Anyone who spends even a few minutes at St. Benedict's would quickly realize that much of this emphasis on a young man's emotional health comes from the top. Fr. Edwin seems to have specialized in a possibly unrecognized branch of cardiology focused on "expanding hearts." Sometimes appearing as "coach-in-chief" at morning convocation, Fr. Edwin's teaching has the feel of a pep talk, urging students to stay focused, to study diligently, and to fulfill their commitments to sports and other activities in the St. Benedict's community. "Hard work beats talent most of the time," he often declares. Students learn early on the value of determination and perseverance proclaimed in an old school motto: "Benedict's hates a quitter." Lapses are pointed out often, but so are improvements, large or small. Individual and group achievements are celebrated enthusiastically by the entire community at convocation or assemblies.

Conclusion: How Do We Measure Success for Our Students?

What proud, if not macho, 14-year-old boy from urban neighborhoods in Newark and its surrounding struggling suburbs would leap at the chance to come to an all-male school that requires him to attend school in the summer and does not have a football team? The question answers itself and points to one of our greatest ongoing challenges, retaining students once they walk in the door for the freshman "overnight," our week-long orientation program that serves as a rite of initiation to the school's structure, academic expectations, and traditions. Our admissions process quite deliberately seeks to understand how strongly a student desires to come, as well as the academic ability to succeed in the college prep curriculum. It asks for teacher recommendations from a core subject area. The admissions team examines the students' transcripts and personal essays. There is no admissions test. Over time, the focus is more and more on how best to keep students in school and working to achieve their potential for success with St. Benedict's. For veteran teachers, it is no shock that soon students realize that they will have to work harder than they ever have just to pass a challenging class. Many have not developed previously the determination to keep going and may tend to just drift along toward failure. Keeping the many "strugglers" trying is the major challenge to keeping them at St. Benedict's. The intentional design of the Freshman Year with the demands of starting with "The Overnight" and ending with "The Backpack Project," in which the entire class hikes the 47-mile section of Appalachian Trail in New Jersey, is to demonstrate as concretely as possible that they can succeed with determination and effort (Holtz, 2016).

While the Headmaster, as well as faculty, are skeptics of the usual measures of student success, they encourage all to take the SAT and the now popular alternative, the ACT, and help them prepare them for the tests. Results of such standardized tests provide some measure of our students' learning and achievement, and also a way of knowing how far they have to go to gain admission to and succeed at a broad range of selective schools that may be available to them and that continue to require high scores. In any given class, SAT scores and now often ACT scores, can range from the bare minimum ("good bowling scores," Fr. Edwin will say) to at or near the top.

St. Benedict's places considerable emphasis on encouraging students to pursue college as a passport for most to a better place than they inherited. Surely that is what their parents, guardians, or grandparents want for them. "We want choices, options for them," as Fr. Edwin stresses. On that measure, St. Benedict's students fare very well indeed. Nearly 100% of the 110 graduating seniors are admitted to at least one and often several of their choice of colleges. And as far back in our recent history as 1979, our top students have been admitted to such highly selective small colleges as Amherst, Bowdoin, and Swarthmore, and more recently, into the Ivies as well. A typical graduating class would show a distribution heaviest among New Jersey schools, with Rutgers predominating, and a very broad range of other schools, with the top 10–20% students admitted to and attending Amherst, Bates, Boston College, Bowdoin, Georgetown, Holy Cross, Lehigh, and Swarthmore, to name the most popular. The Ivies, including Cornell, Harvard, Penn, and Princeton, as well as Stanford, have accepted SBP students of exceptional ability in recent years.

While the school's statistics about recent college admissions success always draw attention, the measure with greater significance for faculty has come from several surveys taken based on rigorous research done of graduates from the last 15 years. That study, originally conducted with the classes of 2005 through 2014 and repeated again in 2016, showed that 84% of alumni from those years had earned degrees or were still pursuing them (Holtz, 2016). A portion of students at the most highly selective colleges and universities indicated that they had to struggle mightily, if not heroically, in their beginning classes but gradually improved their academic standing in the following years leading to graduation.

For Fr. Edwin, these the measures do not matter very much. For him, the most important measure of success is to see these young men go on to navigate adulthood successfully, to begin career paths, and to start families. "I can now call upon students I've served for any kind of advice I need, medical, legal, financial, architectural, you name it," he says to current students. But "to see alumni return to introduce me to their kids, to see that they have become good fathers," he readily says, is the most gratifying sign to him that St. Benedict's works.

As a result of a very powerful story about the school broadcast in 2016 by *60 Minutes*, St. Benedict's has now garnered a national reputation for its unique way of teaching and developing young men. Since *60 Minutes*, St. Benedict's has been much sought after for advice about how to improve schools and school programs across the country and beyond. In response, the school has formed the Vox Institute. The Vox (Latin for "voice") Institute has been established to help schools and other education program leaders develop school models, school leadership structures, and programs to encourage and strengthen student voices in their schools. The Vox Institute has already been contacted by schools and programs in Wisconsin, Maryland, Oklahoma, and New Jersey, to name a few. This system has enabled St. Benedict's to help young men, often at-risk, to develop and magnify their voices, while also providing them with opportunities to grow into themselves and into meaningful roles as leaders. Through the Vox Institute, St. Benedict's Prep is committed to sharing its model with schools on a national level.

Perhaps the following message sent by a former student to Fr. Edwin after a recent young alumni gathering will convey St. Benedict's perspective on success in a meaningful way.

> I probably (definitely) should have said this a long time ago, but last night was as good an inspiration as any to actually let you know how important Benedict's was to me.
>
> I still remember the essay topics we had when we were applying. Even though I didn't write the happy life essay, the fact that Benedict's cared about a happy life stuck with me, especially as I began to learn what a happy life would be. I never remember hearing about making money (although we knew that, when we did make money, a new generation of kids would need our support). Instead, we heard and saw that whatever happiness we would have would be a result of loving each other and the people around us, and doing meaningful things.
>
> On that note, we learned that we had a purpose in life. That we had God-given talents and it was our moral duty to do everything in our power to get the most out of those talents, and to use those talents to make a difference in the world.
>
> I think I'm stubborn and idealistic enough that I was kind of thinking this way before I got to Benedict's, and I know I wasn't always the easiest person to reach, but the Benedict's message has inspired me in everything I do now. As a teacher, I've had some successes and some failures (I think/hope more successes). I know that, when I've been successful, it's been when I stole/adapted what I'd learned about education from Benedict's. While I still have an unhealthy ego, I've come to know that I'm standing on the shoulders of giants, and my success has a lot more to do with my ability to follow your lead than anything I can come up with myself. Or at least adapt your lead and make it work in what is a much different school.
>
> I work at a deeply cynical school. Most of the people around me can't think past a dollar sign. They encourage students to spend as little possible, make as much as possible, keep their mouths shut, and not take chances. Obviously, I'll never buy into that value system, and I've done my best to communicate Benedictine ideals to my students, even if I don't get to call them that.
>
> While I'm not in Benedict's every day, I need Benedict's every day. When I start to question what I'm doing, when I start to wonder if I'm crazy and all the people around me are sane, I remember that, if I'm crazy, so are you, and so is Fr. Al, and Mr. Burokas, and Ms. Flynn, and Fr. Mark and Fr. Boniface certainly were. I know that when I stay late, Mr. Scanlan and Cass are still in the building, and you LIVE in the building. I know that I'm

the person I am because a group of good people trusted that the Rule of St. Benedict was timeless, no matter what the world looked like, and that morality and idealism would always make a difference, no matter how cynical the world became. While too many of the people I talk to every day may disagree, when I need to, I can still hear the lessons I heard in high school, and I try to be the person I wanted to be/you wanted me to be.

Thanks for pushing me to be the best person I could be. Thanks for giving all of us a chance, and for believing in us. On a personal note, thanks for loving me and putting up with me even when I made it difficult. You said last night that alumni were the reminder that Benedict's works. As a teacher, I know the feeling (I also know from experience that Benedict's works A LOT better than damn near every other school). So, as an alumnus, I just wanted to let you know that Benedict's inspires me every day, and I hope/ believe that I'm doing something right with that inspiration.

Thanks, DK '03[2]

NOTES

1. Fr. Edwin no doubt had the Biblical significance of this in mind.
2. *Letter to Fr. Edwin D. Leahy, O.S.B.* (February 3, 2017). Used with permission.

REFERENCES

Chittister, J. (2010). *The Rule of Benedict: A spirituality for the 21st century*. New York, NY: Crossroad.

Holtz, A. T. (Ed.). (2016). *Creating a successful urban school culture: A summary of the principles, programs, and practices of St. Benedict's Preparatory School*. Self-published manual.

McCabe, T. A. (2011). *Miracle on High Street: The rise, fall, and resurrection of St. Benedict's Prep in Newark, NJ*. New York, NY: Fordham University Press.

Payne, M. M., OSB. (1994). *SBP memorandum*. Newark, NJ: St. Benedict's Preparatory School Archives.

St. Benedict's Preparatory School. (2017a). About SBP. Retrieved from https://www.sbp.org/about/about-sbp

St. Benedict's Preparatory School. (2017b). Facts at a glance. Retrieved from https://www.sbp.org/about/facts-at-a-glance

CHAPTER 5

THE CATALYST MODEL

Catholic Inspired Urban Charter

Mike Fehrenbach
Christian Brothers of the Midwest

Ed Siderewicz
Catalyst Schools

History: The Invitation

If the superintendent of the nation's third largest school district approached you and made a request, would you say "no?" We said "no" not once, but on four separate occasions. Paul Vallas was the first Chicago Public Schools' (CPS) superintendent who asked us at San Miguel to consider replication as a charter school. He was followed by Arne Duncan, the former Secretary of Education for President Barack Obama, who continued to make Chicago Public Schools' desire for San Miguel, founded in 1995, to replicate as a charter clearly part of the bureaucracy's agenda (Fehrenbach, 2016).

San Miguel School is sponsored and owned by the De La Salle Christian Brothers, meaning that the school is Catholic and dedicated to the human and Christian education of the young, especially the poor. The fear and, as a result, the hesitation about extension into the charter sector was about a loss of identity. The question was: How can a public charter school fulfill the mission that was initiated in 1680 by the first group of

Responding to the Call for Educational Justice:
Transformative Catholic-Led Initiatives in Urban Education, pp. 73–92
Copyright © 2019 by Information Age Publishing
All rights of reproduction in any form reserved.

Christian brother teachers when that mission has the values of the Gospel as a central component of its raison d'être? This was the key element in the reflection undertaken by the leaders of San Miguel and the leadership of the Christian Brothers of the Midwest.

Superintendent Duncan met with the San Miguel leadership on several occasions and had frank and open conversations around finding a way to join the public school system without compromising our identity. The relationship Duncan built with the brothers was a call to take the request more seriously and not disregard it without further contemplation and dialogue, both internally and with CPS (Fehrenbach, 2016).

Duncan was not offering the invitation out of some naïve belief that it would be free of conflict. Duncan believed that there was one common enemy and that was academic failure; those engaged in educational reform efforts have one common goal and that is academic success for more students (Fehrenbach, 2016). Duncan knew that whoever can create more high quality seats for children, particularly focused on our most disadvantaged, those providers needed to be partners in the education of all our children regardless of sector. Duncan was challenging San Miguel leadership to be innovative, creative, and flexible, to find ways to get to "yes," rather than find ways to get to "no" (Fehrenbach, 2016).

When the possibility of collaborating with the CPS was up for final discussion in the Brothers' Provincial Council, former Superior General, Br. John Johnston laid out a rationale to pursue the experiment. His intervention was an iteration of the words of Pope John Paul II (1979/2014) in the *Catechesi Tradendae* to do what we can in the situations in which we find ourselves. In hindsight, it seems so simple. Yet, it was the First Amendment to the United States Constitution up against our own limited viewpoint regarding Catholic schools that caused us hesitation.

In addition to Johnston's intervention, what finally moved us to action to request collaboration with CPS was the consensus that there was really no way to find out if this could be done in the abstract. The only way we would know if we could fulfill our mission, with integrity, in the public realm was to make an effort to do so.

Six years later, San Miguel leadership agreed to submit an application to CPS for a charter. Duncan agreed that he would be supportive of that effort, given our application satisfied the State requirements governing charters. And so, in 2005, we began a journey toward collaboration with CPS that continues to this day (Fehrenbach, 2016).

A Journey Begins

The first step, with many to follow, was to seek out Catholic or other religious organizations that had attempted the same thing, creating a public school founded on specifically religious values. In 2005, we could find no blueprints, as there were no previously charted courses we could follow. It was up to us to clear away the brush and the rocks and find our own way. If, after giving the effort 100%, we found out that we could not function in the public system while being true to ourselves and our founding inspiration, we would simply withdraw.

The first proposal for charter was crafted in 2005, where the basic principles of the San Miguel model we were going to replicate included: a faith-based school that provided a human and Christian education for the young, especially the poor; an outreach program to families and to the larger community; a graduate support system that followed our graduates into their subsequent educational levels; a strong board focused on development and mission alignment; and a quality educational program that prepared students for life (Brinig & Garnett, 2014).

These principles were replicated from the San Miguel School located in Chicago, a middle school serving grades six through eight. While the San Miguel School was successful at bringing students with significant academic deficits to grade level and beyond, with the proposed charter we hoped to be able to bring children into the system earlier, eliminate the achievement gap before it developed and support them in their advancement. Given this desire to reach students earlier, we decided to request a charter for an elementary school, kindergarten through eighth grade. Beyond the more ambitious grade level spread, the intent was to implement the rest of the San Miguel model as it existed in the middle school with a primary focus on providing a human and Christian education for the young, especially the poor (Fehrenbach, 2016). Reaching the poor would be no problem because the targeted neighborhood was the Austin community that fell into economic and social poverty, in part, because of the white flight that took place in Chicago in the 1960s. The issue which stared us in the face was how to provide the Christian education when the first amendment to the United States Constitution has been interpreted as prohibiting promotion of any specific religion in government sponsored agencies, like public schools. It took several months to write an application and our days were filled with editing, revising, and many conversations with consultants. Ultimately, the charter was granted in 2005 (Fehrenbach, 2016).

The Curve Ball

As part of the approval process, CPS threw us a curve ball when it said we could get the charter we wanted but, they also wanted us to accept a second school. They would give us the charter, but it would not be granted for the Austin community that we knew and where we had anchored relationships because of a San Miguel School that already existed there. Instead, we were invited to open the charter in the North Lawndale community on Chicago's west side. If we opened in North Lawndale first, we would be given a contract for a second school in the Austin neighborhood.

At the time, there were minor differences between charter and contract. The state of Illinois had a small number of charters available because they capped the number they would grant. The contract option was the way CPS managed to open additional schools without the State increasing the cap. We had spent 6 years considering this option and by now spent additional time and money writing the application for charter and in our naiveté said go for it. The consequences of this decision had significant impact for several years into the operation of the small system of schools we were creating (Fehrenbach, 2016).

Desired Outcomes

Our intentions and motivations were pure and innocent: we wanted to bridge the private religious school/public secular school divide. Following years of reflection, it was a mystery to us that there should be conflict between the two worlds. We believed we could bring the values of a private, religious school to the secular world. To bridge the divide, we designed a management structure that would provide administrative and support services to both the San Miguel and the chartered Catalyst corporate structures. La Salle Education Network (LEN) was what we called the independent management structure where we had three 501(c)(3) systems we attempted to bring into collaboration. The independent management structure was an effort to cut administrative costs for both school systems and to keep mission at the core of all the schools' activities and programming (Fehrenbach, 2016).

The Catalyst charter schools would be genuine and authentic public schools that would not violate the separation clause. The culture of the schools would be rooted in the values that have inspired the schools the De La Salle Christian Brothers have operated for more than 300 years, those values being: community, relationship, rigor, respect, results, and hope. There would be no religious teaching, no indoctrination; no evangelization or proselytizing would take place. Rather, a priority component would be character formation through a program called Character Counts that is built on the following six pillars: Trustworthiness, Respect, Responsibility, Fairness, Caring, and Citizenship (Christian Brothers Conference, 2012). As we envisioned the schools, these character traits would infuse the culture, be embedded in all programming, and ultimately become the vehicle through which we nurtured the atmosphere we successfully created in the private schools the Christian Brothers had operated for decades.

The First of Several Surprises

The first Catalyst school opened in 2006 and it was the beginning of many lessons. We quickly discovered a hostile political environment in North Lawndale. Apparently, CPS had asked several charter operators to move into North Lawndale and use the former George Howland School of the Arts as the site for a new charter. Residents of the neighborhood were resentful that the school had been closed and consequently at least two other charter operators were refused access. We were not told this information, possibly because CPS believed that we would be able to bring some calm to the situation and successfully get the community behind us. However, as we worked with the community's Transition Advisory Committee, and engaged other community groups, community forums became contentious. The popular belief permeating elements of the community was that there was a conspiracy between CPS and the Chicago city government to gentrify North Lawndale which sits in the shadows cast by the Willis tower. With more wealth, the tax base of the neighborhood would be more valuable to the city and opposition groups believed bringing in the charter was the first step in the gentrification process (Fehrenbach, 2016). There were times when the police were called to quell the anger of some community members, especially a group called the Voice of the Ex-Con that represented the several thousand Lawndale citizens who had experienced imprisonment.

Fortunately for us, after these contentious meetings we were able to share the San Miguel School as our model. We took North Lawndale residents to our San Miguel campus, let them talk to parents, sit in classrooms, meet teachers, feel the school's climate and culture, and see what we intended with Catalyst. When they witnessed the comportment of our San Miguel students, experienced the calm and politeness of the children with one another and their teachers, they said, "That's what we want for our children too." The residents allowed us to open (Fehrenbach, 2016).

Additional Surprises, Critical Errors, and Challenges

One of the most critical errors we made was making the assumption that the San Miguel Board and the administrative team, charged by the Board with starting Catalyst, shared a common understanding of what the relationship between San Miguel and Catalyst would be. Unfortunately, this was not so, and the difference in the way everyone understood the relationship became a serious problem for Catalyst when it needed stability to create a solid foundation. The San Miguel Board wanted to simply spin Catalyst off and be done with it. Those of us working to develop Catalyst operated under the erroneous assumption that the San Miguel Board wanted a long-term relationship. This placed La Salle Education Network in jeopardy from day 1 and we spent 2 years trying to effectively disengage from a relationship in which the San Miguel Board did not want to participate. This was a serious distraction from the many things involved in a start-up.

We were also naive in thinking we were capable of opening two schools in 2 years as we did not have sufficient administrative and support capacity to take on so much. After the first several months there were only two of us on the administrative staff to get the new school going. The bench was not deep, and the challenges were multiple. These challenges included:

Student Enrollment and Culture

Because San Miguel worked exclusively with middle school children and we were not certain about a primary school curriculum, we decided to begin with fourth and fifth grade and then grow the school at both ends year-by-year, fourth grade down to kindergarten and at the same time fifth up to eighth. That gave us an additional year to plan a primary curriculum. By year 5 we would have 500 students. The mistake we made was that we did not take into account that other local schools might see this as an opportunity to encourage their "problem" children to move to the new school. We received many children with more emotional-behavioral issues and special education needs than anticipated. This immediately made the establishment of the kind of culture we wanted more difficult (Fehrenbach, 2016).

We also determined 30 students per room provided a multitude of issues that made it difficult to grow our culture. It took San Miguel multiple years to establish its culture and reputation in the community and we were trying to do the same within months. We had to find appropriate adjustments that would make it possible to provide better classroom management and teacher satisfaction as we began the journey.

An additional issue with student enrollment was the fact that some parents did not want to split their children between two schools. If they had a fifth-grade child and a second-grade child they preferred a school that could accommodate both. In response to parents' desires, we decided to ramp up more quickly by filling in grades Kindergarten through third grade faster than we initially anticipated. This would give us the advantage of additional time to prepare students and to acculturate them to the values central to the proposed educational system. It also meant, of course, more parents could choose Catalyst for their family.

Testing

State testing was a second issue that had a lasting impact on the development of the first school, Catalyst-Howland (the North Lawndale campus).

Catalyst-Howland had to administer the State of Illinois standardized test (ISAT) only several months into the first year. While we did not have opportunity to teach the inaugural enrollment for even a full year, we had to own the test results of the ISAT and the scores were not good. Given these scores, the CPS oversight increased and the pressure on administrators and teachers multiplied (Fehrenbach, 2016).

Leadership and Staffing

We hired an experienced administrator (35 years in educational administration) who had worked at one of the De La Salle Christian Brothers high schools to be principal of Catalyst-Howland. This person was intimately familiar with our core values, had been to many training programs, was committed to the mission, and had the desire to lead the school. We thought this was a good fit since we needed an anchor for the school's culture. The kind of relationships that needed to be developed with neighborhood organizations and students' families did not happen as required and conflicts emerged that took months to resolve. We learned that a cultural divide existed that proved to be too wide to bridge.

We also learned quickly that staffing patterns used at the San Miguel School did not work effectively at Catalyst-Howland. The San Miguel model proposed thirty students per class with two teachers and an aide. At Catalyst-Howland, we discovered that the two teachers typically found it difficult to create a team and in fact split the workload so that each of them was teaching half time for full time pay. This was not the kind of team teaching we wanted to see develop. In the following year we changed the system so there was one teacher and one aide, which was a more effective use of resources.

Bureaucracy

When operating an independent, private, Catholic school the level of bureaucratic interference is minimal. Of course, there is always the (Arch) diocesan Office of Education that implements standards, but the system is more relational than what we found in the bureaucracy of a very large city educational structure. It took a long time to learn how the system functions, who the key players were, and the internal politics of 125 Clark Street where the Chicago Public Schools offices are located.

Part of the problem was that CPS was not convinced of the way it was going to relate to the charter movement. Charters were tossed from office to office for management and the cast of city players changed regularly. In the first 9 years, we had five superintendents and were assigned multiple liaisons with CPS, none of whom really understood what was going on. With each change, the rules also changed. It was a challenge to learn how the game was going to be played.

Politics

The Chicago Teachers' Union was not shy about expressing its animosity toward the charter movement. Charters are not required to unionize and only a few of the charter networks in Chicago are part of the union. The bargains made between city and state government and the union often puts charters at some disadvantage. For example, the initial charter law allowed charters to self-replicate. One charter could include multiple campuses. This changed by the time we opened and each of our campuses had to have its own charter. This meant applying for a charter each time we wanted to open a new campus. Also, charters do not get the same level of funding as traditional Chicago public schools. To this day, the City of Chicago and the Teachers' Union representatives are engaged in a battle that frequently spills over and everyone in the system including families and children suffer the impact.

We were learning a great deal about ourselves as we entered this process. We were also learning that no relationship is easy and the relationship with Chicago Public Schools amidst the political realities of the city of Chicago could not be built on the initial fervor and the positive motivation of providing good education to students in impoverished neighborhoods. It was clearly going to take work.

What Was Different the Second Time Around?

As we prepared to open a second school (Catalyst-Circle Rock in the Austin neighborhood) in 2007, we were able to apply many things we had learned from the earlier mistakes we made. This included such things as hiring a principal 6 months prior to opening Catalyst-Circle Rock and housing her at Catalyst-Howland where she was able to study the issues we were encountering. An experienced and knowledgeable elementary school teacher and leader who had experience in Chicago Public Schools, she was trained by New Leaders for New Schools. She had sufficient time to plan the curriculum and form a leadership team that could build an effective community of teachers, families, and students in the second school. Given her ability to understand and embrace the mission and values and her ability to design and develop strategies to implement them, the launch of our second school went more smoothly.

The site for Catalyst-Circle Rock was not an abandoned stand-alone public school like Catalyst-Howland; rather it was the home of a small

Christian Academy. The owners liked our sense of mission and our values and because of the De La Salle Brothers' long tradition in running excellent schools around the globe, thought we could run a better school than they were currently operating. They closed their school, which gave us the opportunity to open Catalyst-Circle Rock as a K–8 school.

We also more effectively established the culture of the school from day one because of the leadership team we formed during the 6 months previous to opening and the lessons they learned by observing Catalyst-Howland. We picked up a number of students from the previous Christian Academy who applied to the new contract school. The culture embedded in the school they previously attended was not totally dissimilar from the one we were establishing. They did not experience the same culture shock our first students at Catalyst-Howland experienced and were not resistant to the discipline and the relationships we intended for teachers to have with their students.

In opening a second school, we faced a variety of challenges that ranged from hiring the right teachers to engaging the community. Despite these challenges, which many schools face, in 2012 the third school, Catalyst-Maria, opened in Chicago's Marquette Park-Chicago Lawn community. Catalyst-Maria has just over 1,100 students in grades kindergarten through senior year in high school. We fortunately avoided many of the pitfalls we stumbled into when opening Catalyst-Howland in 2006. When Chicago Public Schools, in their wisdom, determined it benefited the North Lawndale community to build a brand new school on the same block as Catalyst-Howland, we decided to close that school. In our judgment, North Lawndale was once an educational desert but now has more seats than children to fill them. Catalyst schools currently educate more than 1,600 students each year and there has been great interest around the country in the model we created and continue to refine. Among the communities that have begun a faith-inspired charter or are exploring the possibility of doing so are: St. Louis, Tulsa, Sacramento, New York City, Kansas City, MO, and Oakland.

Catalyst's Appeal

What is it about Catalyst that attracts attention? First, we attempt to be transparent about our failures. No one need repeat our mistakes. We are willing to share our experience with anyone who wants to learn about it. Second, we serve the urban poor and statistics show we have done it successfully. For example:

- 100% of the class of 2015 were accepted by colleges and universities;

- The high school graduation rate is 98% compared to the neighbor-hood average of 50% and the city of Chicago Public Schools overall rate of 66% (The Catalyst Schools, 2016b);
- 93% of the freshmen are on track to successfully complete their year and freshmen who are on track are four times more likely to graduate from high school (Roderick, Kelley-Kemple, Johnson, & Beechum, 2014);
- 32% of the high school students are in dual enrollment and are receiving college credit prior to enrolling in a college.

Third, and maybe most important, we come from a more than 300 year old tradition of Catholic education that has been innovative, creative, and true to its founding vision. The inspiration of St. John Baptist de La Salle, who started the movement with his first band of teachers, has captured the imagination of so many educators around the world that they have taken his name and call themselves "Lasallians."

The Tradition

What is central to the Catholic Lasallian tradition that gives shape to the educational enterprise and that we have attempted to embed in the culture at Catalyst? De La Salle was gradually drawn to serve poor unsupervised children who roamed the streets of his home town, Reims, France. They frequently engaged in delinquent behavior, had no one to care about them, lived with dirt and hunger, and had no prospect for a secure future. He was confronted by the cycle of poverty. De La Salle grew in the conviction that education was the way out of poverty and that a human and Christian education was what poor children needed in order to be saved. The schools he helped organize and then founded were dedicated to the salvation of youth. For St. de La Salle, salvation had two distinct yet related components.

First, salvation was not seen as some distant reality that existed in another world. These children needed a way to make a life for themselves in the present. Hunger is real. Homelessness is real. Passing inappropriate and dysfunctional behavior from generation to generation dooms the future for countless numbers. Therefore, salvation meant the school was to provide every opportunity to learn the skills required for gainful employment and the ability to earn an income that would sustain the young as they grew to adulthood. The expectation was that they would become productive, contributing members of society who could care not only for themselves but for their own families. In De La Salle's historical moment such things as accounting, penmanship, math, and reading were critical skills that led to employment and these subjects were taught.

Second, salvation meant that not only would these children learn to do good things with their lives but would become good people. Salvation was about conversion in the sense of turning their lives around and transforming their hearts. Central to the transformation De La Salle envisioned was a relationship with Jesus who embodied the love and passion of God for humanity. He was convinced that in learning the precepts of faith, the poor unsupervised children would be led to the kind of relationship with Jesus that would raise them up and lead them to a life built on the "Golden Rule": Treat others as you would have them treat you. Employable skills and love of God and neighbor would ultimately change the social structure that led to institutionalized poverty in 17th century France. De La Salle believed the school was about excellent and practical content but more than that, it was a school for life. The excellent school addresses the "whole child" in a comprehensive way: physically, intellectually, emotionally, psychologically, socially, and spiritually. To ignore any of these human components is to short change the child and consequently, the society in which the child participates.

In the tradition begun with St. John Baptist de LaSalle, a school has high academic expectations and produces measurable results, is an incubator of faith, a work of justice, and an inclusive community built on mutual respect. It is a living organism built on a network of healthy relationships. The Lasallian community has articulated these values as central to the tradition. They might be stated uniquely in different cultures and settings but the fundamental reality remains.

Core Values

Faith and Gospel Values

These are central to the identity of a Catholic school and present a challenge when operating a public school where we cannot promote religion. We found that telling the story of De La Salle and his early community of teachers, who called themselves brothers, is important. When faculty, administrators, and staff learn the story, they see that they are working with children and families not very different from those encountered by the early brothers. Leadership at Catalyst, a faith-inspired school rising from the Lasallian tradition, nurtures vocation in the members of the educational community it places before the students. Teachers come into the classroom as models of healthy adult living and as whole human beings committed to something beyond self-interest. They convey the message that love is the core of the Gospel and becoming love is the transformation preached by Jesus. At Catalyst, faith-inspired means creating a community in which people know who they are, function with integrity, live for the good of the children entrusted to their care by parents who rely on us to be about their child's well-being. It means leading students to their best selves and to a life built on integrity.

Research (Proehl, Starnes, & Everett, 2015) has shown that Catalyst Schools reflect the essential elements of Catholic schools as enumerated by the Catholic Institute for Education (CIE). These include welcoming everyone, a commitment to diversity and social justice, fostering positive relationships, mutual respect, the formation of the whole child, a strong Gospel-based value system, high expectations for success, and a relevant and broad curriculum. Findings from interviews and reviews of internal documents from this study showed that, except for explicit references to faith, the Catalyst Schools met the other criteria identified by the Catholic Institute of Education. The missing element was worship and prayer.

Academic Excellence

This is key to a successful school. If the school is not providing a quality education, it is not fulfilling its mission. In the established tradition of Lasallian schools, excellence involves curriculum, assessment, preparation for further education, and higher level critical thinking skills. It also involves understanding the context in which the students live and what they bring with them to the classroom each day. Excellence is ultimately about relationship. De La Salle frequently spoke to his teachers about the nature of the relationship they were to have with their students. The early teaching community came to believe they could not effectively teach a student they did not know. It was the relationship that taught the teacher what worked toward the student's advancement, what kind of discipline the student responded to most positively, how to engage the child's family, if the child had food or was consistently hungry, or if the child slept. The relationship also generated trust on the part of the child for the teacher. The teacher-student relationship itself became the sacramental and sacred ground that permitted teaching and learning. In this context, De La Salle convinced his teachers that they were Guardian Angels who protected their children from physical and spiritual harm. It was an intimate relationship that promoted the well-being and the good of the child. After the initial 35 years, the first Lasallian teaching community codified and published in print its best practices in what was called The Conduct of the Christian Schools.

Benefits to Student Achievement

At Catalyst-Circle Rock, in Chicago's west side Austin neighborhood, 515 African American students attend. Of all students who have graduated, 88% have gone on to graduate from high school compared to the 47%

average for the neighborhood and the 66% average for all Chicago Public School students (The Catalyst Schools, 2016a; U.S. Census Bureau, 2010). Moreover, Catalyst's graduation rate is trending upwards as 97% of its graduates over the last 4 years are persevering through high school today.

Also impressive is the 97% daily attendance rate at Catalyst's Circle Rock campus (The Catalyst Schools, 2016a). When it comes to both near- and long-term benefits, these are our best statistical measures of success. Having undergone three major testing rubrics in the last 5 years (from Illinois Standards Achievement Test to Northwest Evaluation Association to Partnership for Assessment of Readiness for College and Careers), there is no better and consistent indication of statistical success.

At Catalyst-Maria, our K–12 school with just over 1,100 students (50% Latino and 49% African American) benefits to students are evidenced by these facts:

- $103,007 average scholarship awards received per student from colleges in 2016 ($13,596,880 total received for 132 students as of March 9, 2016);
- 22% of the class of 2016 received full college scholarships;
- 10 is the average number of college visits for each student during both junior and senior years;
- 69% of Catalyst-Maria's high school graduates are currently attending college (The Catalyst Schools, 2016b).

These accomplishments, which far exceed city-wide averages, tell just part of our students' success stories that unfold over a longer term. For example, Darius's score of 23 on his ACT and involvement in other activities earned him a full ride at the University of Michigan. While he achieved some academic success, he was also a Catalyst college seminar leader, participated in Future Leaders of Chicago, a program sponsored by the University of Chicago, and earned two semesters of dual enrollment credit through a collaboration with Daley College. Darius's mother could not support him as a child and so at age 5, his great grandmother began raising him. This meant he had to move from Chicago to Indiana. She died in 2007 and he had to move back to Chicago to live with his aunt. He wanted to study in a diverse environment and through his investigation of various opportunities, he found Catalyst. Now he credits the college exploration course, ACT Prep, and his senior seminar with helping him get where he is today. He is the first in his family to graduate from high school and the first to go on to college.

Another example is Gloria. She was part of the first group of National Honor Students at Catalyst. She not only focused on academics but was a member of the volleyball team, the yearbook staff, and the book club.

Gloria scored a 23 on the ACT and had a 3.73 cumulative GPA. Her passion for animals led her to the zoology club and animal science and went on to study zoology at Western Illinois University in the fall of 2016. Her family members are not documented but she was born in the United States and is a citizen. When she was in the eighth grade she saw how hard life was for her older sisters and realized she wanted to excel and to benefit from hard work. She has put all of her energy into her study and life at Catalyst and now sees her future as a zookeeper at Brookfield Zoo in the Chicago area where she can work with the big cats. Gloria found in Catalyst a pathway to discover and fulfill her dreams.

Respect

Respect is central to human relationship. De La Salle told his teachers as they formed their practice:

> You should learn to recognize Jesus beneath the rags of the poor children whom you have to teach. Adore him in their person. Cherish poverty and honor the poor, after the example of the Magi, for poverty should be amiable in your eyes since you are engaged in instructing the poor. (Loes & Huether, 1994/2007, p. 99)

The central point of De La Salle's meditation is that the poor deserve respect. They deserve to be properly cared for. He wanted his brother teachers to see each child as worthy of their love and he often asked his brothers to love their students, each one, and to know them and the context in which they were growing up. This is why he embraced poverty and why he wanted his teachers to embrace poverty as well. Because they were teachers in their heart and because they were called first and foremost to serve the poor, they wanted nothing to be between them and those to whom they dedicated their lives (Loes & Huether, 1994/2007). No ambition, no desire to possess things, nothing was more important than the children who needed caring, loving adults who were totally dedicated to their growth in knowledge and spiritual wholeness. His concern was respect. Each and every child deserved to be known, appreciated, taught, disciplined, guided, nurtured, and given every opportunity for a full life (Loes & Huether, 1994/2007).

Respect returns us to the way in which De La Salle understood the values of the Gospel. He constantly called his brothers to remember they lived and breathed the presence of God. If we look closely at the Gospel, that presence throughout is about love. When the school is built on respect, it is infused with love for the students. When it is infused with love for the students it lives in what De La Salle named the presence of God. Whatever we choose to call it, we attempt to the best of our ability to walk into its reality and invite our students to be about love as well.

Malcolm felt the respect at Catalyst. In his own words, he described what it looked like:

I started at Catalyst when I was in the 4th grade, and was part of Catalyst's first graduating class in 2010. Catalyst has helped me to prepare for high school, as they had outstanding teachers and staff who actually cared for us and made sure we got the best education possible. Teachers would stay late after school if you needed extra help. I remember Mrs. Greer who worked with me in math and told me never to be afraid to ask for help when I needed it. This taught me a life lesson, as one will always need help with something in life and it's okay to ask for help when we don't understand something.

During my years in high school, Catalyst staff still stayed in touch with me to ensure I stayed on track and had all the resources I needed to do well. Today I am working for the Boys and Girls Club while I am pursuing my career as a Chicago Police Officer. This has always been my dream. I took my initial Chicago Police Department exam recently and am still in contact with some of the Catalyst staff as I begin this new journey in life.

Community

The school is never an amalgamation of isolated individuals but rather is always about community. Connection, collaboration, and building bonds of trust make a school function well. Healthy communities are built on respect and the trust it engenders. Schools are familial realities much more than they are business enterprises. They are personal experiences to which children bring family and neighborhood drama, in which they live the relationship drama of friendship and learn what it means to have impact in each other's life.

In his Meditations, De La Salle (Loes & Huether, 2007) reflected on the importance of community frequently. He encouraged his teachers with these words:

the virtue that ought to stand out most in community is charity and union of hearts.... What ought to inspire us most to achieve this, as Saint John says, is that those who live in love live in God, and God lives in them. Are you united with your brothers? Do you speak to them and treat them with love? Do you pay too much attention to your dislikes and antipathies? Deepen within you the conviction that in community you ought to live anew the spirit of the first Christians, who were all of one heart and one mind. (p. 211)

Throughout his encouragement to these first brother teachers these sentiments occur. The foundation of community is love. For a school that claims the tradition of the Lasallian movement, the effort to build common bonds of respect and love must be intentional. They are two building blocks that precede academic excellence because without them, excellence is shallow and one dimensional. Community built on genuine concern, compassion, and love ultimately teaches the young student how to be in the world, how to be a good moral and authentically spiritual person.

In a community built upon genuine love for the well-being of others, we learn what it means to be humble servants. This is what Catalyst means when it makes a commitment to forming citizens who give back to their neighborhood, city, and country, agents of change. De La Salle often spoke of humility as one of the cornerstones of love and community. Without humility our relationships can become contentious and filled with irritation and disquiet.

This is how the Lasallian educational community understands salvation. Clearly we provide every opportunity to develop the skills required for a productive and sustaining life but do not stop at that. We hold up the expectation of our vocation that we have been called to teach youth about the demands of love, the importance of giving back, the challenges that can be successfully met as we gradually grow in understanding our unity with all of our brothers and sisters. The school is an incubator that assists families in raising up the next generation who we hope will build a better world.

Germaine's mother offered a reflection on how community is central to the way Catalyst functions and extends to the students' families.

> Because of Catalyst, High Jump, and Daniel Murphy Scholarship, my son is experiencing a life-altering change that is all good. While at Catalyst, the staff got him into the caddie program during the summers. During the past three summers, he has earned money that he is saving for his future. Not only did Catalyst help my son but they have helped me as a mother. Catalyst partners with parents to make sure their children succeed. Germaine writes music, wants to be a producer, and plans to go to Marquette University. This is his dream. I never had these opportunities because my mother was barely able to have a roof over us and food on the table. I am thrilled for my son to have these opportunities that I never had.

De La Salle was no fool. He fully understood the human dynamic and the drama of human relationships. It is why he constantly called his teachers to account and frequently nurtured the sentiments of kindness, self-denial, charity and disinterestedness in them. These qualities build cohesion and peace.

Social Justice

Catalyst schools are a work of justice and as such become one path out of economic poverty that can breed destruction. We have operated the Lasallian Schools, including the San Miguel schools and the Catalyst Schools, because they are where our gift meets the world's need. Education that promotes higher level critical thinking, understanding moral behavior, a sense of community, and respect for others is life- and world-changing. As then Secretary Duncan articulated in a 2009 speech: "I believe that education is the civil rights issue of our generation. And if you care about promoting opportunity and reducing inequality, the classroom is the place to start. Great teaching is about so much more than education; it is a daily fight for social justice."

It is not only part of our Gospel belief, it is even part of the U.S. Conference of Catholic Bishops' (2005) statement on justice through which we are compelled to live and act with justice. Our sense of justice is rooted in the belief that every person has inherent value and worth. Our commitment to justice means we live and work every day in ways that reveal, grow, and enhance human dignity.

Catalyst intentionally targets underserved and economically challenged communities. The Catalyst Schools website (2018) identified the student body in this way: over 90% of the scholar population of Catalyst Schools qualifies for the Federal free and reduced-price meals program, and scholars range in age from 5 to 18. The campuses are serving over 1,600 scholars during the 2017–2018 school year, 98% of the students come from minority populations that have been disenfranchised and abused for generations through discrimination by individuals and systems. Catalyst's mission is to work within communities as a partner in lifting up a new generation so it can effectively build a positive future.

In the article that appeared in *The Journal of Catholic Education* by Proehl and colleagues (2015), they stated:

> While interviewees made recommendations to improve Catalyst Schools, there was universal agreement about one point: The Catalyst Schools provide hope for the children and communities in Chicago's poor neighborhoods. The level of urgency surrounding the need to help the children was palpable for the individuals we interviewed. For example, one young teacher declared, "Our mission is so much greater because literally I feel like our work can be the difference between life and death of some students." She went on to accentuate, "It's too important to be taken lightly or to trivialize by saying our goal is to get kids in college. No, we need to change the world." (p. 149)

Justice is not simply a theory or a dogmatic directive. It is a way of life. At Catalyst it is part of the fabric.

Look at Carlito. He was brought to the United States when he was only nine months old and remains undocumented. He is part of the Dreamer's Club and has great dreams in spite of our political climate. With a 4.78

cumulative GPA and a 30 on the ACT, he should qualify for wonderful opportunities. He has earned dual credits and has a head start on a college career. He hopes to attend the University of Illinois at Chicago after finishing two years at Daley Community College through the STAR scholarship. Carlito and his family lived in a basement when they came to the United States. Finding work was a challenge for his father but eventually he became a landscaper and they have finally found a home. Carlito came to Catalyst from one of the traditional public schools because felt he needed a fresh start if he were to advance in life. He found that start in his relationship with understanding, compassion, and teachers who know education is about more than information. Carlito knows that his opportunities will be limited because of his legal status but wants to be the best he can no matter the circumstances.

Leadership, teachers, and staff do not underestimate the enormity of the task they confront daily. It is emotionally and physically exhausting and any teacher who does not understand his or her life work as vocational will not survive. Without a true supportive community, even committed teachers by vocation will not survive. Unless teachers and staff have real love for the community in which the school exists and for the human persons populating that community, they will not survive. If the educational team is not built on a culture intentionally built on the values that underlie spirituality, the school will never produce the kind of results that justice demands of it.

The history of Catalyst demonstrates that excellent results exceeding expectations can be achieved when the school is committed to the five core values that have formed the Lasallian tradition for more than 300 years. Faith and Gospel Values, Academic Excellence, Community, Respect, and a Commitment to Justice are transformational values. We have made many mistakes, have suffered failures, and continue to learn hard lessons along the way. But we are convinced that this work is a sacred trust and not only transforms communities and children—it transforms us.

Something to Consider

The Catalyst Schools offer one potential solution to the need for faith-inspired education that has a sustainable business model. The model was able to achieve close to break-even financial results by the fourth year. The initial 3-year start-up costs are funded through a combination of incremental grants/funding and a controlled expansion of the student population. The Catalyst network raises 4.5% of its annual budget through grants and donations. Over 95% of the required funding is contributed from a stable funding source.

Over the past several years, the Catalyst Schools have been invited to numerous conversations with other educational leaders, pastors, and Dioceses to consider replicating or at least inviting others into the conversation about sustainable models. These conversations have taken place in Cleveland, New York City, Tulsa, St. Louis, Oakland, Sacramento, and Kansas City. In October 2015, Bishop Barber of Oakland gathered over 50 of the Diocese's priests to learn about and reflect upon the current state of Catholic education in the Diocese and what potential there might be in a faith-inspired model similar to Catalyst.

After intensive strategic planning with Bellwether Education Partners in 2015, a new platform was created to respond to the needs and interests of others to help explore the faith-inspired model. Simply put, Catalyst is not interested in replication of its own schools and would continue to focus on deepening its mission and vision in Chicago. The new platform, Legacy Partners, was created to preserve and amplify the impact of urban Catholic education by supporting the transition of a faith-based model to a faith-inspired charter model where appropriate and where such transition would not threaten existing successful Catholic schools.

To achieve this mission, Legacy Partners work closely with Dioceses and religious orders to help them plan for and navigate the private-to-charter transition. This effort is anchored around three key levers: a faith-inspired charter school day, a faith-based wrap-around program, and strong local organizational and diocesan leadership that exemplifies the core values and ethos of the legacy school being replaced.

To realize the ultimate vision to preserve the spiritual, academic, socioemotional, and civic impact that Catholic school education has on urban populations, Legacy Partners works with religious organizations and Dioceses unable to sustain school operations under a private Catholic school model.

Future of the Faith-Inspired Charter Schools

Numerous conversations are occurring across the country, furthering the possibility of faith-inspired charter schools. When Catalyst was first created, very few Catholic educational leaders were interested in the experiment. Over the past 10 years the interest has grown, research is being conducted, and the dialogue has expanded. We invite critical thinking and open dialogue and hope this model is one way the ethos, values, and contributions private, faith-based schools have given to neighborhoods and communities will not be lost. The search for the magic bullet that will save urban Catholic schools goes on through research and discussion as in the 2008 publication by the Thomas B. Fordham Institute (Hamilton, 2008) titled

Who Will Save America's Urban Catholic Schools that profiled a section on the Catalyst Schools titled "A Partnership with Chicago Public Schools" (p. 65). However, we do not think Catalyst is it. However, it might be one piece in a tapestry of options that allows the Catholic values to continue as a presence in underresourced urban communities.

REFERENCES

Brinig, M. F., & Garnett, N. S. (2014). *Lost classroom, lost community: Catholic schools' importance in urban America*. Chicago, IL: University of Chicago Press

Catalyst Schools, The. (2016a). *Catalyst Circle Rock: Results*. Retrieved from www.catalystschools.org/circle-rock/results

Catalyst Schools, The. (2016b). *Catalyst Maria: Results*. Retrieved from http://www.catalystschools.org/maria/results

Catalyst Schools, The. (2018). *What we do*. Retrieved from http://www.catalystschools.org/what-we-do

Christian Brothers Conference. (2012, Winter). Catalyst: Bringing the Lasallian charism to public schools. *De La Salle Today*, 20–23. Retrieved from http://www.catalystschools.org/files/filemanager_uploads/CB_Conference_DLS_Today_-_Catalyst.pdf

Loes, A., & Huether, F. (Eds.). (2007). *Meditations by John Baptist de La Salle* (R. Arnandez & A. Loes, Trans.). Washington, DC: Lasallian. (Original work published 1994)

Duncan, A. (2009). *A call to teaching: Secretary Arne Duncan's remarks at the Rotunda at the University of Virginia*. Retrieved from https://www2.ed.gov/news/speeches/2009/10/10092009.html

Fehrenbach, M. (2016). *Schools of character: Faith-inspired schools in the Lasallian tradition*. Winona, MN: Saint Mary's Press.

Hamilton, S. W. (Ed.). (2008, April 10). *Who will save America's urban Catholic schools?* Washington, DC: Thomas B. Fordham Institute. Retrieved from https://edexcellence.net/publications/who-will-save-americas-urban.html

John Paul II, St. (2014). *Catechesi tradendae: On catechesis in our time*. Manchester, NH: Sophia Institute Press. (Original work published 1974)

Proehl, R. A., Starnes, H., & Everett, S. (2015). Catalyst schools: The Catholic ethos and public charter schools. *Journal of Catholic Education*, *18*, 125–158. doi:10.15365/joce.1802072015

Roderick, M., Kelley-Kemple, T., Johnson, D. W., & Beechum, N. O. (2014). *Preventable failure: Improvements in long-term outcomes when high schools focused on the ninth grade year. Research summary*. Chicago, IL: University of Chicago Consortium on Chicago School Research.

U.S. Census Bureau. (2010). *U.S. Census 2010*. Retrieved from http://www.census.gov/2010census/

United States Conference of Catholic Bishops. (2005). *Seven themes of Catholic social teaching*. Washington, DC: Author. Retrieved from http://www.usccb.org/beliefs-and-teachings/what-we-believe/catholic-social-teaching/seven-themes-of-catholic-social-teaching.cfm

CHAPTER 6

GRADUATE SUPPORT

Ensuring High Levels of Educational Attainment for NativityMiguel Graduates

L. Mickey Fenzel
Loyola University Maryland

Melodie Wyttenbach
University of Notre Dame

NativityMiguel schools, which formally educate students through the middle school years, readily note that their educational programs extend for additional 4 years or more following students' graduation from eighth grade. As students begin to prepare for the transition from middle to high school, they become involved in the graduate support program (GSP) that supports them throughout their high school years and beyond. Students and their parents or guardians are introduced to the program as early as the sixth or seventh grade year as they begin to learn about high performing high schools that provide a high quality education for each student, as well as the right fit for each graduate based on his or her academic skill level and areas of strength. Graduate support has long been an essential ingredient of the NativityMiguel model and is identified as one of three priority areas of the NativityMiguel Coalition (n.d.-b, "Our Mission"). All schools in the

Responding to the Call for Educational Justice:
Transformative Catholic-Led Initiatives in Urban Education, pp. 93–110
Copyright © 2019 by Information Age Publishing
All rights of reproduction in any form reserved.

NativityMiguel Coalition and the Jesuit Schools Network include a graduate support program as part of their educational commitment and mission to break "the cycle of poverty through faith-based education" (NativityMiguel Coalition, n.d.-b, "Our Mission"). (See Chapter 2 for a fuller description of the NativityMiguel schools.)

NativityMiguel schools provide an accelerated educational program that enables students to improve their academic skills that are 1 or 2 years below grade level upon entry to a level that is at or above grade level when they graduate. Having developed these academic skills, as well as social and cultural competencies to feel confident in the presence of persons higher on the socioeconomic ladder, they enter ninth grade prepared for academic success in high performing Catholic and other independent high schools, as well as high performing traditional, charter, and magnet public high schools. At the same time, most NativityMiguel graduates transition from relatively homogenous middle school programs that serve mostly students of color from high poverty urban neighborhoods to high schools where the vast majority of students are Caucasian and from middle and upper middle-class homes. In addition to the stress that this new and unfamiliar environment brings, students from NativityMiguel schools continue to face the stressors of living in their home communities and commuting to high quality high schools that may lack the competencies to provide them adequate support. Although they graduate from NativityMiguel schools confident of their skills and ability to engage with others who possess greater social and political capital, it is also not unusual for the NativityMiguel students to face personal and institutional racism-related and social class-related stress in high school.

To meet these challenges and succeed in high performing high schools, NativityMiguel graduates continue to receive support, primarily through the graduate support program (GSP). Research (Andrews, 2012; Wright, Masten, & Narayan, 2013) has shown that students of color may require this additional level of support at the time of transition to high school to build resilience, in particular to resist and succeed in the face of racism-related stress in the form of microaggressions, as well as other personal and institutional sources. Lacking the strong circle of familiar peers from the eighth grade, NativityMiguel graduates in predominately White high schools benefit from continued encouragement and the development of skills to address subtle and overt discrimination. Several graduates have remarked in interviews how difficult it is to feel comfortable in schools where very few students look like they do or come from similar neighborhoods (e.g., Fenzel & Richardson, 2017a).

History

One of the objectives of the Nativity Mission Center (NMC) middle school, the flagship NativityMiguel school founded in 1971 for what was to become a network of more than 64 private middle schools that have served urban children placed at risk, was to prepare boys on the Lower East Side of Manhattan for admission to and success at Xavier High School, LaSalle Academy, and other good quality Catholic high schools in New York (Fenzel, 2009). While attending high school, many of the NMC graduates, who referred to their middle school simply as *Nativity*, would return to their middle school for some academic support and to talk with some of the teachers and administrators. In the mid-1980s, according to the NativityMiguel Coalition (n.d.-c) website ("Origin of the Graduate Support Program"), the school's principal, Rev. Jack Podsiadlo, Society of Jesus (SJ), moved to formalize the graduate support process in order to help students stay on track to graduate from high school. At that time, Fr. Jack himself, along with volunteers, reached out to students, their family members, and high school leaders and counselors to keep abreast of graduates' progress. In a 2003 article, Podsiadlo and Philliber identified additional functions of graduate support at NMC that included providing tuition assistance for the private and Catholic high schools, holding regular tutoring sessions, SAT preparation, and monthly support groups at the Center, and hosting a regular Friday night basketball gathering.

Podsiadlo and Philliber (2003) reported that it was not until the mid-1980s that NMC was able to keep track of the progress of its graduates and little was known of the fate of many of the early graduates. They reported that 81% of the students who graduated between 1989 and 1996 completed high school, a rate much higher than that of a comparable set of graduates of New York City public schools. It was during that time that Fr. Jack assigned a volunteer teacher[1] to the graduate support function full time as the school was able to expand the services offered to graduates and their families (NativityMiguel Coalition, n.d.-c, "Origin of the Graduate Support Program"). Nativity Mission Center took a further step in 1998 when Fr. Jack hired Roberto Rodriguez, a 1990 NMC graduate, upon his graduation from college. Roberto, who served in this role until 2006, was able to connect exceptionally well with the graduates and their families, who lived in neighborhoods like the one where he grew up. He kept a close eye on the graduates' high school attendance and progress, oversaw participation in study hall at the Center, introduced some students to the possibility of attending boarding school, and increased the services provided to graduates and their families to help them with college selections and applications for admission and financial aid. He took students on trips to visit colleges on weekends, provided informal counseling to the graduates who were experiencing struggles at home, the neighborhood, or school, and worked closely with family members to help them see the value of their sons attending college, and even leaving home to do so. During an interview with him during the study conducted by the first author of this chapter during the 2003–04 academic year (see Fenzel, 2009), Roberto also indicated that he was spending more time supporting graduates while in college and working to establish an alumni association to help support graduates with high school expenses. Although gentrification on the Lower East Side led to the closing of the school in 2012 (see Chapter 2), the alumni association continues to be active and raises funds to support high school and college tuition expenses for the graduates (J. Podsiadlo, personal communication, April 21, 2017).

As Nativity Mission Center was refining its GSP, other Nativity and San Miguel schools[2] that had opened in the early 1990s were faced with the need to help their students with high school applications and support them during their high school years. The graduate support function was frequently administered by a person already on staff at the school and taken on as a part-time responsibility. As the schools graduated more classes and the leaders saw the need to provide more services to graduates, the position of GSP director usually became a full-time assignment and, in some cases, developed into more than one full-time position. During visits to a number of NativityMiguel schools during the 2012–13 academic year, we encountered two schools that employed two full-time staff members to graduate support and others that had or were about to increase staffing to include one GSP director and a part-time assistant director. Staff members who were responsible for developing graduate support programs would visit Nativity Mission Center or other schools in the growing network to observe their operations and learn of their approach to addressing this function.

National Organizational Support

Graduate support has also been a focus of the national organizations, including the Nativity Educational Centers Network, formed in 2001, and the current NativityMiguel Coalition, established in 2015, following the closing of the NativityMiguel Network in 2012. GSP directors have been afforded the opportunity to meet together to share best practices at national and regional meetings, the first of which was held in Baltimore in 2002. The NativityMiguel Coalition, serving 46 of the schools as of 2018 that follow the model first developed at Nativity Mission Center, has a strong focus on graduate support that includes a Graduate Support Council composed of graduate support directors from several NativityMiguel schools (NativityMiguel Coalition, n.d.-a, "Graduate Support").

The function of the NativityMiguel Coalition's national office is to foster supportive relationships among schools and school leaders to better understand how schools are thriving within the unique and distinct demands of the educational mission and to strengthen competencies of their school leaders (see Chapter 7 on the NativityMiguel Coalition). The NativityMiguel Coalition aims to address common challenges, leverage opportunities, and share learnings at the regional and national level for presidents, principals, development directors, directors of graduate support, and teachers. Levels of support to these audiences range from regular calls among council members to organized regional and national gatherings, all with the common purpose of creating community and exchanging best practices to strengthen one's school and programs. The Graduate Support Council, composed of graduate support directors from several NativityMiguel schools, meets regularly to discuss topics such as the high school admissions process, supporting students in their transitions to high school and college, and how to meaningfully engage parents in the process of transitioning to secondary and post-secondary institutions. As members come to the Council with a range of experience, the networking allows for veteran graduate support directors to challenge and support one another, while educating those new to the role, leveraging the capacities of all involved (NativityMiguel Coalition, n.d.-a, "Graduate Support").

The Graduate Support Function

The graduate support function began to take root as the Nativity Mission Center school graduated its earliest classes and school administrators saw the need to provide a number of services to help graduates stay on track for high school graduation and college admission, as well to maintain their contact information and records of their levels of educational success and attainment. The NativityMiguel Coalition (n.d.-a, "Graduate Support") provides a useful summary of the graduate support function at member schools and describes how the program was developed and refined over the first 15 years of the operation of the Nativity Mission Center school. The webpage devoted to this program mentions that graduate support begins before students complete 8th grade in order to help them access the most appropriate or "rigorous high school or post-secondary opportunity to continue their education" (NativityMiguel Coalition, n.d.-a, "Graduate Support," "GSP is an essential component of our educational design"). The Coalition notes also that, although there may be differences in the services provided by the member schools, the primary focus of the program is to provide services before and after middle school graduation to position graduates for later educational, personal, and professional success.

In earlier research (Fenzel, 2009) conducted during the 2003–04 academic year, we found the essential functions of graduate support to be consistent among the several schools in the former Nativity Educational Centers Network. These functions included working with students and their parents or guardians on choosing a high school, arranging for visits to local high schools or providing other opportunities for students and their families to learn about high school options, overseeing students' academic progress during high school, providing tutoring or homework support, paying personal visits to graduates in the high schools, arranging events to bring graduates together socially, offering retreats that reinforce the spiritual values inherent in NativityMiguel programs, and providing support for college selection and applications. The GSP directors' visits to the graduates in high school enable the directors to follow up on concerns raised by high school counselors, other graduates, and parents or guardians and show graduates that the faculty and administration of their middle school continue to care about each graduate personally and take an interest in their well-being and success. Several GSP directors have reported that their graduates, who return home to their often distressed and stressful homes and neighborhoods during the impressionable high school years, continue to need the support from people who know and care about them to help them avoid the pitfalls of the street and keep them on track to graduate and seek admission to college or consider alternative postsecondary plans.

Helping students and their families with selecting a high school involves discussing the various options and recommendations from school staff that are based on the students' strengths and interests. In this process, the GSP director, who has also come to know each graduating student by teaching him or her in a class or seminar, works with other staff to identify high schools that might provide a good fit for the student. In many schools, graduate support functions are incorporated in the curriculum through a "life skills" class that is taught by the GSP director. Students and their families have opportunities to learn about high school possibilities through school fairs held at the middle school and through school visits, some of which are led by the graduate support director and others arranged by the families. In most cases, Catholic and other independent high schools require applicants to submit scores from standardized tests for which the middle schools help students prepare. Parents and guardians, who are likely unfamiliar with the application process to these selective schools, receive assistance from NativityMiguel school graduate support with the process of applying for admission and financial aid. Several of the schools, primarily located on the East Coast, occasionally encourage particular students to consider attending a boarding school, an issue that is carefully discussed with students' parents or guardians. As we found in interviews with several graduates of different NativityMiguel schools, parents are often resistant to having their children attend a high school or college very far from home.

Because nearly all families are unable to afford tuition at nonpublic schools, the Nativity and NativityMiguel school personnel work with the high schools to negotiate scholarship opportunities for their graduates, which will influence the number of graduates they can encourage to apply to particular schools. Some of the NativityMiguel schools incorporate limited high school tuition support from their own budgets and some provide their graduates with computers and books for use in high school. The growing number of Cristo Rey schools in the U.S. is providing another affordable, high-quality, and college-preparatory avenue for an increasing number of NativityMiguel graduates. (See Chapter 3 regarding the Cristo Rey program and funding model.)

A number of GSP directors indicated to us in interviews that an important function they serve, and which high school college counselors often tend not to address, is working with families to help them see the value of their children attending a 2- or 4-year college. Many parents and guardians, who feel the need for their children to enter the workforce as early as possible to supplement the families' meager finances, often fail to see the long-term benefits of their sons and daughters continuing their studies after high school. One GSP director mentioned how important she saw college attendance to breaking the cycle of poverty that stands as a central goal of the NativityMiguel schools and was pleased to see more of her students seeking 4-year college degrees. Convincing parents and guardians of the importance of their children taking this step is work that requires the building of trust that comes from nurturing relationships over time. Some graduates have chosen to attend college or university close to home in order to provide some financial assistance to the family through part-time work and living at home.

Where there are two or more NativityMiguel schools in the same city, GSP directors often take advantage of their close proximity to coordinate programming for graduates in high school (Fenzel, 2009). Such has been the case for the schools in Baltimore and New York with respect to providing SAT preparation and events such as peer-led discussions of the challenges they face in predominately White high schools. These graduate support directors often meet together and communicate electronically to discuss how their work is progressing, to support one another, to coordinate shared programming, and to offer suggestions for program improvement. In addition, the NativityMiguel Coalition schedules regional as well as national meetings to provide graduate support directors with opportunities to share best practices and support one another.

Personal Relationships

The quality of the GSP directors' personal relationships with graduates and their parents and guardians is very important as they must have the trust of the graduates and their families in order to be effective. Some schools have benefitted by having GSP directors remain in their positions for a number of years to build these relationships and having one or both members of the GSP team who are alumnae/alumni themselves has provided an additional benefit. Such is the case for a school for girls in New York City, which has had an alumna of the school serve as either the GSP Director or Associate Director in recent years (Cornelia Connelly Center, 2017). At a school for boys in the Midwest, an administrator and GSP director who served the school for its first 20 years was well acquainted with the Catholic high schools in the region and developed good relationships with the graduates that helped many of them remain connected to the school and volunteer to participate in the lives of the current students. When he retired, an alumnus of the school took on a leadership role with the GSP team.

Going "above and beyond" for the benefit on graduates is a theme that we have seen expressed frequently in our research (Fenzel, 2009; Fenzel & Richardson, 2017a). For example, a number of students we interviewed at a coeducational NativityMiguel school on the West Coast indicated how they relish the relationship they have with their GSP director, who regularly seeks them out at their high schools or through social media to engage them and listen to whatever concerns they face. Several of these graduates mentioned that they also initiate contact with her for support and advice. Another GSP director of a school for girls mentioned the need for ongoing education for its graduates that includes guiding them in making responsible sexual decisions, an effort that has coincided with a decrease in pregnancies during high school. Our research (Fenzel, 2009; Fenzel & Richardson, 2017a) over the years in NativityMiguel schools has shown how valuable the relationships that GSP directors have with their graduates and graduates' families is to the sense of community, family, sisterhood, and brotherhood that persists for years following eighth grade graduation.

Mentoring

In addition to the common practices seen across NativityMiguel schools, a few, including one for boys in the Midwest, have developed mentoring programs to supplement graduate support whereby a member of the community or increasingly, a graduate of the school, commits to meeting regularly with a graduating eighth grader to check in, provide a listening ear and encouragement, and dispense career guidance where appropriate. This kind of program can provide continuing exposure to adults outside of their home communities and an opportunity to continue to develop their communication skills with adults from different walks of life, including some with social or political influence and strong connections in the community or business world. When conducted well, mentoring relationships can help to reduce the lack of parity that exists with respect to cultural and intergroup social capital between majority and minority young people that affects quality-of-life opportunities and access to persons and institutions of power and higher status and more fulfilling careers (Murrell, 2007). In a recent meeting, one GSP director indicated that these mentoring relationships are successful in approximately two-thirds of the cases, with a third of the mentors giving significantly more time to the graduates than asked for. When successful, life-long friendships develop that can have transformational effects for graduates, and mentors serve as resources not only during in high school and college, but also as they enter the workforce and navigate adult life.

Organizing mentoring programs places additional responsibilities on the shoulders of the graduate support director who must recruit, train, and assign mentors, follow up on their activities, and assess the contributions that the program makes to the lives of graduates. Careful screening of potential mentors and proper training and follow-up is needed to ensure that mentors are working with graduates in a way that is consistent with the mission of the NativityMiguel schools and benefits the continued development of their mentees.

At a school for girls in the Northeast, mentors and mentees commit to working together from the 7th to 12th grade. These mentors provide support and advice to the young women as they face the challenges of a private high school education and prepare to take the next step into college, vocational training, or career. The school's website indicates that the goal of the program is "to help close the opportunity gap for current students and alumnae in high school by providing an additional female adult role model who is positive, caring, and willing to share professional/ life experiences, encourage success and explore educational and career options" (Mother Caroline Academy and Education Center, n.d., Mentoring: Program: The Goal"). Having been started by a long-time volunteer at the school, the program coordinator is now an alumna of the school.

Many graduates are returning the favor of having been mentored by serving as mentors themselves in both formal and informal ways (Fenzel & Richardson, 2017a). A number of graduates of a single-sex school for boys in the Midwest have been joining its school's mentoring program to serve students who are graduating and heading into high school. A graduate of a coeducational school on the East Coast, who later received a law degree and became a member of the school's Board of Trustees, acknowledged in an interview that he was serving as a mentor to a number of graduates of his NativityMiguel school. Some single-sex schools for girls also recruit alumnae to serve in a number of roles that include serving as one-on-one mentors and leading formal and informal talks with current students. GSP directors have found that alumnae can provide strong role models for the students and reinforce the phenomenon of sisterhood and a community of mutual support that has been an important hallmark of NativityMiguel schools.

A mentor extraordinaire to a large number of Nativity Mission Center graduates is Rev. Jack Podsiadlo, SJ, who has served in a number of formal and informal roles at the school, from teacher to president, as well as mission director for a consortium of three New York City Nativity-model schools. Fr. Jack has maintained regular contact with scores of graduates over the years, recruiting some of them to return to the school after college graduation to serve as teachers and administrators. Danny Perez is one of Fr. Jack's mentees who has taught and served in administrative roles at the Nativity Mission Center and other New York City schools. Mr. Perez's commitment to give back to the students of his and other NativityMiguel schools was most recently evidenced in his appointment as Executive Director of the NativityMiguel Coalition (NativityMiguel Coalition, 2017). Now serving the Latino community in Richmond, Virginia, Fr. Jack frequently travels to New York for gatherings of alumni of the school and to attend special events in the lives of the graduates that include weddings and baptisms. He has noted several of his personal visits with graduates, including special events in their lives, on social media.

Postsecondary Support

Supporting graduates as they begin their studies in 2- and 4-year colleges and universities can make a difference in a student persisting through graduation, as the college experience brings about additional challenges related to race and finances, as well as those that emanate from becoming a smaller fish in a larger pond and dealing with a schedule and level of independence different from what they encountered in high school. While the college matriculation and graduation rates of NativityMiguel graduates has been quite high compared to those of other young people from similar backgrounds (Fenzel, 2009; Podsiadlo & Philliber, 2003), additional support in the form of individual mentoring and opportunities for involvement in service and other activities during the college years can make a difference for many students who might otherwise end up dropping out (Gamble, Kim, & An, 2012; Kim & Hargrove, 2013).

One of the NativityMiguel schools for girls on the east coast has initiated a GSP 2.0 program, taking the graduate support role to a new level (Cornelia Connelly Center, 2017). This aspect of the GSP focuses on supporting graduates who are attending college, going so far as visiting them at their colleges. This school serves as one example of how the schools that have established themselves in the community over a number of years have used careful planning and building of community relationships to solidify its financial standing. Doing so has enabled the school to expand and strengthen its support of graduates through increased staffing, along with the provision of additional services and a larger space that can accommodate more of its graduates for academic support and seminars on preparing for college, in addition to being able to provide financial assistance to support high school and college attendance. Seeing the importance of providing emotional and instrumental support after high school to their graduates, most of whom are the first in their families to attend college, has led a number of NativityMiguel schools to expand their services to include personal visits and other services to graduates attending college. Although many colleges and universities now have offices that support students of color and provide them with programs that can enrich their college experience, an important role for the GSP director as a caring supporter, encourager, and resource continues.

Although the NativityMiguel schools are focused on providing a strong college preparatory curriculum, they also have sought to support those students for whom college has not been their choice. NativityMiguel graduates often pursue specialized training in community colleges and technical institutes, and others may decide to enter the military or join the workforce. Effective GSP directors make use of community resources, including other graduates and friends of the schools, to help guide these students and provide them with an understanding of some of the options available to them. The purpose of the program is primarily to help graduates pursue a stable life path guided by the values learned and a commitment to help other graduates succeed in breaking the cycle of poverty for themselves.

Recent Research Findings

Survey Findings

During the 2013–14 academic year, the first author of this chapter conducted a mixed methods study of graduates' perceptions of the long-term benefits of a NativityMiguel education and the role that graduate support has played in their academic and career success, as well as their development as leaders and service providers. In addition, both authors have continued to consult with a number of school leaders, graduate support directors, and graduates to learn about recent developments in the schools. With respect to findings from an online survey of 151 graduates from seven different middle school programs who finished eighth grade between 1991 and 2011, respondents reported that they took advantage of an average of 7.0 (SD = 2.9) different services offered through graduate support from a provided list of 12 possible services (Fenzel & Richardson, 2017b). The vast majority of respondents identified the most frequently utilized services as the four that involved selecting and applying to high performing secondary schools. These included individual and group advising meetings, involvement of parents and guardians in the process, assisting them with preparing high school applications, and preparing them for the high school admissions tests. Approximately half of respondents acknowledged meetings with the GSP director about applying to college and attending alumni/alumnae events and approximately a third noted that they participated in college visits and took part in meetings related to applying for financial aid. Approximately three-fourths of respondents reported having check-in meetings with the GSP director during their high school years and approximately one-third reported receiving tutoring support while in high school. For the services identified by the fewest number of respondents, most notable were tutoring help and college preparation meetings. One factor that may have made it difficult for some students to take advantage of these services at the NativityMiguel school is the distances between home, the NativityMiguel school, and the student's high school, as several of the Coalition schools have enrolled more students throughout the city, and less so from the neighborhoods very near the school. Although very few schools supported a formal mentoring program for graduates, responses to the survey showed that where there was not a formal program, some students were mentored by an older adult during high school and beyond, many of whom were not a part of the school staff. Interview findings (Fenzel & Richardson, 2017a, 2017b) also showed this to be the case. In many instances, long-term mentors were committed community members the graduates would have met through a number of the events and programs sponsored by the schools that brought them into contact with donors and other influential community members.

Graduate Interview Findings

With respect to interviews, the first author of this chapter interviewed NativityMiguel graduates from six different schools, most of which were held with small groups of two to five graduates (see Fenzel & Richardson,

2017a, 2017b). The mean age of those interviewed was 19.5 ($SD = 4.4$) with a range of 14 to 30 years. The majority of those interviewed (70%) were males and 54% had attended a single-sex NativityMiguel middle school. The oldest graduates interviewed were from three single-sex schools for boys, including graduates of the original Nativity Mission Center ($N = 7$) and two schools both of which had graduated nearly 20 classes ($N = 16$ each; both founded in 1993). These three schools had also been a part of a large study conducted by the first author 9 years earlier (see Fenzel, 2009).

In an analysis of the interviews from the latter two single-sex schools identified above, two researchers (Fenzel & Richardson, 2017a) identified the central theme that described the benefit of the NativityMiguel education they received as *community*. Five derivative themes emerged that included Developing Academic Self-Efficacy, Building Resilience, Becoming Leaders and Servants ("Men for others"), Brotherhood/Peer Support; Mentoring and Support. Graduates indicated that, through high school, college, and beyond the college years, they knew that the GSP director and other former faculty, as well as other graduates, whether or not they were part of their graduating class, were just a phone call, text message, or e-mail message away. Having shared the NativityMiguel educational experience together, including time spent with tutoring, college preparation, or social gatherings that were a part of the graduate support program, the graduates had developed a special and very real bond of brotherhood and family and took responsibility to make the most of their full Nativity educational experience to provide leadership and service to younger students and people in need in the communities where they lived and worked. Some graduates noted that the more than 7 or 8 years of a Nativity educational experience was a gift that they received to help move them out of economic poverty and one that came with a responsibility to help others who are underserved in the society.

These themes of sisterhood, community, resilience, and building academic self-confidence were also evidenced in the interviews conducted with alumnae and GSP directors of several NativityMiguel schools. For example, three young women, graduates of a West Coast NativityMiguel school for girls and boys who were college students at the time of the interviews, provided several examples of the caring support provided by the graduate support director, a young woman herself. These alumnae testified that the GSP director, who provided highly valued and patient support and outreach during their high school years, was an important factor in their success in high school and into college. One alumna particularly appreciated the help she received in preparing for high school tests, meeting other academic needs, and adjusting to the experience of attending a college where the vast majority of students were Caucasian. Another alumna, who was working part-time at her NativityMiguel school while attending college, appreciated the math and writing support she received from volunteers at NativityMiguel that contributed to her high school success and mentioned the commitment she has to the success of current students and recent graduates by taking the time to share her experiences and learning. Alumnae of a NativityMiguel school on the East Coast reported similar appreciation for the assistance they received from their GSP director over and above the services, such as tutoring and learning about options for college, provided by their high school, a Cristo Rey school. In some cases, graduates who attend Cristo Rey high schools continue to grow in an educational environment in which the teachers and administrators are particularly committed to urban education and provide support services that the students require for continued success. In all cases, the personal relationship of caring and trust that the graduates had developed with their GSP director was particularly noteworthy.

Administrator Interview Findings

Findings from recent interviews with the graduate support directors and other administrators from a number of NativityMiguel schools conducted by each of us independently showed similarities and differences in the graduate support function among the schools. One universal finding was that, as the schools graduate more classes and the number of alumni and alumnae continues to increase, the number of staff hours needed to perform the same graduate support functions increases and additional staff devoted to them is needed. When asked if there was more that they would like to do if they had additional time or staff, all responded with ideas of more ways in which they would like to engage graduates in high school and college or better maintain databases with up-to-date information on graduates. Most noted also that they are often asked for information on graduates' high school performance, graduation rates from high school, and college admission and graduation rates for use by board members and development directors who look for grant funds to support the school.

In addition, the GSP directors and other school leaders have recognized the importance providing support to graduates attending college given the challenges that many of them face living independently, securing sufficient financial resources, especially as tuition and living costs rise each year, and addressing new sources of stress they encounter in the larger and more complex environment that offers more choices for spending time and financial resources. GSP directors are finding that, as the graduates leave high school and move to college or other pursuits, there are still many needs that could be addressed with adequate resources. Maintaining regular contact with them at this point in their development is difficult when so much of their time is devoted to working with their graduates throughout high school. Making use of social media to locate graduates with whom they may have lost touch and to invite graduates to events at the school has helped reengage graduates and keep them involved. Although they encourage graduates to continue to reach out to them when they encounter difficulties or just to check in, a number of the GSP directors have felt discouraged about the times when they learn after the fact that they could have provided some assistance to help graduates stay in college if they had only known. A number of the GSP directors indicated that cultural norms lead many graduates and their parents or guardians to hesitate to reach out when they could use some assistance.

Also important to underscore is the importance of the work of the GSP staff member while their graduates are in high school, as most high schools lack the staff, and sometimes the understanding, to work effectively with young people whose parents are not well educated and tend not to contact the school about their concerns. Language can be an additional barrier as well, since a sizable number of the parents and guardians NativityMiguel schools serve have very limited English language proficiency and information sent home by most high schools is written in English only. Legal documentation has also been cited as an issue for which high school college counselors tend not to even think of when presenting information to the NativityMiguel graduates who are undocumented. Some GSP directors have had to step in to help these graduates understand their possible paths to postsecondary education and scholarship aid and also to obtain legal status in the United States.

A certain percentage of the NativityMiguel graduates, perhaps as much as 10% or more, find that the first high school they attend is not a good fit and seek to transfer; some may even attend three or four high schools before either graduating or completing a GED. By scheduling regular high school visits and making other contacts with the graduates through social media, texting, phone calls, and the like, as well as maintaining contact with high school counselors, the GSP directors are able to anticipate many of the difficulties that arise and take some steps to address issues of concern. Many of the issues that the graduates encounter stem more from their home lives and not the high school, since many of the NativityMiguel students and graduates face issues of parents in prison, overcrowding in the home, neighbors who harass them for going to "White schools," parental discord or drug addiction, and the like. One of the schools we visited had a 2-day-a-week social work intern who had five such high school students on her case load that required nearly all of her time meeting with the graduates individually and making phone calls to secure needed services or seek the involvement of parents or guardians.

Conclusions and Implications

The social justice mission of NativityMiguel schools to help break the cycle of poverty through faith-based education would not be complete without graduate support, an essential component of the NativityMiguel educational model. Our research, much of which is summarized here, shows clearly that graduate support helps historically underserved young people continue on a successful and fulfilling path of educational attainment and career opportunities that would otherwise not be available to them. Most high-performing public and independent high schools who welcome NativityMiguel graduates, more than 90% of whom are students of color who qualify for the federal free and reduced meals program, often lack the personnel or understanding necessary to help guide and support them through their college-preparatory curriculums and into college. Navigating this path, which is laden with racism-related stressors, financial challenges, and other difficulties that stem from economic poverty, requires the guiding hand and receptive ear of one or more caring and knowledgeable adults such as those who oversee graduate support.

High schools, as well as colleges, who are willing to admit historically underserved and academically talented students from NativityMiguel and other middle school programs must find the resources needed to participate meaningfully in the goal of achieving greater educational equity and access. As we have seen in our work, these resources extend beyond providing adequate academic support to responding sensitively to the stressors of racial prejudice, family difficulties, and distressed neighborhoods that often contribute to declines in academic engagement and performance and emotional well-being. Since NativityMiguel schools graduate only small numbers of historically underserved and talented students, more high schools, including Catholic and other faith-based ones, might consider taking the lessons of graduate support and partner with one or more urban middle schools to identify more talented students placed at risk and design programs to challenge and support them at levels similar to what NativityMiguel schools provide.

There are also a number of national and state organizations that support higher levels of educational attainment for historically underserved students by providing tutoring and counseling during the high school years to prepare more students for college success, as well as support during college (e.g., Lawyers' Committee for Civil Rights Under Law, 2014). Several Catholic sponsored organizations have also been involved in these efforts that support the work of schools for students placed at risk (e.g., see Chapter 8 on Notre Dame Mission Volunteers). In addition, charter schools such as Knowledge is Power Program (KIPP) have devoted considerable resources to help students prepare for high school and college success with its KIPP Through College program (KIPP Foundation, n.d.). The expanse of graduate support services across NativityMiguel and other schools and networks is a sign of commitment to the academic and life success of marginalized students and hope for the betterment of our diverse and evolving world.

NOTES

1. It is not unusual for one of more volunteers from the community or from a volunteer organization, such as AmeriCorps or Jesuit Volunteer Corps (JVC), to serve as teachers or other support persons in a NativityMiguel school for a period of 2 to 3 years, or longer. Compensation for JVC and AmeriCorps volunteers usually include housing, a living allowance, medical insurance, and an education award. At the end of the commitment period, some volunteers, having earned a teaching certificate, continue as full-time fully compensated teachers.
2. See Chapter 2 for the history of NativityMiguel schools that came about when schools in the original Nativity and San Miguel networks of schools merged in 2006. The term, NativityMiguel is used in this chapter to refer to the schools that have been a part of any of these networks.

REFERENCES

Andrews, D. C. (2012). Black achievers' experiences with racial spotlighting and ignoring in a predominately white high school. *Teachers College Record, 114,* 1–46. Retrieved from http://www.tcrecord.org

Cornelia Connelly Center. (2017). *Graduate support program.* Retrieved from http://www.connellycenter.org/our-programs/graduate-support-program

Fenzel, L. M. (2009). *Improving urban middle schools: Lessons from the Nativity schools.* Albany, NY: State University of New York Press.

Fenzel, L. M., & Richardson, K. D. (2017a, April). *Supporting continued academic success, resilience, and agency of urban boys in Catholic alternative middle schools.* Paper presented at the annual meeting of the American Educational Research Association, San Antonio, TX.

Fenzel, L. M., & Richardson, K. D. (2017b, October). *Accompanying underserved urban students along the path to higher education: Graduate support in NativityMiguel schools.* Paper presented at the annual meeting of the International Society for Educational Planning, Toronto, Ontario, Canada.

Gamble, B., Kim, S., & An, S. (2012). Impact of a middle school math academy on learning and attitudes of minority male students in an urban district. *Journal of Urban Learning, Teaching, and Research, 8,* 13–25. Retrieved from http://www.aera-ultr.org/journal.html

Kim, E., & Hargrove, D. (2013). Deficient or resilient: A critical review of Black male academic success and persistence in higher education. *The Journal of Negro Education, 82*(3), 300–311. Retrieved from www.journalnegroed.org/

KIPP Foundation. (n.d.). *KIPP through college.* Retrieved from http://www.kipp.org/approach/kipp-through-college/

Lawyers' Committee for Civil Rights Under Law. (2014). *First gen nonprofits.* Retrieved from http://firstgenfellows.org/first-generation-college-student-links/

Mother Caroline Academy and Education Center. (n.d.). *Mentoring: Program: The goal.* Retrieved from http://www.mcaec.org/mentoring/mentoring-overview/

Murrell, P. C., Jr. (2007). *Race, culture, and schooling: Identities of achievement in multicultural urban schools.* New York, NY: Lawrence Erlbaum.

NativityMiguel Coalition. (n.d.-a). *Graduate support.* Retrieved from http://nativitymiguel.org

NativityMiguel Coalition. (n.d.-b). *Our mission.* Retrieved from http://nativitymiguel.org

NativityMiguel Coalition. (n.d.-c). *Origin of the graduate support program.* Retrieved from http://nativitymiguel.org

NativityMiguel Coalition. (2017, June 9). *Perez named as Coalition's executive director.* Retrieved from http://nativitymiguel.org

Podsiadlo, J. J., & Philliber, W. W. (2003). The Nativity Mission Center: A successful approach to the education of Latino boys. *Journal of Education for Students Placed At Risk, 8,* 419–428. doi:10.1207/S15327671ESPR0804_3

Wright, M. O., Masten, A. S., & Narayan, A. J. (2013). Resilience processes in development: Four waves of research on positive adaptation in the context of adversity. In S. Goldstein & R. B. Brooks (Eds.), *Handbook of resilience in children* (2nd ed., pp. 15–37). New York, NY: Springer.

CHAPTER 7

LEARNING TO THRIVE THROUGH A COALITION OF MISSION-ALIGNED SCHOOLS

Terry Shields
The Bement School

As various models of private, public charter, and public district schools have emerged over the last 20 years, various support organizations have also been established to accelerate the growth and maximize the effectiveness of these schools. The evolution of these organizations, known as networks, Charter Management Organizations (CMOs), or District initiatives, have required time, resources, and talent to establish a function, structure, and strategy appropriate for the particular group of schools. Decisions about standardization of the model and responsibilities of control within the model have been central to the ongoing and fluid development of these organizations (Bradach, 2003).

While much research has been done on CMOs and District initiatives, minimal study has been done on private, faith-based networks. Robson and Smarick (2016) stated:

Among the most prevalent of the new-wave reforms are school consortia. They are being used to mitigate the downsides of parochial schools' traditional island-like status. For generations, most Catholic schools have been

Responding to the Call for Educational Justice:
Transformative Catholic-Led Initiatives in Urban Education, pp. 111–128
Copyright © 2019 by Information Age Publishing
All rights of reproduction in any form reserved.

highly independent, each the charge of an individual parish. In a consortium, a small group of schools team up to meet common needs and capitalize on economies of scale. For those familiar with chartering, consortia might be thought of as proto-networks, somewhere between a standalone charter and a charter management organization (CMO). ("Developing School Consortia," para. 1)

This chapter will study one such consortia, the NativityMiguel Coalition (the "Coalition"), which was established to support the educational mission and model of the NativityMiguel Schools across the United States. The NativityMiguel Coalition operates on the belief that an excellent education is delivered most effectively when: (a) schools have independent control and autonomy of essential decisions impacting mission, and (b) schools collaborate with other aligned-schools in a coordinated, targeted process of improvement and accountability that cannot exist within in a single school. This chapter will look inside the Coalition and provide a systems-level view to illustrate how these two beliefs were core to the founding of NativityMiguel schools and continue to drive program development in member schools.

Founding Stories

Through the 1950s and 60s, the Nativity Mission Center provided a number of youth services to area Puerto Rican families on the Lower East Side of Manhattan that included an academic tutoring program for boys designed to prepare them for admission to and success at city Catholic high schools. In the 1960s, the Center began to provide a summer leadership camp for the boys in Lake Placid that was incorporated as part of the extended year program of the middle school that opened at the site in 1971. As successful as the school was, it was not until 1990 that a second school that followed the Nativity Mission approach opened in Boston led by the efforts of a former Nativity Mission teacher (Fenzel, 2009; also see Chapter 2). A year later, the middle school model was incorporated into a Catholic K–8 school in Harlem that was identified as the Gonzaga Program.

Rather than a franchise model of growth, groups interested in founding a school followed a "Replication by Observation" model. Founders spent time observing existing schools, replicated the best of what they saw, and at the same time, not bound by a rigid set of standards and practices, adapted the model as needed for their local community. In 1993, inspired by the trajectory of students on the Lower East Side school and reassured by the founding of Nativity Prep Boston and the Gonzaga Program, groups founded schools in Baltimore, Boston, New York, Providence, and Milwaukee. Notably, the De La Salle Christian Brothers led by

Bro. Lawrence Goyette, FSC, founded and sponsored the San Miguel School of Providence, Rhode Island and several religious congregations of women sponsored the first schools for girls in New York and Boston. One coeducational school in Baltimore was among this new group of schools.

Unlike other school networks, the growth of what became known as NativityMiguel Schools did not depend on a singular founder who was franchising a standard school model and training leaders to execute on certain practices and design principles. Nor did the growth rely on a central office that standardized manuals and templates or formalized procedures and systems. Instead NativityMiguel schools were started by a founding group with strong connections to the local community who well understood the educational needs of historically underserved children that were not being addressed and could assemble the people and resources to address this need.

To this day, each NativityMiguel school remains independently governed by local boards of directors who are responsible for fidelity to the mission and fiduciary oversight. (Some schools employ a two-tiered board structure with a board of members holding certain reserved powers on behalf of the sponsoring congregation or congregations serving on the board of directors.) A NativityMiguel School ultimately survives and thrives on the commitment, investment, and function of the local board and leadership. The board is responsible for hiring and firing the head of school, for overseeing that key policies for mission are defined and followed, and for ensuring that the school has the resources it needs to thrive. The board is most effective when it collectively represents the local community, contributes a broad range of skills, and has the autonomy to make decisions based on the needs of the school and available resources and personnel.

The NativityMiguel Network: An Initial Attempt at a Formal Association

In 2000, B.J. Cassin, a venture capitalist from Menlo Park, California and then a trustee at St. Mary's College in Moraga, California, was invited to visit the San Miguel School of Chicago by an alumnus of St. Mary's who was teaching at the school. The San Miguel School had been founded by two De La Salle Christian Brothers in 1995. Upon touring the school, Cassin committed to fund capacity grants to the San Miguel School and other existing schools. He also committed to fund feasibility studies for groups interested in starting a school and provide start-up grants of $150,000 to groups that developed a sound and feasible plan.

Additionally, Cassin funded the formation of a formal association that would connect all of the schools. Prior to 2000, school leaders would gather informally to discuss a range of challenges. These meetings were driven by school leaders learning from one another by asking: "What are you doing about …? What does … look like in your school?" On one occasion in January 1998 at Fordham University in the Bronx, New York, students from the schools played in a basketball tournament as school leaders met to discuss curriculum, discipline, fundraising, and facilities. School leaders organized to explore more extensive structures and channels of collaboration, especially as the number of schools increased. Spurred by Cassin's gift and understanding the value of this sharing and exchange, a formal association was established in the spring of 2001. This organization, which took various forms until it would ultimately become the NativityMiguel Network in 2006, would be charged with leading this collaboration until it dissolved in June 2012.

To better understand why it dissolved, we return to the independence and autonomy that have been the hallmark of the founding of more than 70 NativityMiguel Schools since 1971, 65 of which remain in operation today. NativityMiguel schools believe that students are best served when each school has the authority and ability to deliver an education based on local need, resources, and personnel. This independence allows a school to be nimble and fluid in responding to needs of its community and not restrained by the approval or direction of upward or external forces. Naturally, when the NativityMiguel Network moved to standardize the NativityMiguel model, it was often met with hesitancy, ambivalence, or reluctance. Schools asked critical questions: Who is making the decisions? Is it in the best interest of *our* students, families, school, and community? What if our school has an alternative approach that works for us? This last question was especially true of schools that had started prior to the establishment of a formal association.

The NativityMiguel Network found itself in a difficult position. The growth of the national office and its funding was predicated on a more formal definition of the educational model that was being prescribed for schools and accountability to a more extensive set of performance metrics. This definition and accountability, unfortunately, was counterintuitive to how NativityMiguel Schools were founded and operated and required more substantial time and resources from schools that were not in a position to offer them.

The NativityMiguel Coalition: Reimagining a Formal Association

The demands of founding, leading, and sustaining a NativityMiguel School are great. School leaders are responsible for preserving a strong fidelity to mission with a financial model that is not funded by tuition nor dependent on public funding. The demands require both an urgent internal focus to ensure strong school culture, curriculum, instruction, and assessment and a persistent external focus to ensure the necessary funding, resources, personnel, and partnerships. School leadership often liken these demands to "pushing a rock up the hill."

After the NativityMiguel Network dissolved in the spring of 2012, many schools were missing the more formal connection that they shared with mission-aligned and like-minded schools for the 11 years prior. Forty school leaders gathered together again, but without the umbrella of a national organization, in the fall of 2013 at the University of Notre Dame. Sessions focused on school leadership and development and the conversation returned to reenvisioning a more formal association.

In the spring of 2014, the NativityMiguel Coalition was established by school leaders who believed that they are stronger "pushing the rock together" than they were as a single school and that collaborative relationships directly and clearly accelerated the progress of a school to deliver on its mission. This is very similar to the intent of school leaders who pursued a more formal association the late 1990s.

Naturally, the decision of any group of individuals, organizations, or, in this case, schools to formally associate with one another requires a level of definition to their identity. What unites them? What characteristics do they share in common? Learning from the strengths and weaknesses of the former NativityMiguel Network, the NativityMiguel Coalition attempted to answer these questions *without* resorting to strictly-defined standard practices and a system of accountability to the model. Rather, member schools are similarly aligned in mission, governance, core beliefs, and outcomes and it is the responsibility of the local board of directors and leadership team to implement practices that adhere to this alignment. When the new Coalition's Board of Directors, comprised of school leaders from member schools, met in 2014, they adopted an identity framework, which emphasized providing an education for students placed at risk that would be explicitly faith-based. Perhaps the best test of the Coalition's identity is when school leaders gather at national and regional conferences. Are they seeing themselves in the mission, realities, challenges, and success of other schools?

It must be emphasized that the NativityMiguel Coalition is not void of measures of accountability. The main difference is that schools are not accountable to a central office in preservation of an educational model; instead schools are accountable locally to their students, families, and communities to deliver on the promise of their mission. Data are collected at the national level to support a national narrative of success, to identify and learn from schools that are consistently demonstrating strong student outcomes, and to help all schools identify areas for improvement. Rather than a system of evaluation and judgment, accountability in the NativityMiguel Coalition relies on a collaborative spirit of improvement that pushes each school to become better.

Explicitly Faith-Based: Alignment in Mission

One way that member schools of the NativityMiguel Coalition are aligned in mission is that all schools *deliver an explicitly faith-based education*. This faith is foundational to the NativityMiguel schools' mission in that it drives *how* they deliver this mission, not necessarily *who* they deliver it to. NativityMiguel schools are inclusive communities embracing persons from all faith traditions and from no faith traditions. Many schools do not ask about religious preference, so it is not possible to accurately know the percentage of students and families in the Coalition identifying with certain faith traditions, if any. Informally, schools report religious preferences typical for the populations served by the school (i.e., schools serving a predominantly Latino neighborhood tend to educate more Catholic students, schools in African American neighborhoods tend to educate more Protestant or Muslim students.)

Regardless of the religious preferences of its students, the concept of faith is central to NativityMiguel Schools which ultimately aim to instill a sense of hope and belief in a vision that is not clearly visible today. Asking any stakeholder, whether it be board members, donors, faculty, staff, students or families, to trust in a future that seldom resembles their present reality requires an unwavering faith. An explicitly-faith based education therefore provides a bedrock foundation for how NativityMiguel schools talk about, envision, and deliver upon their mission. For example, the seven Principles of Catholic Social Teaching, which are fully embodied in NativityMiguel schools, allow individuals and the collective school community to reflect on the school's mission and its sacred and secular impact in our society. For schools that prioritize preferential options for the poor, Catholic Social Teaching becomes a seminal framework to reinforce why this mission is necessary.

Most member schools in the NativityMiguel Coalition are sponsored or endorsed by various religious congregations: Jesuits, De La Salle Christian Brothers, School Sisters of Notre Dame (SSND), Episcopal congregations, and several other religious communities of women and men. A smaller subset of nondenominational NativityMiguel schools identify also as faith-based.

For schools founded by a religious congregation, the charism of the congregation has been critical to the founding of each school. Each school's feasibility study outlines how the congregation's tradition is an ideal response to a compelling, urgent need. In this way, the growth of the NativityMiguel Schools has "refounded" the educational mission of these congregations in communities often void of their presence. This synergy of the tradition giving birth to new schools which in turn reanimates the tradition is illustrated and contextualized in the following educational mission statement that appears in a number of documents of the Brothers of the Christian Schools (as cited in Proehl & Suzuki, 2009).

> We are aware that our educational service of the poor cannot presume to solve all the problems of poverty in the world, but only specifically those which are related to education. As a group we follow the path which leads to the poor, acknowledging that God calls us to bring creative and generous responses to the world of the poor today, through fidelity to our founding charism. (p. 457)

Sponsorship of the religious congregation necessitates the formation of mostly lay board members, supporters, leaders, faculty, staff, students, and families in the particular spirituality, values, language, stories, and tradition of each congregation. Trainings and retreats for various stakeholders are often framed with the principles, statements, letters, research, and writings of the religious order's founder and subsequent clergy, brothers, sisters, scholars, and/or leaders. Posters and messaging visible in the school reflect and promote a shared understanding common to the particular congregation. Through professional development and school review process, each religious congregation spends great resources and time to ensure that the school truly embodies and lives out the charism of the congregation and that the growth and development of the school is animated by the charism.

This formation drives the learning and teaching culture in each school. When I was a teacher at St. Ignatius Loyola Academy in Baltimore, Maryland from 1997–2000, Ignatian spirituality and the Jesuit approach to education was a fundamental component of professional and personal development for the faculty and staff. In a memo dated January 1999, the principal stated:

> The spiritual dimension of the Academy is the most important. I use "spiritual" meaning what is not of the body, what is not measurable (at least in any scientific sense)—and especially what is sacred, or holy or most important.... The essence of our spirituality ought to be "Jesuit" with a special emphasis on the Jesuit credo of *persons for others* and (for the staff) the Jesuit pedagogical goal of *cura personalis*. These simple phrases embody the sense of mission and sacrifice and devotion that ought to comprise the core of each staff member's commitment to the boys and also embody the spirit

of selflessness, service and determination to "make a difference" that we
hope will characterize our students and graduates. (Sindler, 1999, para. 1)

While these characteristics are common in any Jesuit school, in Jesuit-sponsored NativityMiguel schools they are refounding a presence in communities who otherwise would have thought such a spiritual approach to education was inaccessible for their children.

Similarly, upon visiting several Lasallian-sponsored schools that had opened, Bro. Lawrence Goyette, FSC (2002), founder of the San Miguel School of Providence, wrote a reflection titled "If De La Salle Walked into A Miguel School Today." He framed the reflection around core Lasallian principles such as the importance of Welcome and Hospitality, of the Awareness of God's Presence, and of Faith, Zeal, and Community and highlighted how those principles animate these relatively recently-founded schools.

While fidelity to several different religious congregations can be an unfortunate risk to divisive or divergent camps in the Coalition, there is typically much convergence in message when schools gather, meet, discuss, share, listen, and reflect. For example, the Lasallian "Let us remember that we are in the holy presence of God" and the Jesuit "Seeing God in all things" are both born from a similar spiritual mindset and encourage school leaders, faculty, and staff to focus on the sacred goodness in each person they encounter. Similarly, the Lasallian "Touching the hearts and minds of your students" and the Jesuit "cura personalis" both advocate for education of the whole child which all of our schools deliver.

Perhaps one of the best illustrations of this was told to me on several occasions by the Rev. John Finley, Executive Director of Epiphany School in Dorchester, Massachusetts and an Episcopal priest. As a teacher at Nativity Prep in Boston in the 1990s, he was asked to develop a framework to capture the spiritual identity of the school. He was told by Jesuit representatives that his final version beautifully captured Ignatian spirituality. When he founded Epiphany a few years later, he used the same piece to propose the school's spiritual identity and reviewers said it perfectly articulated the Episcopal identity.

Member schools in the NativityMiguel Coalition deliver an explicitly faith-based education and these schools believe that they would not be able to accomplish the same results in any other context and environment. There is a definite, though difficult to measure, value to this open expression of faith that drives the formation of students and how they view themselves and their relation to others, the world, and their future. By sharing resources, facilitating discussion, and extending invitations to observe schools, the Coalition provides a venue to discuss and learn how the distinction of an inclusive faith-based education contributes to the growth and development of students.

Serves the Economically Poor: Alignment in Mission

Option for the Poor and Vulnerable as a principle of Catholic Social Teaching states: "A basic moral test is how our most vulnerable members are faring" (United States Conference of Catholic Bishops [USCCB], 2018, Option for the Poor and Vulnerable section). In addition, the Catholic tradition "instructs us to put the needs of the poor and vulnerable first" (USCCB, 2018, "Option for the Poor and Vulnerable"). Unfortunately, this principle is strongly tested and weakly fragile when it is applied to Catholic education and private, faith-based schools overall.

If it is said that education is the great equalizer in our country, it could also be said that tuition is one of the great dividers. The typical financial model for private schools is based on the ability of families to pay tuition. While all students must meet admissions criteria, a private education is more readily accessible for families who are able to pay tuition. A family that can afford tuition can enroll a student in the school; a family that is unable to afford tuition is typically deterred unless a scholarship is available. As the cost of school operations continues to increase, tuition also increases. It is necessary to state the obvious: if a private, faith-based education is to remain accessible to the economically poor, charging and increasing tuition to finance the school is not a viable path.

Private schools with a priority to educate poor and marginalized families face significant financing and funding obstacles and need to rely on revenue sources other than tuition. NativityMiguel schools are a radical and audacious attempt to overcome those obstacles and keep the educational tradition of the religious congregation that have operated excellent faith-based schools for many years accessible to students and families who otherwise could not consider or afford a private, faith-based education.

It is important to note that NativityMiguel Schools do not define access as offering a limited number of scholarships that allow economically-poor students, often a small percentage of a typically more affluent overall student body, to attend the school. Since Nativity Mission Center opened in 1971, NativityMiguel schools have focused on the question: How do you design a private, faith-based school that is financially accessible for the poor and designed to be academically- and formatively-accessible to address the needs of the poor? Research (e.g., Evans, 2004; Evans & Kim, 2013; Fenzel, 2009) has documented how poverty is a disruptive force to a child's education and how effective schools add necessary supports to counter that force. These supports are foundational to NativityMiguel schools and often not a priority in private, faith-based schools with a tradition and design of educating students from more affluent families.

Over time, NativityMiguel schools have learned, developed, and adapted a philanthropic model to remain financially accessible and sustain a nontuition-driven school. Typically, 95% of their yearly operating revenue is derived from the generosity of mission-driven donors and only 5% from tuition. Private schools that serve a more affluent population ask parents and alumni to consider gifts to fund annual funds and capital campaigns; the parents and alumni of NativityMiguel Schools are unable to make any significant gift to the school at this time. While NativityMiguel Schools may adopt similar fundraising strategies as other private schools, their philanthropic model resembles other service agencies. All NativityMiguel schools rely on some equation of board giving, major gifts, annual fund, special events, foundational grants, student sponsorships, and corporate partnerships in some form or another, though the percentages of support differ for each school.

Schools learn practices from one another at regional and national conferences and webinars, visit other development teams when possible, and share resources and materials such as annual reports, annual appeal letters, development plans, and calendars. As a testament to that collaboration of sharing and learning, many NativityMiguel schools are reaching milestones of 15+ and 20+ years and, collectively, schools raise over $60 million dollars annually. While the demands of fundraising are still extensive each year and questions remain as to how a nontuition driven financial model can be sustained in the long term, most NativityMiguel schools are operating from a position of greater strength each year: raising more funds in revenue than they are spending, growing reserves and an endowment, and increasing the percentage of the operating budget that has been received or pledged as the year begins. (It is important to note that while the question of sustainability may be more pronounced in the NativityMiguel financial model, it is a familiar conversation to all private schools who rely on tuition as well.)

Commitment Beyond Graduation: Alignment in Core Beliefs

Each NativityMiguel School offers a Graduate Support Program (GSP). Graduate Support has been developed over many years not as a mandate that is prescribed by a national team in a central office but through ongoing adapting, learning, and sharing by a network of Graduate Support professionals with a shared purpose who convene and connect regularly.

While the origin of the GSP, which dates back to the fall of 1985 at Nativity Mission Center in New York City, is explained in greater detail in Chapter 2 in this book, it is noted here as an excellent example of local independence and national alignment in the NativityMiguel Coalition.

Similar to the founding of NativityMiguel Schools, the concept of graduate support spread from Nativity Mission Center to other schools through a process of replication by observation. When Larry Siewert was helping found Nativity Jesuit Middle School (NJMS) in Milwaukee, Wisconsin, he visited Nativity Prep in Boston and remembers Barry Hynes saying that when you reach the age of having graduates, a graduate support program is "part of the package, part of what you do." He heard a similar message at Mother Caroline Academy in Boston and at Nativity Mission Center in New York City. Even in the year before they started, Siewert and others were interested in what happened to Nativity students when they graduated, and it was evident that Fr. Jack Podsiadlo, school principal, remained connected with every alumnus to assist with the transition to and through high school.

By the early 1990s, it was clear to Fr. Jack that supporting graduates would be best served by a full-time person rather than as additional responsibilities on the Principal. For the first few years, graduate support was staffed by a full-time intern who would develop the program rather than teach. When a grant was secured to fund the program, Roberto Rodriguez, a Nativity Mission Center graduate, became the first full-time paid director of Graduate Support. In this capacity over several years, Roberto refined the program and instituted more parent engagement and more structure such as requirements for scholarship funding.

When Fr. Jack was tapped to formalize the network of schools in 2001, he was able to shape the growth and development of the GSP at the national level. He hosted the first gathering of Graduate Support Directors in Baltimore in the spring of 2002 to share challenges, opportunities, knowledge, and resources. Larry was present at the meeting and presented on his Mentoring Program which other schools adopted and adapted within their GSP. In the next school year, a manual was developed to compile best practices, resources, and a fuller understanding of Graduate Support.

Since that initial gathering, the GSP continues to take shape based on local need, resources, and personnel and through sharing the learnings of one program with others. A prime example is in the decision of whether a NativityMiguel School will fund a portion of a student's high school tuition. Families have often relied on gap funding to cover tuition and/or fees in the next level of education and to access extracurricular activities by covering associated costs.

The Value of the NativityMiguel Coalition

In addition to knowing how they are aligned with one another, it is important that member schools can clearly name the value of belonging to the Coalition. A school will continuously assess the value of membership:

Are they stronger together with other aligned schools than they would be figuring it out as a single school? The Coalition's collective strength is not school management. Management decisions are made at the local level. The Coalition's value is focused on school improvement.

Learning to Improve

While every school has a desire to improve (and if one does not, new leadership is needed!), a desire to become better is not enough. School improvement requires stamina, determination, and discipline on the part of the school leader and school community. Even with this mindset, improvement can frustrate any school or organization without the proper process supported by the appropriate tools.

The frustration of school improvement can be especially pronounced in NativityMiguel schools which typically are organizations with small staffs and fledgling systems dealing with complex operational needs. More so, students are fully engaged in student formation and academic achievement for an average of 9 hours a day. In order for a maturing school to improve, the full team needs to reserve time that is not readily available to be strategic and purposeful in getting better. School leadership, therefore, needs to be efficient in using any time wisely and focused in what needs to be accomplished.

The principles of improvement science, outlined in the book *Learning to Improve* by Anthony Bryk of the Carnegie Foundation and colleagues (Byrk, Gomez, Grunow, & LeMahieu, 2015), frame how a NativityMiguel school (and other schools) can make the most of this time. The Carnegie Foundation has extensively researched the concept of improvement science and trained practitioners in recent years, especially as it applies to schools and supporting organizations.

Bryk and colleagues (2015) have contended that any organization seeking to improve first identify the specific problem to be addressed, the change or changes to be implemented and the measurements to assess whether the change led to improvement. Furthermore, improvement science recommends several principles to guide the process such as identifying specific, user-centered problems, determining what is working and what is not working, seeing the systems that yield the results, and observing the results of introducing small changes.

Accelerate Improvements Through Networked Communities

Most importantly for our matters, this final principle of improvement science offers an alternative lens for how supporting organizations, such as the NativityMiguel Coalition, can behave in order to support each member school in improvement efforts. A typical behavior of supporting organizations is to develop, plan, and implement large-scale, singular-focused initiatives that are rolled out to all schools. Even if these initiatives are developed in conjunction with the schools, deciding which singular initiative most blankets all schools is a difficult task. Even if there is a broad focus, say governance or curriculum, each school may need to solve a different problem within that focus and may resent an irrelevant or nonapplicable "solution" that is being mandated.

Within the improvement science framework, the appropriate function of supporting organizations is to help identify the work that each school needs to be engaged in and allow each school to own and be invested in the work. The supporting organization's role is to track the problems that schools are attempting to solve and to connect common threads across the organization. If two or more schools are engaged in the same problem, the function of the supporting organization takes on a heightened role as improvement spreads much more rapidly through networked communities.

Bryk and colleagues (Bryk, Gomez, & Grunow, 2010; Bryk et al., 2015) used the term Network Improvement Community (NIC) to describe this function. Within a NIC, schools share with other schools how they are adapting practice and improving systems in response to specific problems. NICs embrace the wisdom of crowds: we can accomplish more together than the best of us can accomplish alone. Improvement is accelerated when organizations are connected and sharing success and challenges. If one organization is able to learn from the improvement (or obstacles that impaired improvement) of other organizations, then they are able to more rapidly, efficiently, and effectively move beyond their challenges.

The Carnegie Foundation (Bryk et al., 2010, 2015) conceptualizes the NIC in the following way and it fits the NativityMiguel Coalition well. In this structure, the Coalition acts as the hub, connecting schools in person and virtually, identifying and communicating common challenges, and leveraging opportunities for growth. This role is especially important when the improvement communities that are being networked are lean organizations with minimal personnel, resources, and time to devote to valuable yet peripheral tasks. The schools are led by mission-driven practitioners who are doing what it takes in pursuit of excellence. These practitioners are not beholden to external mandates, programs, pressures, or directives from the hub and are free and open to experiment and innovate. When a practice in another school is proving to work, leaders, faculty, and staff are eager to learn and adapt from their colleagues in other schools. This framework harnesses the balance of independence and collaboration in the NativityMiguel Coalition. The Coalition is a member-driven organization which heightens the role of the members as the developers, carriers, and

deliverers of expertise, whereas in more standardized, centralized structures, the home office has this role.

At this time, the Executive Director is the sole staff member of the
NativityMiguel Coalition and is employed by the Board of Directors, which
is comprised of at least nine school leaders who represent the needs and
expectations of all schools. The Executive Director's role is to ensure a
working system that leverages the collective strength to accelerate progress
in member schools. Through this system, the Coalition fosters supportive
relationships among schools and school leaders, better understands how
schools are thriving within distinct demands of this education mission, and
strengthens competencies moving forward.

The effectiveness of this system relies on the active participation of the
members who are always learning, adapting, innovating, and ready to
share. Schools understand their obligation to other member schools, to the
hub, and to betterment of their shared mission, and practitioners understand that value is measured not only in what is being given to them but
also in what they are giving to the community. This is empowering to practitioners who realize that they can impact a broader educational system in
addition to their students, families, and immediate community.

Programs in the NativityMiguel Coalition develop and evolve over time,
not as a mandate but as a desire to improve and excel in a collaborative
structure of learning and improvement, as was examined above in the GSP
and nontuition driven financial model. Not wanting to reinvent the wheel,
and open to the contributions of others, NativityMiguel school leaders look
to others for direction and resources to overcome challenges; to adapt,
create, and innovate as appropriate for local needs, resources, and personnel, and then share progress and advancement with others who are seeking
similar ideas.

As stated above, schools in the NativityMiguel Coalition are outcome-
aligned. Member schools are committed to certain outcomes yet believe
there are different ways of getting there, again reinforcing the value
of local independence and decision making. Overall, the Coalition is
more concerned about upholding a school's outcomes in mission than
ensuring particular inputs of a standardized model. The preferred focus
is on how each student and all students are doing in terms of retention,
academic growth and proficiency, high school transition and graduation,
postsecondary placement and success, and other measures.

The collection of data by the hub is a critical task. Each member school
tracks and submits data that support a set of outcomes measured by key
performance indicators. These data position member schools within a
scale of impact not possible with one school. The purpose of collecting
and reporting these data is not to evaluate a school as passing or failing
or to uphold a strictly defined standardized model. Rather, the purpose is

to identify what can be learned from schools that are performing well and equip all schools with the tools and knowledge to improve. This allows the NativityMiguel Coalition to better target supports and professional development. Accountability at the Coalition level drives excellence by learning and communicating best practices of schools that are consistently meeting outcomes.

A Crowded Marketplace

Education is a crowded market these days. Charter schools, independent schools, independent faith-based schools, alternative district initiatives, homeschooling, and unschooling all provide options for parents beyond the traditional district school. All of these school options need to define their mission, frame their model, build school culture, hire talented teachers and leaders, and promote their results to attract and retain families, funders, and other partners.

To meet the sophisticated needs of schools in this crowded educational market, supporting organizations such as a diocesan Catholic school's office or the education office of sponsoring congregations have had to adapt to more extensively address critical issues in addition to faith formation. Both the Jesuits and the De La Salle Christian Brothers, two religious congregations that sponsor nearly half of all NativityMiguel Schools, provide national and regional services such as spiritual formation, leadership development and recruitment, board development, and professional development for other positions through the Jesuit Schools Network and Christian Brothers Conference, respectively. Similarly, the National Association of Episcopal Schools offer similar support for Episcopal affiliated schools.

The NativityMiguel Coalition maintains a relationship with these organizations and is developing a partnership to increase efficiency and maximize learning in areas such as data collection and leadership formation. The aim is for each supporting organization to know and deliver its unique expertise in a collaborative structure that allows well-informed schools to efficiently and effectively access what they need to improve. The best interests of schools are served when supporting organizations are able to minimize confusion and avoid redundancy in overlapping supports, services, programs, and communication.

Similarly, numerous supporting organizations similar to the NativityMiguel Coalition have also emerged to pay attention to shifting markets and emerging needs and leverage collective strength in a way that one school cannot. Several schools belong to supporting organizations that address critical educational challenges and opportunities across sectors. For example, Schools that Can (STC) is a national network of high-performing district, charter and private schools in urban areas that unites leaders "to expand quality urban education and close the opportunity and skills gap" (STC, 2015, "Our Mission"). Similar to NativityMiguel Coalition, STC (2015) creates "a safe space where teachers and school leaders from urban schools, education innovators, and industry leaders can work together to advance school improvement" ("Our Ecosystem"). STC has conducted a review of several NativityMiguel schools and invited them to join.

Another example is The Drexel Fund which "invests and partners in the growth of high-quality, financially sustainable networks of faith-based and other private schools to create transformational outcomes for all students and families" (The Drexel Fund, 2017, "Our Mission"). The Drexel Fund (2017) has accelerated the growth of schools in states with favorable school choice policy by offering leadership development and strategic planning to successful schools looking to replicate its model and networks seeking to increase their scale. Schools that were once members of the NativityMiguel Network, such as Academy Prep of St. Petersburg and Tampa and Good Shepherd Nativity Mission School in New Orleans, LA, have benefitted from the support and expertise offered through The Drexel Fund. While geographically limited at this time, the Drexel Fund has highlighted the educational opportunity and impact of school choice as a compelling catalyst for legislative change in other states as well.

Advocating for school choice legislation and collaborative learning across sectors in a competitive and crowded education market are both challenges and opportunities that NativityMiguel schools will face in the years ahead. The NativityMiguel Coalition recognizes that schools have abundant choices for supporting organizations and that other organizations may be more adept with certain expertise and supports. Rather than compromising its mission and value by overextending its focus, the Coalition seeks partnership with these organizations to deliver expertise and supports that will benefit its member school. The Coalition also realizes that some NativityMiguel Schools may prioritize involvement with other support organization given specific needs and limited time and resource.

Conclusion: Challenges and Opportunities Ahead

NativityMiguel schools were founded to serve children of economically-poor families who desire a quality, faith-based education for their children yet are unable to afford or access such an education. NativityMiguel schools, with a mission of "breaking the cycle of poverty through a faith-based education" (NativityMiguel Coalition, n.d.) are designed to specifically serve this demographic of students and prepare them for success at the next level of education and for professional and personal achievement.

When Nativity Mission Center started in 1971, it would have been impossible to imagine starting 65 similar schools across the country. Even 25 years ago when Nativity Prep of Boston first replicated the model, it would have been difficult to envision 63 founding groups attempting and accomplishing a similar venture. In many ways, NativityMiguel Schools are a refounding of a mission that is rooted in the strong faith and educational tradition of religious communities and congregations who have served similar populations for generations and have made an intentional decision to remain present and relevant in the lives of the poor. This movement was not founded on standardization and centralization of an educational model, rather investment in and prioritization of a critical educational mission that relies on local personnel and partners to respond to local needs with local resources.

The question driving the formation of the Coalition, that is, how can we uphold a priority of local independence and achieve the strongest system of regional and national collaboration to facilitate learning and accelerate improvement, is an important question moving forward for all engaged in thinking about systems that will assure the accessibility of private, faith-based schools to the economically poor and marginalized.

If the movement forward is characterized by inward, internal judgment with divisive territorial boundaries then private, faith-based education risks being accessible only to families who are able to pay tuition. Rather, all private, faith-based schools and supporting organizations need to be challenged to continuously consider how models of local strength can contribute to broader growth and how learnings in one diocese, sponsoring congregation, college/university, or school can be harnessed as an opportunity to spur innovation elsewhere.

Given their history and tradition, private faith-based schools are uniquely positioned to deliver an academically excellent and holistically formative education that can impact students, families, and communities. Can private, faith-based schools and the dioceses, sponsoring congregations, funders, families, alumni, and other organizations that support them map what the next 25 or 50 years will hold for a mission of providing a high-quality, faith-based education that is accessible to marginalized students from economically-poor families? Such an endeavor may be ambitious in an ever-changing educational market on both the public and private side and any map would need to be flexible to rapidly-evolving variables. In their control, however, is leading with a mindset that prioritizes being present, relevant, and accessible in the lives and education of all students and families, and defining, advocating, paying attention, and being open to opportunities to do so. Whether it be school choice, charter schools, higher education partnerships, teacher formation or leadership development to name a few, space and time is needed to allow for conversations and research to inform how others are engaged in this mission in certain communities and to inspire others to take action elsewhere.

REFERENCES

Bradach, J. L. (2003, Spring). Going to scale: The challenge of replicating social programs. *Stanford Social Innovation Review*. Retrieved from https://ssir.org/articles/entry/going_to_scale

Bryk, A. S., Gomez L. M., & Grunow A. (2010). *Getting ideas into action: Building networked improvement communities in education*. Stanford, CA: Carnegie Foundation for the Advancement of Teaching. Retrieved from http://www.carnegiefoundation.org/spotlight/webinar-bryk-gomez-building-networkedimprovement-communities-in-education

Bryk, A. S., Gomez, L. M., Grunow, A., & LeMahieu, P. G. (2015). *Learning to improve: How America's schools can get better at getting better*. Cambridge, MA: Harvard Education Press.

Drexel Fund, The. (2017). *Our mission*. Retrieved from http://www.drexelfund.org

Evans, G. W. (2004). The environment of childhood poverty. *American Psychologist, 59*, 77–92. doi:10.1037/0003-066X.59.2.77

Evans, G. W., & Kim, P. (2013). Childhood poverty, chronic stress, self-regulation, and coping, *Child Development Perspectives, 7*(1), 43–48. doi:10.1111/cdep.12013

Fenzel, L. M. (2009). *Improving urban middle schools: Lessons from the Nativity schools*. Albany, NY: State University of New York Press.

Goyette, L., Bro., FSC. (2002). *If De La Salle walked into a Miguel school today*. Unpublished manuscript.

NativityMiguel Coalition. (n.d.). *Our mission*. Retrieved from http://www.nativitymiguel.org

Proehl, R. A., & Suzuki, S. (2009). Transferring social justice initiatives into Lasallian schools. *Catholic Education: A Journal of Inquiry and Practice, 12*, 457–474. Retrieved from http://digitalcommons.lmu.edu/ce/vol12/iss4/8

Robson, K., & Smarick, A. (2016, March 29). Innovation in Catholic education: New approaches to instruction and governance may revitalize the sector. *Education Next*. Retrieved from http://educationnext.org/innovation-in-catholic-education-instruction-governance/#

Schools That Can. (2015). *Who we are*. Retrieved from http://www.schoolsthatcan.org/who-we-are

Sindler, J. (1999, January 8). *Memo* (unpublished manuscript). Baltimore, MD: St. Ignatius Loyola Academy.

United States Conference of Catholic Bishops. (2018). *Seven themes of Catholic Social Teaching*. Retrieved from http://www.usccb.org/beliefs-and-teachings/what-we-believe/catholic-social-teaching/seven-themes-of-catholic-social-teaching.cfm

CHAPTER 8

NOTRE DAME MISSION VOLUNTEERS AMERICORPS

Deploying Volunteers to Improve Education of Urban Children

Peter Litchka
Loyola University Maryland

The purpose of this chapter is to explore and examine the impact that the Notre Dame Mission Volunteers AmeriCorps (NDMVA) is having on the achievement and success of students through a national network of service. NDMVA has been a grantee of AmeriCorps since 1995 and currently provides educational services in 23 cities across the United States. This examination will be viewed through the integration of Catholic Social Teaching (CST), the mission of Notre Dame Mission Volunteers AmeriCorps (NDMVA), and national service initiatives that help to support the needs of students placed at risk.

Responding to the Call for Educational Justice:
Transformative Catholic-Led Initiatives in Urban Education, pp. 129–145
Copyright © 2019 by Information Age Publishing
All rights of reproduction in any form reserved.

Catholic Social Teaching

The mission of NDMVA is consistent with the principles of Catholic Social Teaching (CST) and the preferential option for the poor. Anchored in the belief in the dignity of every human person, CST supports as a fundamental right access to adequate education (United States Conference of Catholic Bishops [USCCB], 2005). CST calls upon Catholics to focus their service and work alongside the oppressed in a way that will ultimately put an end to poverty and oppression, as well as restrictive structures found in society to preserve the life and dignity of every human person (Kirylo, 2006; USCCB, 2005).

Volunteerism and National Service

AmeriCorps

AmeriCorps, which is administered by the Corporation for National and Community Service (CNCS), provides grants to both public and non-profit organizations that support community service at the local, state, and national level. The primary goals for AmeriCorps are:

- *Satisfy Unmet Social Needs*: primary purpose is to help communities solve human social and economic problems.
- *Develop Corps Members*: provide opportunities for members to develop character and job preparation in terms of learning and experiences.
- *Enhance Civic Ethics*: create opportunities for members to develop civic consciousness as they help to build (rebuild) communities and develop partnerships as well. (CNCS, 2017)

According to CNCS, the AmeriCorps programs both enhance the communities in which they serve as well as create experiential learning opportunities for young adults who are preparing to enter the workforce. AmeriCorps has placed thousands of such young adults into positions in which they learn about service and apply such skills to local communities around the country. Finally, these young adults are paid for their training and experiences in service, with the hope that each develops an awareness of civic responsibilities (CNCS, 2017).

Full-time AmeriCorps members (volunteers) complete up to 1,700 hours of service during a year and receive a living stipend, health benefits, and a residence to share with fellow members to assist in helping the elderly, the disabled, and students in schools, often in conjunction with nonprofits such as Habitat for Humanity, Boys and Girls Clubs, the American Red Cross, as well as numerous faith-based and community initiatives. Since 1994, almost 1 million AmeriCorps members have provided more than 1.4 billion hours in service across the United States, taking on the various social and economic problems found in communities across the nation (CNCS, 2017).

Improving student achievement in underserved schools has been a strong focus for AmeriCorps since its founding. Although the studies of the effectiveness of AmeriCorps efforts are few, a summary of research findings by Magee and Marshall (2005) concluded that AmeriCorps programs supporting students placed at risk provide a solid return on investment. In a review of seven studies, which include Aguirre International (1997), Magee and Marshall (2005) reported that gains in student reading and math achievement generally were greater than would be obtained without such assistance.

Notre Dame Mission Volunteers AmeriCorps

The Notre Dame Mission Volunteers (NDMV) was established as a nonprofit volunteer organization in 1990 by the Sisters of Notre Dame de Namur (SNDdeN), a Catholic religious order founded in 1804. The Sisters of Notre Dame de Namur, like many other Catholic religious communities of men and women, have long been committed to social justice work as an integral part of their Catholic identity. Founded in Belgium, a small group of the sisters came to the United States in the middle of the 19th century committed to the education of young people at the margins of society (Sisters of Notre Dame de Namur, 2015).

The Order, which includes approximately 900 Sisters across the United States, has a mission of providing educational and other services to the poor. The Sisters fulfill their social justice mission through serving as teachers and administrators in Catholic schools from preschool through college and serving children, adults, and families in parishes and community centers. In 1995, the Notre Dame Mission Volunteers AmeriCorps (NDMVA) received its first AmeriCorps grant, and currently has 116 service sites across the United States, with 389 members (volunteers), serving more than 13,000 students (NDMVA, 2017).

The mission of NDMVA (2017) stated:

> Notre Dame Mission Volunteers believes that education is the central tool in the struggle of the poor for human dignity, self-esteem, and willpower. We seek to build community among our members, as well as the people with whom we work by reaching out across culture and class. We are committed to helping people help themselves. Our goal is to promote and

encourage education, community empowerment, leadership development and multicultural harmony. ("Learn: Mission Statement")

There is a clear and defined connection between the mission of NDMVA with that of the Catholic Social Teaching, AmeriCorps, and volunteerism in general. The mission and actions of NDMVA focus on providing educational support to those within society who are often not provided with equitable opportunities, and as a result, may become even more vulnerable, more marginalized, and ultimately fall prey to the vicious cycle of helplessness and hopelessness. In addition, NDMVA members develop their own personal capacities to become more productive members of society in terms of education, building communities, and providing others with opportunities to reach their God-given potential. Particularly noteworthy of the NDMVA program is the provision for community building and spiritual formation for the members through the training and retreat program (NDMVA, 2017). These aspects of the program help to ground members in the Catholic nature of service as solidarity with those who are served.

Within the individual program sites, the NDMVA site director oversees the members' services, coordinates with local partnering sites where the members serve, and is the primary liaison between the national office in Baltimore and the members. Partnering sites include public schools, charter schools, private religious schools, and other community agencies in economically disadvantaged communities. NDMVA members provide services to students by serving as teachers' assistants, providing one-on-one or small group instruction and supporting after-school programs, and helping to coordinate education and youth development activities.

Most of the members are based at operating sites around the country, being assigned to local partnering sites that include schools as well as community and faith-based organizations. Members are supervised by operating site directors, who are overseen by the NDMVA national office. Most of the operating sites are found in urban centers where the needs are greatest.

To address injustice, schools can play a vital role in creating a culture where all are welcomed, regardless of socioeconomic or cultural background, and where everyone is transformed through idealized influences, inspirational motivation, intellectual stimulation, individualized consideration, and empowerment; thus, NDMVA has developed collaborative partnerships with schools within its network.

NDMVA focuses much of its efforts and resources on increasing the academic achievement levels of children who are involved in the program activities. Academic and social support are provided during the regular school day and after school as well, depending on the needs and available resources found at the various partnering sites. At the various school sites, NDMVA members engage in activities such as:

- Providing in-school and after-school academic tutoring and small group instruction for children in elementary, middle, and high school, focusing on reading and math.
- Creating and managing out-of-school enrichment programs in areas such as sports, drama, visual arts, creative writing, environmental education, and debating.
- Providing intern teaching services for small groups of students, typically 6–12 in number, under the direction of a master teacher.
- Providing general classroom assistance to teachers.

Previous Evaluations

To ensure continuous funding for their program, NDMVA began to contract independent evaluations of the effectiveness of the programs in 2008. Findings from the first evaluation (Fenzel& Dean, 2011) of 109 students in grades 3 through 10 enrolled in after-school programs at five urban school sites showed positive correlations between the frequency of participation in three activities, obtaining homework assistance, engaging in independent reading, and working independently on homework, and increases in both their school engagement and academic performance. Receiving after-school tutoring was also strongly related to these positive changes in perceptions for students in grades 7 through 10. This study also showed that school principals acknowledged the value of the work of the NDMVA members who provided most of the after-school services in their urban schools for students placed at risk, many of which were Catholic schools that followed the NativityMiguel model.

In a subsequent evaluation, Litchka (2013) completed a mixed-method examination to assess the impact of member support on student attitudes and achievement. Both pre- (fall) and post- (spring) surveys were conducted as well as on-site interviews and focus groups involving both elementary and secondary students, with positive and significant changes found in both attitudes and achievement, specifically by gender, ethnicity, and type of service. Of note, further analysis showed that in-school programs supported by NDMVA had a much more significant impact than did the after-school program.

The Present Study

An independent assessment of the Notre Dame Mission Volunteer AmeriCorps informs the foundation of this study. The author was asked by the Executive Director of the NDMVA to develop, implement, and report on the level of effectiveness of the program as part of NDMVA's continued involvement with AmeriCorps, and was completed in 2015. The 2015 assessment focused on an in-depth evaluation of the Chicago site. Chicago was selected as a model for the entire network, in that it represented both the urban nature of where NDMVA provides services as well as student demographics. For this assessment, the construct of student engagement was used as the foundation for measuring the effectiveness of the program on students.

Student Engagement

During the past couple of decades, the concept of student engagement has emerged as a focal point among researchers, policymakers, educators, and others (Fredericks, 2013; Kuh, 2009; Parsons, Nuland, & Parsons, 2014; Skinner, Kindermann, & Furrer, 2009). The research is very clear that if students are not engaged in their school work, there is a significant chance of them not being successful, both in the short-term and long-term. The goal is to ensure that programs that are being utilized in this context are successful to the extent that student engagement is improving because of these programs, ultimately improving student academic success.

Having students who are engaged in their learning is a critical component for consideration as schools are under constant pressure to have both high standards and achievement for all its students, but also to ensure that students have the resources and support to be successful (Fredericks, Blumenfeld, & Paris, 2004). Students who are engaged in their school are more likely to be successful and become productive members of society (Lehr, Hansen, Sinclair, & Christenson, 2003; National Research Council, 2004).

Researchers have found significant links of high levels of student engagement to improved achievement within both academic and nonacademic school contexts(Skinner et al., 2009). Consequently, students who are more engaged in their school life are more likely to earn higher grades and score better on standardized tests and less likely to drop out of school, regardless of ethnicity and/or socioeconomic status. In contrast, however, students who are not engaged in positive aspects of their school life are more likely to be less successful and become involved in negative behaviors, and are less likely to stay in school or graduate (Christenson & Thurlow, 2004).

Researchers have also examined student engagement from a longitudinal perspective (Sinclair, Christenson, Lehr, & Anderson, 2003). In other words, researchers wanted to find out if variables exist that impact whether a student can become more or less engaged, and if so, under what circumstances. Much of the research implies that, as students progress from elementary to the middle years and on to high school, engagement often decreases (Marks, 2000; Steinberg, 1996). At one time, it was proposed that a major reason for students being disengaged was the comprehensive and impersonal high schools that students were often faced with. However, some researchers have suggested that this disengagement often starts as early as the elementary years, when meaningless instructional activities or an overemphasis on standardized test preparation occur, and schools are unable or unwilling to create learning environments that emphasize the individuality of students, high expectations for success, and a more positive family/community environment. This type of context often follows students from their early years well into high school. To further exacerbate this situation, researchers have found that disengagement is significantly higher in students of color living in high-poverty urban areas (Yazzie-Mintz, 2007).

Regardless of the school level, student engagement is a strong predictor of student success. McPartland (1994) suggested that schools who have programs aimed at improving student engagement should consider four factors:

1. Providing opportunities for students to be successful in their schoolwork;
2. Creating a caring and supportive school culture among both students *and* teachers;
3. Ensuring that students are provided with relevant, interesting, challenging, and appropriate curriculum and instruction driven to meet the needs and interests of the students;
4. Providing resources for students and families that are at-risk, particularly during the formative years.

One of the primary aspects of the NDMVA program is that of having individualized and small group instruction, both during regular school hours and after-school. This format has been researched extensively over the past several decades, suggesting greater student engagement and higher achievement, particularly with students who face socioeconomic inequities and other issues of social injustice (Achilles, Finn, & Bain, 1997; Biddle & Berliner, 2002).

Chicago Site

In Chicago, NDMVA supports several unique educational settings, including a network of charter schools that emphasize free enrollment and a college preparatory curriculum across numerous campuses. NDMVA members serve at the ACHIEVE, ADVANCE, and SUCCESS campuses found within Chicago.[1] NDMVA members serve as academic intervention-ists working one-on-one and in small groups with students performing below grade level in reading and writing. Members also assist in the class-room and provide support during after-school activities. In addition, centers offer programs and services to children, teens, families and seniors, including an after-school program that helps students with homework, mentoring, and other small group activities. NDMVA members serve in classrooms as teaching assistants, assist students in the process of applying to high school, and provide graduate support to alumni who have moved on to high school and college.

The three sites that were selected as part of this evaluation were the ACHIEVE, ADVANCE, and SUCCEED sites. Two of the schools, ACHIEVE and SUCCEED, were located on the west side of Chicago and were public schools, while ADVANCE was a charter school located on the south side of the city. Both ACHIEVE and SUCCEED had a long history of less-than-sat-isfactory results in terms of academic achievement, and had gone through significant reconstitution prior to the evaluation in terms of personnel and leadership. ADVANCE became a charter school 3 years earlier and was being run by an outside agency in affiliation with the city's board of education.

As shown in Table 8.1 the enrollment in these schools range from 200 to almost 500 students, and each has very high levels of students living in poverty, as measured by the participation rates in the federally funded free and reduced meals (FARMs) program.

Table 8.1.
Individual School Sites-Student Demographics

School	Grades	Enrollment	FARMs
ACHIEVE	6–8	200	97%
ADVANCE	K–6	440	97%
SUCCESS	K–7	439	94%

Note. FARMs=Percent of Students Receiving Free/Reduced Meals

Quantitative Survey

The quantitative portion of the evaluation was conducted by using a pre-and post-survey, *The Engagement versus Disaffection with Learning Scale*

(Skinner et al., 2009). This instrument was designed to assess student motivation that includes the construct of engagement versus disengagement in terms of the impact that such motivation can have on student learning, success, and achievement. The conceptual framework of student motivation suggests that student engagement in the learning process is enhanced when the social setting supports students' basic needs, both in a behavioral as well as emotional manner. When met, such needs provide students with a sense of support, structure, involvement, and opportunity. Conversely, when such needs are not met, often students feel neglected, not supported, or "forced to learn," which can have a serious impact on student learning and achievement.

The instrument contains 24 items, divided into four subscales:

- Behavioral Engagement (5 items): tries, pays attention, and is persistent.
- Emotional Engagement (5 items): motivated, taps emotions, and enjoys learning.
- Behavioral Disaffection (5 items): lack of effort, withdraws, and pretends to pay attention.
- Emotional Disaffection (5 items): feeling discouraged, dislikes learning, feels frustrated during the learning process. (Skinner et al., pp. 495–496)

For each item, the response scale ranges include 1 (not at all true), 2 (not very true), 3 (sort of true), to 4 (very true). Thus, the higher the ratings for Behavioral Engagement and Emotional Engagement, the more positive the student is motivated in school. Conversely, the higher the ratings for Behavioral Disaffection and Emotional Disaffection, the less motivated the student feels about school. Structural analyses conducted by Skinner and colleagues (2009) submitted that the items can be analyzed in various combinations, including separating the four subscales, combining both engagement subscales in comparison to both disaffection subscales.

Below are examples of items for each domain:

- Behavioral Engagement: "When in class, I listen very carefully."
- Emotional Engagement: "I enjoy learning new things in class."
- Behavioral Disaffection: "When in class, I just act like I am learning."
- Emotional Disaffection: "When we work on something in class, I feel discouraged."

Skinner and colleagues (2009) reported internal reliabilities from a sample of students in grades 3–6 of .61 to .85. In addition, when combining behavioral and emotional engagement items, levels of consistency were found to be from .79 to .86 for student reporting. Finally, factor analyses found that the four-factor model was the best fit and correlated as expected: the behavioral and emotional subscales correlated positively, and the engagement and disaffection subscales correlated negatively (Skinner et al., 2009).

The pre-survey was administered in late September, while the post-survey was administered in mid-May. Students who had access to computers and the Internet could take both surveys during school time via the online survey tool, Survey Monkey. For those students who did not have access to computers and/or the internet, a paper-pencil version of the survey was provided under the supervision of a teacher or NDMVA member. The site director transformed these into the web-based format and, additionally, made copies of the paper results and sent them onto the evaluator. A 2-week window was provided to each site for completion of the survey both in the fall and spring.

To analyze differences in the perceptions of both engagement and disaffection as well as to provide anonymity of students, demographic items (sex, grade, ethnicity, name of school/center) were added to the survey. In addition, each student was provided with a unique identification number.

Qualitative: Focus Groups

The purpose of the qualitative portion of the evaluation was to develop a better understanding of the meanings constructed by students who participate in the NDMVA program in the three Chicago sites. Unlike the quantitative portion, this part of the evaluation sought to interpret, translate, and assess student experiences, particularly as it relates to the context of this study.

The evaluator contacted the site director to set up focus group interviews with the selected students from the treatment groups (those who are receiving services). The focus group interviews were conducted via Skype, an online telecommunications application software produce that provides video chatting and conference calling from computers, tablets, and mobile devices via the Internet. The discussions were semi-structured in their format, in that the interviews included a mix of predetermined quested and less structured questions, which allowed for the evaluator to probe deeper, and for the interviewees to provide examples and share experiences. The structured portion focused around the following questions for students:

1. Please describe the services you receive as a student from the NDMVA staff?
2. What do you see as the benefits of receiving such services?

3. What concerns do you have about the program?
4. What would your life as a student be like if you were not part of the program?

Interviews were recorded and then transcribed for analysis purposes.

Data Presentation

Descriptive Data

More than 300 students from the ACHIEVE, ADVANCE, and SUCCESS schools took both the fall and spring surveys. There was a decrease in the number of students taking the survey in the spring as compared to the fall, with the treatment group decreasing from 154 to 128. One of the reasons for this decrease is that some of the students had become proficient in reading and had reached their grade-level, thus no longer requiring academic support from NDMVA members. Overall, the percentage of students in the treatment group as compared to the comparison group from fall to spring did not change significantly.

Data collected showed that 50.5% of the students self-identified as female and 49.5% as male. Regarding grade levels, there were 79 students in third grade who participated, 87 students in fourth grade, 69 students in fifth grade, and 76 students in sixth grade, for a total of 311 students. The final demographic data collected was that of student ethnicity, with more than 90% of the student self-identifying as African American ($n = 284$).

Survey Data and Analysis

To examine the differences in student perceptions between the fall and spring surveys, mean scores and standard deviations were computed according to each of the subscales and grouping of students (comparison and treatment). As shown in Table 8.2, the treatment group's difference in the mean ratings between the fall and spring was more positive in each of the four subscales.

Results of the initial statistical analysis demonstrates the impact that the NDMVA program is having on students in three selected sites in Chicago. In comparing the change in student perceptions over time (early fall to late spring) between the comparison group (those students not receiving services) and the treatment group (those receiving services) among all three schools together, the treatment group's change from fall to spring was more positive for each of the four subscales.

Table 8.2.
All Schools Fall/Spring Survey Results by Subscale and Groups

Subscale	Comparison Group (n = 134)			Treatment Group (n = 177)		
	Fall Mean (SD)	Spring Mean (SD)	Difference	Fall Mean (SD)	Spring Mean (SD)	Difference
Behavioral Engagement	3.02 (.54)	3.16 (.50)	.13	2.95 (.57)	3.24 (.63)	.29
Emotional Engagement	2.52 (.53)	2.75(.63)	.23	2.40 (.58)	2.97 (.71)	.57
Behavioral Disaffection	2.14 (.60)	1.99 (.58)	(–.15)	2.15 (.54)	175 (.60)	(–.40)
Emotional Disaffection	2.42 (.64)	2.27 (.66)	(–.15)	2.43 (.57)	2.13 (.60)	(–.30)

Subsequently a multivariate analysis of variance (MANOVA) was used to determine if statistically significant differences were between the multiple independent groups (those receiving services and those not receiving services) and the multiple dependent groups (Behavioral Engagement, Emotional Engagement, Behavioral Disaffection, and Emotional Disaffection), with grade, school, gender and ethnicity as covariates. Results found that scores from the treatment group were higher than those of the comparison group, and in each of the four areas, the difference was statistically significant, $F(2, 311) = 6.979$, $p < .001$. Post hoc analysis of the covariates did not reveal differences that were statistically significant.

Interviews and Observations

A sample of students receiving the services from AmeriCorps were interviewed by the evaluator as part of the qualitative portion of the evaluation. Students were interviewed in small focus groups at the school which they attended, and the results of the interviews are presented in Table 8.3.

During the focus group interviews, students provided evidence of the services received, how often the services occurred and the benefits from receiving services from NDMVA. Below is a sample of quotes from students regarding the benefits of their participation in this program:

Without the help of Miss ___ [NDMVA member], I would not be passing onto the next grade. She understood me, helped me with my reading and some math, and helped me deal with some of my problems I had with my teacher and other students. (Male student R, fifth grader)

Table 8.3.
Student Interview Comments by Categories

Grade	Services	How Often	Benefits
3	Help with reading and sometimes other subjects. (3) Individual help. (3) Small groups. (2) Pull-out. (2)	Every day. 20–30 minutes per day. (4)	Better grades. (5) Working harder. (5) Having adults who care. (4) Enjoying school. (5)
4	Help with reading. (4) Fun activities with other students. (3) Group work. (2) Pull-out. (3)	Usually 4 days per week; 20–30 minutes per day. (4)	Better grades. (5) Getting along with others. (3) Learning how to study better. (4) Feel better about myself. (4)
5	One-on-one Reading and math help. (2) Small reading groups and help with homework. (3) Pull-out. (2)	4–5 days per week, 30–40 minutes each day. (3)	Being in a smaller class for part of the day makes school better. (3) Help with problems. (4) More positive about school (3).
6	Small groups and individual help with reading and homework. (4) Pull-out. (4)	Everyday. 20–30 minutes per day; sometimes longer. (6)	Adult support. (3) People who care about us. (3) More friends (3). Feel better about school. (3) Helping us be better to ourselves and others. (4)

I was pulled-out of my class every day. In the beginning, I didn't want to go but then I began to like it. Miss ___ [NDMVA member] gave me lots of help that many of my friends in other classes were not able to get. I didn't like school, but I like it better now. My grades are better, and I am getting along better with others. (Female student R, fifth grader)

We really trust Miss ___ [NDMVA member]. We have been with her for the whole year and she really believes in us-not all our teachers do. We all think school is very good place to be and we want to be good students. (Female student T, Male student L, Male student K, all sixth graders)

I was not doing well in school, but Miss ___ [NDMVA member] made reading and math fun for me. I like school much better now and I really want to do well. My reading is getting better, and math is too…but I like reading with Miss ___ [NDMVA member] the most. (Female student Z, sixth grader)

These comments articulate the relationships that have developed between the volunteers and the students in a professional, nurturing, and sustainable manner. There is a thread among these and other comments collected during the research that is at the heart of what NDMVA does: serving others through education by not only meeting the needs of the students, but by treating each student with love, empathy, and a sense of solidarity.

Discussion

Creating a sustainable educational model for all students is, at its very core, an issue of social justice in that the educational system should provide an educational experience for *all* young people with a full, just, and equi-table experience. Yet, as the achievement gap continues to widen between those with access to quality public education and those who do not, it has become obvious that many students, particularly students of color and students with little social capital, are still being left behind. As this study shows, there exist pockets of success for these students within the frame-work of social justice, Catholic Social Teaching (CST), and the federal government's ability to support programs such as AmeriCorps. Entities, such as NDMVA, are providing support as society continues to grapple with issues of poverty, access, economic, and social organization that public schools cannot address without additional support.

This study, part of a series of evaluations, examines the impact that the Notre Dame Mission Volunteers AmeriCorps (NDMVA) has had on student success in providing both in-school and after-school support and demonstrates what local institutions, with support from a larger organization such as NDMVA, can achieve. In the case of NDMVA, it cannot be said that what the organization provides is just another in-school or after-school program for children placed at risk. The uniqueness of NDMVA is that its members live and serve alongside the communities where educational and social services are provided. In addition, members and volunteers provide a range of learning activities that support students' educational and social growth. Since NDMVA is an organization that has sites across the nation, there is a focus on ensuring that all directors and members are trained and supported, according the mission of the organization. Several times each year, directors and members come together at a central location to learn, to share, and to plan on how best to deliver the services in a consistent and effective manner. These work sessions also include time for reflection on the principles of CST and prayer, services that NDMVA also provide for its members living in community in areas where they work.

At first glance, the success of the NDMVA program with the schools in Chicago and elsewhere appears to emanate from the synergy created between the members with students, faculty, parents, and the community. These harmonious relationships are key to the success, but, in a sense, it goes much deeper than what shows on the surface. It is the confluence of not only NDMVA and the work it does, but the spiritual tenets of CST and the doctrine of volunteerism as well, resulting in a deepening sense of value and the dignity of all persons, regardless of the conditions of economic poverty and racism. In fact, one could argue that this confluence represents a perspective on how we, as Americans, think of ourselves and think of others, in terms of what we, in a moral and civic manner, are obligated to provide each other.

What this author has discovered is that this obligation goes beyond the personal into what CST, volunteerism, and NDMVA offer is for each who is involved: to go beyond personal self-interest and provide a foundation for every individual to become, in fact, a leader—not only for those who are providing the services, but for those who are receiving the services.

This type of service and commitment to others can be learned and applied, as we have seen in this examination of the work of Notre Dame Mission Volunteer AmeriCorps. There exists a basic yet critical perspective that NDMVA and its volunteers have regarding their work with students, which is a respect for all and a fortitude to never use their authority for privilege or to oppress. In fact, there is a clear emphasis on the part of NDMVA and its volunteers to view the students within the asset model (seeing what is good in a child, family, and/or community), rather than the oft-used deficit model (seeing only what they supposedly lack, do not have, or are not doing). As the director of NDMVA once told this author, "We are here to serve, not save!"

By incorporating its own beliefs and mission with those of CST and the concept of volunteerism, NDMVA members in fact serve others, serve society, and serve themselves as well. The results strongly suggest that this is a model of social justice that fulfills the commitment for an educational experience devoted to providing a complete, just, and rightful educational opportunity for everyone, especially those who have been marginalized.

NOTE

1. The names of each of the centers have been changed to respect the anonymity of each school and its center.

REFERENCES

Achilles, C., Finn, J., & Bain, H. (1997, December–1998, January). Using class size to reduce the equity gap. *Educational Leadership, 55*(4), 40–43.

Aguirre International. (1997). *AmeriCorps state/national programs impact evaluation: First year report.* Washington, DC: Corporation for National Service.

Biddle, B., & Berliner, D. (2002). *What research says about unequal funding: In pursuit of better schools—What research says.* New York, NY: Education Policy Studies Laboratory.

Christenson, S., & Thurlow, M. (2004). School dropouts: Prevention consideration, interventions, and challenges. *Current Directions in Psychological Science, 13*(1), 36–39.

Corporation for National and Community Service. (2017). *AmeriCorps.* Retrieved from https://www.nationalservice.gov/programs/americorps

Fenzel, L. M., & Dean, R. J. (2011, April). *Multi-site evaluation of AmeriCorps-staffed after-school programs.* Paper presented at the Annual Meeting of the American Educational Research Association, New Orleans, LA.

Fredericks, J. (2013). Behavior engagement in learning. In J. Hattie & E. M. Anderman (Eds.), *International guide to student achievement* (pp. 42–45). New York, NY: Routledge.

Fredericks, J., Blumenfeld, P., & Paris, A. (2004). School engagement: Potential of the concept: State of the evidence. *Review of Educational Research, 74*, 59–119.

Kirylo, J. D. (2006). Preferential option for the poor: Making a pedagogical choice. *Childhood Education, 82*, 266–270. doi:10.1080/00094056.2006.10522839

Kuh, G. (2009). The national survey of student engagement: Conceptual and empirical foundations. *New Directions for Institutional Research, 141*, 5–20.

Lehr, C., Sinclair, M., & Christenson, S. (2003). Addressing student engagement and truancy during the elementary school years: A replication study of the check & connect model. *Journal of Education for Students Placed at Risk, 9*(3), 279–301.

Litchka, P. (2013). *Evaluation report of the Notre Dame Mission Volunteers AmeriCorps Program.* Unpublished manuscript.

Magee, M. P., & Marshall, W. (2005). Has AmeriCorps lived up to its promise? In W. Marshall & M. P. Magee (Eds.), *The AmeriCorps experiment and the future of national service* (pp. 1–50). Washington, DC: The Progressive Policy Institute.

Marks, H. (2000). Student engagement in instructional activity: Patterns in the elementary, middle, and high school years. *American Education Research Journal, 37*, 153–184.

McPartland, J. (1994). Dropout prevention in theory and change. In R. Rossi (Ed.), *Schools and students at risk: Context and framework for positive change* (pp. 255–276). New York, NY: Teachers College.

National Research Council and the Institute of Medicine. (2004). *Engaging schools: Fostering high school students' motivation to learn.* Washington, DC: The National Academic Press.

Notre Dame Mission Volunteers AmeriCorps. (2017). *Learn: Mission statement.* Retrieved from http://www.ndmva.org/learn

Parsons, S., Nuland, L., & Parsons, A. (2014). The ABCs of student engagement. *Kappan, 95*(8), 23–27.

Sinclair, M., Christenson, C., Lehr, C., & Anderson, A. (2003). Facilitating student engagement; Lessons learned from check and connect longitudinal studies. *The California School Psychologist, 8*(1), 29–41.

Sisters of Notre Dame de Namur. (2015). *Where we are.* Retrieved from https://www.sndden.org/who-we-are/where-we-are/north-america/

Skinner, E., Kindermann, T., & Furrer, C. (2008). A motivational perspective on engagement and disaffection: Conceptualization and assessment of children's behavioral and emotional participation in academic activities in the classroom. *Educational and Psychological Measurement, 69*, 493–525.

Steinberg, L. (1996). *Beyond the classroom: Why school reform has failed and what parents need to do.* New York, NY: Simon and Schuster.

United States Conference of Catholic Bishops. (2005). *Themes of Catholic social teaching.* Retrieved from http://usccb.org/beliefs-and-teachings/what-we-believe/catholic-social-teaching/seven-themes-ofcatholic-social-teaching.cfm

Yazzie-Mintz, E. (2007). *Voices of students on engagement: A report on the 2006 high school survey of student engagement.* Bloomington, IN: Indiana University, Center for Evaluation and Education Policy. Retrieved from http://www.indiana.edu/~ceep/hssse/images/HSSE%20Overview%20Report%20-%202006.pdf

EDITOR'S INTRODUCTION TO FE Y ALEGRÍA

L. Mickey Fenzel
Loyola University Maryland

Founded prior to some of the Jesuit educational initiatives in the United States, most notably Nativity Mission Center, NativityMiguel schools, and Cristo Rey schools, Fe y Alegrìa is the outgrowth of an educational project begun in Caracas, Venezuela by Fr. Josè Marìa Vélaz, Society of Jesus (SJ), who had begun work with the poor and marginalized children and families there in the late 1940s. Together with local residents, most notably Abraham and Patricia Reyes, Fr. Vélaz founded a school at the Reyes home in 1955 for the children in a high poverty barrio outside of Caracas. Catholic nuns came to teach the children and members of the community worked together so that their children could receive an education that had been denied them. This small but liberating endeavor soon led to other similar initiatives in Venezuela and neighboring countries and the formation of the Fe y Alegrìa network in 1960 (Federaciòn Internacional Fe y Alegrìa, 2016a; Podsiadlo, 1998; Suñol, 2014).

The spark provided by Fr. Vélaz and the Reyeses empowered and emboldened communities at the margins of society to establish schools and thereby become agents in overcoming exploitive conditions and oppression and ensure a better future for their children through high quality educa-

---

Responding to the Call for Educational Justice:
Transformative Catholic-Led Initiatives in Urban Education, pp. 147–149

tion. The efforts of the men and women of these marginalized communities reflected the commitment of the Latin American Church to realizing the *preferential option for the poor* and an example of the growing prophetic voice of the Church that exposed the contradictions of the oppressive social conditions that had denied the residents of the impoverished barrios of Caracas and other urban and rural communities of an education that could support a life of dignity (Freire, 1986).

Today, Fe y Alegrìa is educating over 1.5 million children, adolescents, and adults in 1500 educational centers in 21 countries in South and Central America, the Caribbean, Africa, and Europe. It remains a strong Catholic initiative with 14 of the 21 national directors who are members of the Society of Jesus and more than 900 religious men and women serving in various roles in the education centers and offices (Federaciòn Internacional Fe y Alegrìa, 2016a; Memoria Federaciòn Internacional Fe y Alegrìa 2016b). Entreculturas (n.d., "Know us: Our identity"), a nongovernmental organization (NGO) of the Jesuits headquartered in Madrid, Spain, together with the Friends of Fe y Alegrìa in the United States (n.d.), support the work of Fe y Alegrìa to provide transformative education to marginalized people of Latin America, the Caribbean, and Africa through fund raising and advocacy initiatives.

Begun with community support and participation to provide children with a formal education, Fe y Alegrìa has developed a number of different educational initiatives for children, adolescents, and adults that include vocational training in agriculture, computers, carpentry, and other fields, adult literacy, and special education. The latter includes job skills training for young people with disabilities in a workplace inclusion project, as well as programs to adapt classrooms to better educate children and youth with disabilities (Federaciòn Internacional Fe y Alegrìa, 2016c).

In this volume we present a chapter on the contribution of Fe y Alegrìa to communities in South America. It describes the process Fe y Alegría uses to ensure quality education, one I was able to observe personally on a recent visit to Fe y Alegría schools in Bogatà, Columbia. This chapter was originally written in Spanish by an individual involved in the work of this organization and then translated into English.

REFERENCES

Entreculturas. (n.d.). Know us: Our identity. Retrieved from https://www.entreculturas.org/es/conocenos/nuestra-identidad

Federaciòn Internacional Fe y Alegrìa. (2016a). *History*. Retrieved from http://www.feyalegria.org/en/history

Federaciòn Internacional Fe y Alegrìa. (2016b). *Memoria Federaciòn Internacional Fe y Alegrìa 2016*. Bogatà, Columbia: Author. Retrieved from http://www.feyalegria.org/es/node/7069

Federaciòn Internacional Fe y Alegrìa. (2016c). *More than 200 youth receive job skills training*. Retrieved from http://www.feyalegria.org/en/news/more-200-youth-receive-job-skills-training

Freire, P. (1986). Education, liberation and the church. *Religious Education, 79,* 524–545.

Friends of Fe y Alegrìa in the United States. (n.d.). Identity. Washington, DC: Author. Retrieved from https://feyalegria.us/who-we-are/identity/

Podsiadlo, J. J. (1998, May 23). Schools for the poor in Venezuela. *America, 178,* 8–12.

Suñol, I. (2014). Our work. In *Memoirs 2014*. Bogatà, Columbia: Federaciòn Internacional Fe y Alegrìa. Retrieved from http://www.feyalegria.org/es

CHAPTER 9

THE SYSTEM OF QUALITY IMPROVEMENT OF FE Y ALEGRÍA

Elizabeth Riveros Serrato
Federación Internacional Fe y Alegría
(Translated by Holly A. Schneider)

Introduction

In the year 2004, Fe y Alegría began to develop a System of Quality Improvement that allows educational institutions to foster an atmosphere of learning and continual improvement. The purpose of the system is to cultivate a permanent culture of improving educational quality. In this way, Fe y Alegría intends to contribute from its own experience to the betterment of quality in public education systems of countries in Latin America and the Caribbean.

The application of the quality improvement system in a Fe y Alegría education center begins with an evaluation that has an integrative and multidimensional focus in order to proceed with a process of reflection that is based on the results obtained, bringing them together with an analysis of the context. The process continues with the creation and implementation of improvement plans and systematizing thereafter. Finally, after a few

Responding to the Call for Educational Justice:
Transformative Catholic-Led Initiatives in Urban Education, pp. 151–171
Copyright © 2019 by Information Age Publishing

years a new comparative evaluation is carried out to allow for each center to recognize its progress and to make necessary adjustments and begin a new cycle of improvement.

The first evaluation was carried out in 2007, the second in 2011, and the third in 2015. In this chapter we will first briefly present what exactly is the Fe y Alegría Movement and its concept of quality education, and then continue by concisely detailing the principal characteristics of the improvement system, some data that sheds light on the work, and concrete examples of its application to two Fe y Alegría educational centers that we hope help to better understand our experience.

Fe y Alegría: A Global Movement

Fe y Alegría is "Un Movimiento de Educación Popular Integral y Promoción Social" (Federaciòn Internacional Fe y Alegría, 2016, "Quienes Somos"), a movement of inclusive education and social advancement, directed toward impoverished and excluded populations in order to empower their personal development and social participation. It was founded in 1955 in the marginalized communities of Caracas. Today, there are 21 countries in Latin America and the Caribbean, Europe, and Africa where there are national organizations associated with Fe y Alegría, forming an International Federation: Argentina, Bolivia, Brazil, Chad, Chile, Colombia, Ecuador, El Salvador, Spain, Guatemala, Haiti, Honduras, Italy, Madagascar, Nicaragua, Panamá, Paraguay, Peru, Dominican Republic, Uruguay, and Venezuela.

The Movement unites more than 40,000 educators that carry out their work in schools, radio stations, and centers dedicated to alternative programs, serving more than 1.5 million people. Fe y Alegría works in the following areas: preschool, primary and secondary education, technical training, radio stations, adult education, continuing education, co-ops and small businesses, community development, health, teacher training and professional development, editing educational materials, educational technology, organization of experiences and public action, and more.

The contexts in which Fe y Alegría carries out its work are varied, geographically, socially, and culturally speaking, but there is one common denominator, which is vulnerable populations: urban and rural areas, neighborhoods, and countries with high rates of poverty and marginalized communities, areas with high crime rates and drug trafficking, areas affected by gangs, and populations displaced due to violent conflict.

Fe y Alegría promotes the right to a quality education for everyone, which means recognizing that all people must and should be educated in order to realize their full potential and fully participate in society. Education is a crucial right because it gives one access to other basic human rights. In other words, the consequences of the lack of education, or a poor education, can lead an individual to be excluded from society.

As in Objective Four of the agenda of Global Sustainable Development (Thomson, 2015) approved by the international community, we at Fe y Alegría commit to guaranteeing an inclusive and fair quality education and to promote learning opportunities throughout life. Seeing that education is a fundamental human right for personal development and society's well-being, Fe y Alegría understands that this right should be guaranteed by the state. Fe y Alegría takes on the option of working on and for public education, coming from an understanding of "public" as a place for all citizens, accessible to all, from which the common good is built. For Fe y Alegría, the existence of a quality public education enables societal development and strengthens democracy.

Fostering the right to a quality education means eliminating all barriers that limit access to education or to the continuation of studies, be it barriers of discrimination or those that limit education by socioeconomic class. It means supporting an inclusive and fair quality education: understanding that quality education is inseparable from equality.

Fe y Alegría is aware that the educational gap continues to grow in the world, particularly in Latin America, which is one of the most unequal regions in the world; while some improvements have been seen, countries face significant challenges to guaranteeing the right to a quality education for all people.

Although an average of 95% of children in the region have access to schooling, the quality is very deficient. More than 40% of the student population does not reach the minimum capabilities of reading or mathematics (Organización para la Cooperación y el Desarrollo Económicos [OCDE], 2015).

There is a series of elements that contribute to producing educational inequality (Reimers, 1993):

- differential access to different levels of education for people with limited economic resources and those with greater wealth;
- differential treatment in school, which results in more advantages for students coming from households with greater financial means;
- social segregation in schools, by which the majority of students learn at school to interact with and relate to only those classmates of a similar socioeconomic class;
- significant differences in the individual efforts made by each family to support their children (in the direct transmission of cultural knowledge); and

- content and educational processes that are not directed specifically at dealing with inequality as a problem worth studying.

Overcoming inequality is not achieved simply through the distribution of material resources. It is essential to take into account each individual's sociocultural, political, and personal matters. It is necessary to offer education as a means of expanding individual and collective capabilities. The pedagogical approach must be anchored in the belief that all people have capabilities; it should be an interplay between the reality of each individual and each person's understanding of his or her situation, and should offer relevant alternatives that are attractive and rouse that individual's innate skills and talents.

For that reason, Fe y Alegría supports the improvement of educational quality from its daily practice in contexts of poverty and exclusion as a means to the betterment of public education systems and the transformation of communities and society in general.

How Fe y Alegría Works for a Quality Education for All People

Educational quality is a complex notion that can take on a variety of meanings, including contradicting meanings, depending on who is defining it. Part of the complexity is due to the fact that it is a multidimensional concept, since educational processes occur on multiple levels (educational system, school, classroom, students' families, among others) and are affected by a multitude of factors—some within the schools, some outside.

This amounts to the fact that the quality of education is an ideological notion that rests on a political or social project, in other words, what is understood as a quality education is based on the vision that each society has regarding its future and of the people who are to be developed in order to make that vision a reality. In this sense, value systems and ethical codes underlie the concept of quality education.

Quality education, for Fe y Alegría (2008), is that which:

> Forms the wholeness of the person, making possible the full development of all dimensions of an individual, that values one's unique individuality and socio-cultural belonging, favoring the appropriation and construction—personal and collective—of knowledge, attitudes, and abilities; is that which makes possible the betterment of quality of life of the individual and community of which he or she is part, committing to people in the construction of a more just and humane society.

> It is characterized by an educational practice and societal development understood as a process that is awareness-raising, transformative, participa-

tive, based on solidarity, reflexive, relevant, creative, fair, efficient, created from and with those who are typically excluded, that promotes group leadership without exclusion, where each person has a place in the community's mission. (pp. 268–269)

Quality implies the transformation of those involved, of the school and the communities, for Fe y Alegría quality is directly related to the ability of the school to understand the reality of each student it forms:

- A student who is critical, empowered, able to propose and commit to his/her reality, with leadership, able to debate and construct.
- A school that is open, without stereotypes, heterogeneous, eager; that goes from planning to action and is guided by context.
- An empowered community, that constructs social designs and structures, that recognizes the importance of public establishments and is committed to them, and that develops projects to stimulate processes of justice and equality.

For Fe y Alegría a quality school is one that:

- Is familiar with problems and opportunities in the community in which it resides and contributes to community development.
- Entails a community educational project and is constructed with the community.
- Develops a democratic administration that is participatory and transparent.
- Promotes a good scholarly environment and group resolution of conflicts.
- Cultivates the disposition to learn, reflection about the task of learning and the situation of the school, the mutual respect and collaborative work among educators.
- Evaluates for educational purposes.
- Understands that its mission goes beyond its own walls.
- Works with other schools and the educational authorities in order to achieve a quality public education.

Sistema de Mejora de la Calidad de Fe y Alegría (SMCFyA; System of Quality Improvement of Fe y Alegría)

Adopting the definition of educational quality, the values, commitments, and criteria set forth, the Sistema de Mejora de la Calidad de Fe y Alegría (SMCFyA) is structured as a tool that organizes the school and provides elements to put in place a culture of improvement inspired by public education. It involves a permanent process of revision, assessment, evaluation, and interpretation of the reality of the educational center and its surroundings to make decisions and adequate strategies for change.

This system, designed and put into practice as a comprehensive and multidimensional system of evaluation and improvement, operates as a collection of elements that enable the educational institutions to organize themselves around processes of improvement supported through time, that aim for the goal of reflection and action to be pedagogy. It is proposed that the school be constructed in a democratic meeting space, that contextualized educational projects are designed and implemented in accordance with the reality of the community in which they are put into practice, that classroom strategies that are inclusive and participative are promoted, that students are evaluated with a systematic and formative perspective, that social participation and the exercise of citizenship are promoted, that knowledge is built from the school, and that deep bonds of solidarity are formed with the local communities.

To achieve these objectives, a rationale of cycles is presented, divided into four phases that are presented in the following paragraphs.

Phase 1: The Evaluation of Educational Centers

Evaluation is an action of collective rating of a reality that is carried out for the purpose of identifying, understanding, discussing, learning, and improving the quality of those educational procedures. The evaluation should not be reduced to an exercise of control over the object of evaluation that consists of comparison, classification, hierarchical organization, or even discrimination. Rather, the evaluation should be directed to the betterment of educational practices and founded in the commitment of all those with knowledge and reflection. Only if the evaluation generates comprehension and participation is it possible to obtain educational improvements. From this perspective, it is a pedagogical and ethical challenge, rather than a mere technical deed.

Furthermore, evaluation should be oriented towards autonomy; the educational community should have a clear authority and ability to determine for itself so that it can make decisions that have a positive effect on its own center, and, in the long term, on the efficiency of the educational system. The evaluation as a diagnostic and systematic process should provoke impacts as much as the thinking of teachers, students, administration, and the community.

All of that is reflected in the impact that is produced in the contexts, practices of intervention, and in the organizational culture.

Fe y Alegría prefers a *focus on evaluation* characterized by:

- being multidimensional: taking into consideration the results, educational processes, structure and resources of the center and of the context;
- being of a self-evaluating nature: requiring the participation of the subjects being evaluated (with external participants);
- being directed towards improvement: utilizing information gathered from the evaluation to understand what changes are necessary to improve;
- being participatory: requiring the involvement of all in the analysis of this information;
- being democratic and transparent: it is fundamental to agree upon interpretations and priorities;
- making the educational center the protagonist in decision making: each one identifies the actions and command lines necessary for improvement;
- being contextualized;
- not intending to classify or hierarchically order the educational centers.

What is evaluated in the system of improvement of Fe y Alegría?

From a multidimensional and comprehensive focus, the evaluation's objective is to measure quantitatively or qualitatively aspects of the administrative processes, including leadership styles, optimal use of resources, and professional development training, and teaching and learning, including lesson planning, curriculum development, and student learning. Also assessed are a number of factors related to citizen formation, including a collective development of school standards of conduct, the establishment of a just and supportive social environment, the formation of values, participation of all school personnel in decision making, control of resources, and the openness of the school to the community. Important to this educational approach is the focus on human rights with a particular emphasis on those of women. Finally, academic exam scores and students' attitudes are assessed as outcomes.

The measurements are strictly interrelated and each one generates information that sheds light on the rest and paints a complete picture of the situation at the educational center.

The context defines, limits, and guides the intention with which the center works. One could say that a center is of quality when it responds to the context in which it finds itself, with its interests and needs, and from there develops strategies to transform that reality.

The way in which resources are used influences the education provided. The educational processes and their interaction are determinants of the quality of the education. Because of this, the evaluation of these processes is what will then guide the possible courses of action for the improvement of the centers.

Lastly, the results of the evaluation are considered one of the dimensions used to form a center, to the extent that the other dimensions come together. In accordance with the value attributed to a comprehensive education, the evaluation measures the students' cognitive learning in mathematics and language, and also their attitudes and values with respect to sexuality and care for the body, violence, justice, and solidarity.

To achieve effectiveness of this phase and direct the evaluation from this perspective of a culture of improvement, it becomes necessary to start intentionally developing the ability to:

- Self-reflect, stopping along the way to recognize the practices that the centers carry out.
- Re-familiarize with the context, make sense of the reality that we see and know day-to-day, analyze and relate these realities to the learning and development possibilities of the person that we want to form.
- Understand and read the diverse perceptions in the school about the realities and practices that are carried out.
- Compare practices with other realities to edit and adjust it

Phase 2: Reflection.

Once the results are received, the educational center begins a process of reflection that continues throughout the entire cycle of improvement. For this, *center teams* are organized, with representation from all figures in the educational community, which then reflect on and discuss the results.

During this phase, it is intended that the educational center comes to understand its strengths and weaknesses discovered in the evaluation and then to identify the *central problems* it faces. Once the problems are identified, the teams prioritize them and define the *courses of action* to intervene.

All of this involves developing the abilities to:

- Discuss, participate, and interact with different people;
- Reconstruct and adjust practices based on reflection;
- Confront and question the reality in which the school exists;
- Realize what the practices are.

Reflection involves a time-consuming process and is not without challenges, but with effort it translates to the acquisition of qualities by the educational community, understanding of their own reality, collective learning, forming agreements, and adopting strategies for improvement, which is fundamental to achieve a culture of educational improvement.

Phase 3: Development and Implementation of Improvement Plans

Once the courses of action are defined, the project teams enter a phase of organizing and planning. Then, they focus their actions in a prioritized, sequential, and deliberate way. This organization is carried through the *development of the improvement plan,* projected to take three years, that expresses objectives and results to pursue.

The improvement plan begins its implementation with the accompaniment of the Pedagogical Coordinators of Fe y Alegría and with the participation of all members of the educational community. During the implementation, the school should periodically assess the progress of the plan to make necessary adjustments as they go.

All of this assumes that the educational center continues strengthening its ability to assess and transform itself, producing a new educational culture. The underlying idea of the improvement plan is that *the school should be open to change* and comprehends that progressing is improving and improving is growing and growing is achieving.

Phase 4: Systematization

Finally, each educational center develops a systematization of the process of evaluation and improvement. Systematizing consists of making a critical interpretation of one or many experiences, based on their organization and reconstruction, in order to discover the logic behind the process and the factors that are involved.

The objective within the System of Quality Improvement of Fe y Alegría is paying attention to the processes of improvement and reconstructing their implementation (such relevant players, factors that aid or impede, the context in which it takes place, etc.) in order to learn and begin to leave a trail showing how the changes took place. This way, we build understanding within the center and it aids learning for future experiences of improvement for the school, as well as in other schools that are in a similar situation.

This phase, which begins from the start of implementing the improvement plan, demands additional effort for the educational center that should be planned and systematized, to make room for reflection and time for the organizational team to collect and organize the information that is obtained.

The developing knowledge through the systematization process should be disseminated in a wide and varied way, such as virtual means, publications, or in public spaces, so that the whole educational community and other institutions can become familiar with the center's improvement experience.

Quality improvement implies the transformation of practices that we have identified that we want to transform and, at the same time, reflection on the practices and actions that we are implementing to transform the practice. Table 9.1 summarizes the quality improvement components.

Table 9.1.
Quality Improvement Process Components

Transforming Practices	Reflecting on Practices
• Define the problem	• Define the origin of the experience
• Define the goal	• Define the reason for systematizing
• Define the practices to transform	• Define what needs to be communicated
• Define the actions	• Narrate the actions
• Implement the actions	• Narrate what occurs with the subjects as a result of actions
• Identify the progress	• Discover lessons
• Adjust the practices	• Build knowledge

Essential Elements After More Than 10 Years of Development and Consolidation of an Improvement System

Since we started to define the System of Quality Improvement of Fe y Alegría (SMCFyA) up until the present, the procedures have become more contextualized with the realities of the countries and the education centers. A CONCEPT OF QUALITY, historical and contextualized, has been proposed, which involves the development and creation of new abilities, new organizations, and new viewpoints and the construction of a NEW ACADEMIC CULTURE, in a CYCLE OF QUALITY that allows for creation and transformation. It is a culture that involves continually questioning and hypothesizing what is done and experienced, a quality that makes the school a place of building and exploring and a culture that makes us participants in the process of transforming each one of ourselves, of the school, and the communities.

The model has been implemented in the last 10 years in more than 500 Fe y Alegría centers in 15 countries and in 60 publicly managed centers of 6 countries with an agreement of collaboration between the International Federation of Fe y Alegría and the Telefónica Foundation (Fundación Telefónica).

Here we provide some data that helps us see the degree of work that has been done.

First Cycle

The application of the SYSTEM OF IMPROVEMENT began in 2007 with the first evaluation that took place in 419 Fe y Alegría education centers in 15 countries in Latin America and the Caribbean. In overall figures, that included over 24,000 students, 13,600 faculty, and 2,700 community leaders.

This first cycle was led by the Program of Quality of the International Federation of Fe y Alegría with an international team, which from its headquarters in Colombia accompanied the teams that were slowly created in each national Fe y Alegría that had decided to apply the Quality Improvement System.

Second and Third Cycles

In 2011 the implementation of the second cycle began in 440 educational centers in 13 countries, 279 centers of contrast, meaning that they had participated in the first cycle, and 161 new centers that would begin the application of the system at that time. A second contrast evaluation was carried out in 2015.

From the experience of the work carried out in the education centers during these years we can extract some elements that have turned out to be essential to improving quality, listed here:

1. Collegial leadership and management: the importance of a leader committed to the improvement of quality and education. Although it need not be the administration of that school, it should be supported by the school.
2. Organizing the school with action teams: In the schools that advanced, different action teams were established giving continuity to the process.

3. Organizing the school for improvement: Schools that respect the planning and timeline and that created times and spaces for improvement.
4. The centers that advanced the most practiced reflection in order to be able to narrate, reconstruct what was being done, developing abilities to self-reflect, recognizing its advances and blocks, and proposing permanent transformations and adjustments.
5. Improved school dynamic: In these schools, what was proposed in the improvement plan and the procedures and conditions of the SMCFyA Improvement Plan was in fact achieved with the day-to-day, the context, and/or with processes of the Administration.
6. Identifying the direction of the school: The education centers that advanced had a clear sense of direction in what they were doing and the goal they were pursuing, which meant the work was completed in a logical and connected process rather than disjointed parts.
7. The processes of training in the content being improved: Those schools that implemented training given by the program or by external support achieved transformations.
8. The schools that advanced the most had the participation and commitment of a high number of faculty.
9. The schools that advanced the most were characterized by having good or improved relationships, and trust and communication, among the various figures in the educational community.
10. The education centers that took responsibility for their improvement and for the challenges that came up or challenges that they posed themselves, achieved the greatest improvement.

Some Achievements Since the Application of the SMCFyA Improvement Plan

Below we list some achievements.

With respect to the *Management Teams*:

• The members of the management teams of the educational centers achieved skills in leadership and decision making. The results of the second contrast evaluation showed significant quantifiable advances, especially from the perspectives of families and the community, regarding improvement in the way in which the educational centers were led and in the way in which the centers have opened themselves to group participation and decision making.

- The processes of participation in the school improved: 46.8% of the Centers went from being centers where the administration drove all decision making to being a center that engaged in group decision making.

With respect to the *Faculty*:

- Throughout the process, new skills were developed in the faculty in the way in which they evaluated learners and based their planning on the educational goals of the centers. These changes were reflected in positive changes in families' views of the schools' educational objectives.

With respect to the *Students*:

- Students developed leadership skills and the ability to develop and initiate projects.
- The administrators' opinions of the students' level of empowerment improved by 4% between 2011 and 2015.

Transformations in the *School*:

- 115 Centers not only developed new forms of communication and commitment, but also organized themselves differently such that their improvement plans and training processes were implemented and showed improvements.
- 40% of the Centers (164 of 410) carried out the improvement process under the leadership of their own teams: administrative, quality, and systematizing. This shows achievement in the goal of empowering and developing skills in their subjects.
- Significant improvement in the continuation of students and faculty at the school, with a 22% difference.
- The formation of values improved by 2.6% between 2011 and 2015.

With regard to *student learning*:

- On average, student performance changed positively, more between 2007 and 2011 but also significantly between 2011 and 2015.

In general, since the implementation of the SMCFyA Improvement Plan, a new culture has developed in the school, recognizing the importance of participation, socialization, and formation; and where it fosters guidance and follow-through and it begins building a path toward the organization of a new school that produces better results in impoverished and unsettled areas.

Some Lessons and Challenges

1. In order to implement the SMCFyA Improvement Plan, it is necessary to ensure that schools have in place the conditions necessary for the successful implementation of needed improvements.
2. External guidance for the process that is familiar with the school, the assessment system, and the educational and social politics of the country is needed.
3. Generating a culture of assessment and developing skills and practices in the improvement teams are important.
4. It is necessary to adjust the timing of the phases, such that the evaluation is shorter and less complex, emphasizes reflection, and gives more time to implement the improvement plan from the start.
5. We must develop continual formation processes included in the implementation of the SMCFyA improvement plan to maximize the benefits.

Examples: The Voice of the Key Players

In Fe y Alegría we believe that the best way for one to understand our work is to hear from its protagonists. Below, two education centers discuss their experiences of the application of the SMCFyA Improvement Plan:

1. Critical reading at the center of a process of change. "Hogar de Jesús Mariano Roque Alonso" School, Paraguay
2. Quality begins in the context. "Las Cumbres" School, Ecuador

Critical Reading at the Center of a Process of Change: Escuela Hogar de Jesús, Mariano Roque Alonso, Paraguay

The Context. In the central region of Paraguay, a few kilometers from the capital, lies the town of Mariano Roque Alonso. Our education center, Hogar de Jesús, founded in 1992, is located in the neighborhood "Barrio Universo," an area primarily formed by immigrants from rural areas. In recent years, it has experienced an exponential and chaotic growth in its population as a result of the occupation of public land by families without homes.

The students come from families with scarce economic resources. The parents work in the fishing industry, street sales, construction, or in neighboring factories. Very few manage to earn a minimum monthly salary (U.S.$395). Many students live only with their mothers who are housekeepers or housemaids.

In spite of this difficult context, our Center has managed to preserve an environment favorable to teaching and learning, offering some minimal accommodations in infrastructure and in organization with a group of committed teachers, parents who participate in the center, and students who are motivated to succeed. Nonetheless, there are plenty of problems and serious needs.

Starting Point. During the last Quality Improvement System evaluation, our team detected serious weaknesses in students' reading comprehension. This resulted in difficulties expressing themselves in writing and in correctly understanding what they read.

> *We analyzed the results of the self evaluation and we concurred that there was difficulty in making inferences in reading comprehension and in students' written comprehension that was reflected in various disciplines. We reviewed the possible causes: on one hand, the lack of reading habits and little contextualized written production by the students; on the other hand, it was necessary to adjust the methodological criteria to teach Language in a coordinated way in all disciplines. In order to go beyond the students' literal reading and writing, we had to change our strategy and develop in them more critical reading and writing skills in a more intentional way. (Nery Gómez, Vice Principal)*

The school staff and assessment team recognized that instruction was excessively formal and focused on syntax and morphology, but hardly at all on making sure that the children understood what they were reading or writing. Each instructor had his or her own background and few had knowledge of common education. Additionally, there was no continuity or follow-up between what was learned from one year to the next.

We arrived at these conclusions as a group: teachers, administrators, and parents of the families. The students also participated in the analysis, helping the team understand that our young people barely read at home. So, to improve the quality of their education, we saw that we needed to focus on making our students critical readers by changing the way we taught and the way they learned. We came up with a plan with a few basic principles:

> **Principle 1:** We adopted a communicative focus on the language that is based on students' context and prior knowledge. This focus

aimed to make possible the development of competencies to read for understanding, write different types of texts, and speak and listen better.

Principle 2: We put into effect a methodology based on interdisciplinary projects that would be addressed from different disciplines or classes. In this way, we taught the children to write by reflecting on things that happen day-to-day in the classroom. An example of this methodology was the ninth-grade project, "Water Pollution in the Universo Neighborhood." We analyzed the causes and consequences on the environment (natural and health sciences), environmental laws and the social impact (social sciences), statistical data about the pollution (mathematics), and the structure and writing of an article (Spanish language and literature).

Principle 3: In all areas and levels, language use had to become a tool for peaceful coexistence and communication. In all disciplines, the aim was to develop linguistic abilities.

Principle 4: The standardized use of "Checks" for pedagogical support in reading and writing practice.

Principle 5: Record and systematize the process. This way we could start becoming aware of our achievements and challenges and learn from them. Each teacher documents his or her process of implementing classroom projects. Then, in the Learning Circles, together with the Quality Team, the progress is reviewed for executing the different projects in different grades. Now we meet to discuss our practices, think together about strategies, and tweak our teaching plans. This process had contributed to significant improvements in our teaching.

Point of Arrival. Some of the most significant changes resulting from applying the improvement plan include:

- 91% of the 22 instructors at our center (20 people) have planned and implemented, in a coordinated way, class projects that emphasize inferential reading and contextualized writing. It was expected to be only 60%.
- 92% of all students (887 people) utilized reading strategies and 86% utilized writing strategies in their learning process. It was expected to be only 60%.
- Language performance is also improving. The percentage of failures has decreased by 3.5% from 2011 to 2015. Likewise, in 2015,

we have documented a 3.5% increase in students at the school who pass in Spanish language courses.

With respect to anecdotal findings, we have noticed that students enjoy reading more and interacting more with the texts. We notice improvement in diction and fluidity, as well as in their writing. In addition, we have observed that students are more interested in what is happening around them. They are beginning to better understand the problems in their community and awaken a greater interest in transforming their environment.

During the second cycle, Arami, a sixth-grade student, reported: "There are some stories that teach you to respect your parents, to value the environment, to take care of our planet, to value our friends." With respect to the water pollution project, ninth-grader, Gustavo, noted: "This project helps us to understand. We read, we understand, we know how to explain, and to summarize. We make outlines, and we know how to explain those outlines again. This was the goal of the teachers, for us to understand what we read…. I believe that there is progress."

In comparing the present to the past, one parent testified: "I believe that what was happening a few years ago was that the children would read but without thinking, or maybe they read because they had to but that's it. Or maybe they didn't manage to think about or understand what they were reading."

Quality Begins in the Context: "Las Cumbres" School, Ecuador

Problem to be Addressed. In 1972, to fight the high rates of illiteracy in the San Pablo neighborhood, Fr. Díez, Society of Jesus, together with a group of pioneers, drove the creation of the school that we know today as Las Cumbres, in the Portoviejo quarter in Ecuador.

Many social problems have been accumulating in the community. The neighborhood had grown but the infrastructures had not grown at the same pace to support it. The lack of basic services is the source of health problems and poor nutrition, employment is scarce, broken families are a threat, and drug sales and crime are growing. Meanwhile, the community has struggled to organize itself to resolve such problems. There are institutions working there for the people's rights, but little progress is being made to improve living conditions of the people living in this community.

Amidst this accumulation of problems, we observed that those living in San Pablo did not sufficiently value access to an education. Facing this situation, as educators, we asked ourselves what stance to take. The process of innovation that we are engaged in today began in 2011. At that time, the second cycle of Fe y Alegría's Improvement System was beginning its implementation in our education center in Ecuador. This was a great challenge for us.

The implementation of the Improvement System required constant meetings for reflection and planning with the groups of parents, students, leaders, faculty, and the management team. Following this push, we went into the community, talked with people, and reflected on the growing challenges that affected our community. We could then confirm that many parents were not sending their children to school and, in some cases, the parents' lack of education was contributing to their children's lack of interest. The students lacked support to do their homework, and the options for recreation for the youngest ones were very limited and not at all educational. Overall, the performance of our students was below that of other schools in a similar context; this worried us.

Community Context. In the Las Cumbres Center, we thought that if we did not do anything to influence the context, we would never get out of the unstable situation we are in and we would be hard-pressed to reach the level of quality that we desire. In other words, we believed that the school should take a much more serious leadership role in the community to transform the neighborhood's culture and begin to unite forces of all those who, until now, have worked separately for the wellness of the community. This way, we begin to work in an organized way with the Health Center to inform parents about the importance of vaccinations and making time for medical appointments for their children. We also coordinate with the PRONIÑO Program that aims to eliminate child labor, since many of our students skip school in order to go work at the local factory. In this sense, our primary means of improving the school has developed outside of the school, not within: we have focused on coordinating basic community services to strengthen the agencies and organizations directly and indirectly. For example, we have worked with the police, coordinating educational movements with them and bringing them closer to the school. We believe that the police and the community should not be against each other and that we can play a role in bringing them together.

The Most Vulnerable. Our efforts to improve educational quality are centered primarily on the students who present the most difficulties or are the most vulnerable. Also, we allowed ourselves to be guided by the context. Because of this, we created the Department of Comprehensive and Inclusive Educational Wellness (Bienestar Educativo Integral e Inclusivo, BEII), guided by a psychologist, a social worker, and a supporting teacher. The end goal of this task force is supporting the challenges that come up in the classroom and preventing any student from being left behind.

The procedure that we follow with these children is simple but efficient: when a child is noticed to be having difficulties with challenging material, the teacher calls upon the BEII Department, where professionals, according to their field, use tools and techniques to come up with a preliminary assessment of the situation. Following this, the social worker corresponds with the student's family to make them aware of the special needs of the child. If necessary, the professionals call upon the Institute of Special Education to carry out a psycho-pedagogical assessment and obtain a full report about the student and the recommended suggestions for curricular adaptation in accordance with the recommendations submitted by the supporting professionals.

On the other hand, in recent years we have fostered continuing development for administrators and curricular adaptation workshops for teachers. The latter is focused on making our curriculum flexible and making teachers adaptable to conditions that our students have.

The Culture of Peace Is for Everyone. In the Las Cumbres Center, we put a great deal of importance on the school climate. We have had problems with discipline, especially in the higher grades. We are noting that currently young people have become more aggressive. The violence and aggression in their environment reaches beyond our walls and seeps in. Furthermore, there are new ways of misbehaving that generate new challenges for teachers. But here we have the opportunity to transform that aggression into positive energy. As a first step, we have revised the agreement that we give to the students, the agreement that we have between colleagues, and also the agreement that we have with the administration of the school. This has brought us to launch campaigns and a process of participatory development of the Code of Coexistence of the center. However, we understood that above all, we needed to have an opportunity for reflection and assessment of the levels of aggression and in order to change them. So we called upon the whole educational community: mothers, fathers, students, teachers, and administrators. As a result of these conversations, designs, and agreements, the Code of Coexistence emerged and was approved by the educational district's administration. It is not a stationary tool. As new situations come up, we see ourselves needing to rethink and redesign it.

Process of Participatory Management. What we want for Las Cumbres is to achieve a collegial administration that promotes pedagogical leadership. So, what we did first was to call upon the different educational figures in the community to get to know our plans and invite them to take responsibility.

Then a management team was formed with the Director as leader, the representative of the BEII department, and three teachers to support the shared leadership and responsibility. Each member of the team acts as a partner to the task forces consisting of teachers, which, in turn, work with parent committees. Making this structure work took time, but since the second year of our Plan, we have established task forces, which our management team oversaw. With teachers and administration working together, we have a management team that promoted this shared leadership.

Point of Arrival. Today when we take a look back, we can say that we have improved thanks to the fact that the plans were brought forth from the Institutional Improvement Plan and the fact that it has put the context at the center of our educational performance:

- We have participatory parents who believe that the reality can change. They are participating much more in the Classroom Committees. We have gone from a 4% to a 43% participation rate in various activities for parents of children with scholarships.
- 60% of teachers are committed to adapting their teaching to the specific needs of their students.
- The Committee of Parents has arranged initiatives to improve the infrastructure of the environment, such as fumigations to prevent insects and planting trees in the exterior patio of the school.
- From the period of 2013–2014 to 2014–2015, there has been a decrease in the number of students who need extra help. The first year there were 71 and in the second year there were 45.
- There is improvement in reading and writing. The children are reading more. To motivate reading, 15 minutes of the first hour of class each day of the week is dedicated to reading.

These are just two examples that illustrate the challenges that Fe y Alegría schools are overcoming to help improve the educational and health outcomes for children and their families in some of the world's most economically impoverished communities. They underscore the importance of school personnel working together internally and with the community in which a school is situated.

REFERENCES

Fe y Alegría. (2008). *Pensamiento de Fe y Alegría: Documentos de los Congresos Internacionales, 1984-2007. La calidad de la educación popular, una aproximación desde Fe y Alegría.* XXXIV Congreso Internacional. Colombia 2003. Retrieved from http://www.feyalegria.org/images/acrobat/PensamientoFyAvf.pdf

Federaciòn Internacional Fe y Alegría. (2016). Quiènes somos. Retrieved from http://www.feyalegria.org/es/quienessomos

Organización para la Cooperación y el Desarrollo Económicos (OCDE). (2015). *Informe PISA: Resultados Clave.* París, COUNTRY. Retrieved from http://www.ocde.org/pisa

Reimers, F. (1993). Una innovatión educativa para proporcionar educatión básica con calidad y equidad. *Revista de Pedagogía*, *XIV*, 31-49.

Thomson, S. (2015, September 16). *What are the sustainable development goals?* Retrieved from https://www.weforum.org/agenda/2015/09/what-are-the-sustainable-development-goals/

CHAPTER 10

"HOMEBOYS IS HOPE"

Mauricio Arocha and Jill Bickett
Loyola Marymount University

Homeboy Industries is the largest gang intervention program in the nation (Homeboy Industries, 2016). Its response to the call for social justice in education is rooted in the Ignatian paradigm and Catholic social teaching. Its philosophy is operationalized through a culture of solidarity, acceptance, and redemption with the participation of former gang members who staff social enterprise programs and business ventures that serve the community and other gang members. The core vision of Homeboy Industries aligns with the tenets of Catholic Social Teaching in its focus on the dignity of the human person and its emphasis on community, family, and the dignity of work. Homeboy demonstrates an unwavering commitment to the poor and vulnerable by providing employment, acceptance, and opportunity for those seeking refuge from gang life.

The voices of former gang members confirm the transformative power of this Catholic-based educational model. "Homeboys is hope," said one former gang member. Others praise the educational opportunities, the community building, and the redemption they felt through affiliation with this spiritually based program (Arocha, 2015). Homeboy demonstrates the success that is possible in a program modeled on the Christian paradigm of social justice. Sociologists who have studied gang life in California (Klein, 1995; Rios, 2011; Tita et al., 2003) have suggested that gangs are

Responding to the Call for Educational Justice:
Transformative Catholic-Led Initiatives in Urban Education, pp. 173–189
Copyright © 2019 by Information Age Publishing

grounded in institutional racism, poverty, and urban marginality. Yet, few scholars have focused on gang recovery programs (Flores & Hondagneu-Sotelo, 2012) such as Homeboy, and none has focused on rehabilitation programs with Catholic Jesuit spirituality as its model. Recent research (Arocha, 2015), which operates as the foundation for this chapter, validates the impact of the alternative education space of the Homeboy Industries model, and uses the underpinnings of the Catholic faith and the alignment of Catholic Social Teaching to serve this most marginalized population.

Setting the Context: The Founding and History of Homeboy Industries

Father Greg Boyle, founder of Homeboy Industries, is a member of the Catholic religious order of the Society of Jesus (SJ). Ordained in 1984, Father Greg was first introduced to urban Los Angeles in his assignment at the parish of Dolores Mission in 1986. He soon encountered escalating gang violence and burgeoning gang membership, a period that Father Boyle calls the "Decade of Death," which was tearing the community apart (Homeboy Industries, 2016). The need he saw inspired him to listen to those who were hurt, hopeless, and angry. He resolved to find jobs for gang members, starting with simple jobs at Dolores Mission. He soon developed various programs for at-risk youth in the Boyle Heights community and, eventually, in 2001, united them all under one banner, Homeboy Industries (Boyle, 2010a). Father Greg's mission, and the mission of Homeboys Industries (n.d., "Frequently Asked Questions"), is to assist at-risk and formerly gang-involved youth in becoming positive and contributing members of society through job placement, training, and education. Scholarship has characterized the work at Homeboy Industries as integrative redemption (Flores & Hondagneu-Sotelo, 2012), whereby eclectic spirituality and clinical rehabilitation seek to integrate members into segments of the local community.

Despite the promise and success of Homeboy, and other similar rehabilitative programs, law enforcement policies continue to focus on suppression and sanctions to prevent gang violence (Tita et al., 2003). Social justice advocates insist that funds provided to law enforcement for gang violence prevention have not achieved the same long-term results as integrative prevention programs. Suppression and sanctions lead to arrests and imprisonment (Rodriguez, 2005). Homeboy helps to preserve families, to create and provide jobs that motivate and inspire former gang members, and to lead them to a spiritually engaged life that promotes their sense of human dignity and self-worth (Arocha, 2015).

Educating the Head, the Heart, and the Hands: Services at Homeboy Industries

Homeboy Industries has been in existence for 3 decades. In the beginning years it was nestled between two public housing projects, Pico Gardens and Aliso Village. Today, Homeboy Industries operates in its new location in downtown Los Angeles. Each year, thousands of former gang members from 700 different gangs and 45 different zip codes across Los Angeles visit Homeboy Industries hoping to make a change in their lives (Boyle, 2010a). Former gang members can access a variety of services at Homeboy Industries, which strives to provide healing and hope for the whole person: an education for the head, the heart, and the hands.

Educational Services

Homeboy provides educational initiatives that allow former gang members to obtain certification and degrees and to acquire training for life after the gang. Through a partnership with Learning Works Charter High School, former gang members can earn a high school diploma, or enroll in postsecondary classes in a "Pathways to College" program (Homeboy Industries, n.d., "Educational Services"). In 2016, the Learning Works@ Homeboy Charter High School had an average monthly enrollment of 96 students and approximately 60 clients in college for the first time. Further, Homeboy Industries (2016) facilitated more than 250 certifications in First Aid/CPR, Forklift, OSHA-10, and more, including 73 individual graduates from the Solar Panel Training program. These programs allow Homeboy clients to envision themselves beyond the identity of *former gang member* to become contributing members of society, with skills to engage as citizens and family members in communities they build.

Life Skills Training

Other educational services help former gang members reintegrate into the community and stem the behaviors and attitudes that first drove them into the gang lifestyle. These services are as important as traditional schooling and diploma-granting pathways. Programs such as parenting classes, anger management, speech classes, substance abuse prevention programming, and yoga provide life skills that are critical to escaping gang life. Homeboy also offers mental health support, with over 3,800 therapy sessions provided yearly by mental health clinicians. In 2016, this broad array of support services helped 11 Homeboy clients regain parental custody of their children (Homeboy Industries, 2016). In total, the academic, life skills, arts/enrichment, and work-readiness classes logged a total attendance of 22,195 in 2016 (Homeboy Industries, 2016).

Homeboy also offers tattoo removal—free to minors and community clients—of visible tattoos on the face, neck, and hands. Narratives of former gang members have indicated that tattoos are a major obstacle in acquiring employment and reintegrating into school and society (Arocha, 2015). With four tattoo-removal machines, and a multitude of volunteer doctors and physician assistants, Homeboy provided 11,236 laser tattoo removal treatments in 2016 (Homeboy Industries, 2016). Homeboy reported that the tattoo removal service is often a "gateway" service that clients initially utilize, and then become further engaged in programming and services that can provide the "way out" of the gang lifestyle. In 2016, 1,696 new clients came to Homeboy Industries to have their tattoos removed (Homeboy Industries, 2016).

Social Enterprise

Although Homeboy Industries is known primarily as a job training facility, the above descriptions attest that it is much more. Because Homeboy Industries (n.d., "Why We Do It") believes that 80% of what clients need to redirect their lives is job training and that 20% is therapeutic and other services, from the very beginning Father Greg focused on getting jobs and job training for the individuals under his care. He recognized that even those in the direst circumstances could rise to meet their full potential, if given a second chance. To do this, however, they needed a way out, an "exit ramp off the freeway of violence" (Homeboy Industries, n.d., "Why We Do It," para. 6), which is precisely what Homeboy Industries provides. In the early days, few businesses would offer jobs to former gang members, and so Father Greg began to develop in-house industries to employ these individuals himself. From this effort has grown a robust business model that employs over 200 former gang members a year, in 10 separate social enterprises. These businesses have given rise to Homeboy's two mottos, "Jobs not Jail" and "Nothing Stops a Bullet Like a Job," and provide a vital training ground for clients who have never held a job before (Homeboy Industries, 2016).

One of the most visible and the longest-standing businesses of Homeboy Industries is the Homeboy Bakery. Begun in 1992 after the Watts uprising, Homeboy Bakery epitomizes Father Greg's ministry of putting troubled teens and gang members to work, giving them hands-on work experience, and generating profits to fund other necessary services for this population (Choi & Kiesner, 2007). As Father Greg has said, "We don't hire homies to bake bread. We bake bread to hire homies" (Homeboy Industries, n.d., "Frequently Asked Questions"). With this philosophical foundation, nine other businesses have emerged, including a silkscreen and embroidery shop, Homegirl Café (on the premises of Homeboy headquarters in downtown Los Angeles), Homeboy gear (featuring shirts and other items emblazoned with the Homeboy logo), a catering company, an online market, a diner at Los Angeles City Hall, and a presence in grocery stores and at farmers' markets in Los Angeles. The most recent addition to the enterprises at Homeboy is the recycling venture, including renting out recycled items as prop rentals. These innovative ideas stem from the notion that all individuals have worth, and that all individuals have a right to dignified work, especially the most poor and vulnerable.

Job Training Program

Clients who come though the Homeboy doors feel unworthy and anxious and may be experiencing both housing and food insecurity. None has a job. Many clients at Homeboy have been abused or abandoned as children and have been witnesses to serious violence; most are at a beginning reading level. The majority of clients has experienced serious trauma, whether abandonment and/or sexual or physical abuse, and many have a family history of violence and drug involvement (Homeboy Industries, n.d., "Frequently Asked Questions"). Thus, to be prepared to become contributing citizens, these young men and women need training and support services to heal wounds and provide structure for the vision of a future work life. This process takes place at Homeboys through a four-step, 18-month transformation program, which all clients complete before being sent into the work world. Descriptions of these four steps follow.

Step 1: Reception. In this first step, clients are welcomed and assessed for the services they may need, both personal and professional. In particular, Homeboy Industries makes sure that basic needs like food and housing are secure. Trainees participate in 20 hours of "work therapy," which accustoms them to various work environments, and provides a mentor to help them navigate the early days of transition (Homeboy Industries, 2016).

Step 2: Relationship. Clients, who now become "trainees," work more intensively with support services, become more enmeshed in the Homeboy community, and take academic and life skills classes. They begin to work with employment counselors to think about life beyond Homeboy Industries. Most importantly, though, they continue to develop a sense of community and belongingness, something that many have never experienced (Homeboy Industries, 2016).

Step 3: Reidentification. Counselors develop an individualized employment plan for each trainee, and clients begin classroom instruction and on-the-job training. Extra support services are always available, as needed, to lift up those who are at risk of dropping out of the program (Homeboy Industries, 2016).

Step 4: Transformation. After 18 months of training and work on the self, trainees are ready to begin the task of entering the work force. Without a new narrative, and a way forward as a contributing member of society, clients often fall back into feeling that they are not good enough, that they are the "bad son." Father Greg tells this story at many of his speaking engagements:

> I keep telling them over and over, "You are the son that any parents would be proud to claim as their own." That's the truth. That's not some fantasy. As soon as they know that they are exactly what God had in mind when God made them, then they become that. Then they like who they are. Once they can do that—love themselves—they're not inclined to shoot somebody or hurt somebody, or be out there gang banging. (Morrow, 1999, "Imagining a Future," para. 5).

Following the 1992 Watts uprising, Father Greg began to give simple church jobs to the homies in his neighborhood—but he did something more important before offering a job. He listened to their stories. He discovered the truth of who they really are (Desmond, 2012), and that has made all the difference. When former gang members can discover the truth of who they really are, and know that others can see that too, they are on their way to being whole and healed members of society.

Facilitating an Encounter With the Poor: Father Greg and the Ignatian Compact

The alternative educational space of Homeboy Industries does not identify specifically with the Catholic faith, or any particular religion, but characterizes its spiritual position as "in line with the Jesuit practice of social justice" (Homeboy Industries, n.d., "Frequently Asked Questions"). However, in a 2010 talk to the Catholic Higher Education Collaborative about the Homeboy initiative, Father Greg's message was distinctly Christian, building on Ignatian sentiment and Catholic Social Teaching principles.

He began by describing a sense of God defined by St. Ignatius, as a "God who is always greater, and who cannot take his eyes off you … the God who is too busy loving you to be disappointed" (Boyle, 2010a, p. 381). He continued by asking the question, "Where does God want to be found?"

(p. 381), and answered that God must be encountered in Jesus. In Jesus's becoming flesh, we know that God wants us to encounter him in God's Son. And God's Son came to be an advocate for those at the margins. This is how Jesus facilitates God's encounter with the poor and marginalized. Father Greg (Boyle, 2010a) asserted:

> God wants to be encountered with the poor and powerless and the voiceless, with the people who are excluded and who are easily despised and left out. God wants to be met with the culturally despaired, with those whose burdens are more than they can bear. God wants to be encountered in the demonized precisely so that the demonizing will stop. God wants to be met in the disposable so that daylight will come when we stop throwing people away. (pp. 381–382)

Father Greg has insisted that it is not merely being "men and women for others," as the Jesuit motto indicates, but that it is discovering that we are called to be "one with others" (Boyle, 2010a, p. 382). Valuing kinship and community above all else, prioritizing community above the notion of "service," leads directly to the bedrock philosophy of Homeboy Industries.

Father Greg has offered other evidence of St. Ignatius's advocacy for standing with the demonized. He alluded to the Spiritual Exercises of St. Ignatius, in which St. Ignatius (1914) asked believers to consider "How Christ our Lord puts Himself in a great field of that region of Jerusalem, in a lowly place" Father Greg (Boyle, 2010a) said:

> He [St. Ignatius] sees Jesus standing in a lowly place, and that is what we are called to do. We must stand in a lowly place for the least; for all those that are found in the margins and whose burdens are no longer bearable ... the goal is always the same: how can you stand at the margins? We can only do so if we rely on the model of kinship that was provided to humanity by Jesus. (p. 383)

This model of kinship, derived from the Ignatian spiritual exercises, and built into Catholic social teaching, is operationalized every day in the work being done at Homeboy Industries.

Communities of Practice: Homeboys and Situated Learning

Wenger's (1998) communities of practice theory aligns well with this educational context, for several reasons. First, with its focus on community, it honors the belongingness that is a necessary part of recovery for former gang members. Being "in community" is part of being "in recovery," with all the attendant responsibilities to self and others that this requires.

Second, Lave and Wenger (1991) have asserted that persons are the sum total of their experiences, and that they learn no matter the situation that they are in; hence, the term "situated learning." Wenger insisted that "we are always learning" (p. 30); thus, being in community means learning from community, which is exactly the model at Homeboy Industries.

> Communities of practice present a theory of learning that starts with this assumption: engagement in social practice is the fundamental process by which we learn and so become who we are. The primary unit of analysis is neither the individual nor social institution, but rather the informal communities of practice that people form as they carry out shared experiences over time. In order to give a social account of learning, the theory explores in a systematic way the intersection of issues of community, social practice, meaning, and identity. (Wenger, 1998, p. 1)

The former gang members at Homeboy Industries seek community, engage in daily social practice with each other, attempt to create new meaning in their lives—and, from these experiences, reshape their identities, creating new narratives about who they are and what they will become. Lastly, situated learning in communities of practice is premised on the notion that we are always in the process of becoming. Being in any situation, and belonging to any group, creates a learning experience for the individual that has the possibility of creating meaning and identity. Thus, it is a theory that is both rooted in the present and looks toward the future and the new experiences that are created from the connections made in community. Father Greg quoted an African aphorism in his 2010 book, *Tattoos on the Heart*, "A person becomes a person through other people" (Boyle, 2010b, p. xiv). And meaning, or our ability to experience the world and our engagement with it as meaningful, is ultimately what learning is (Lave & Wenger, 1991). These two concepts, community and the respect for it, and man's search for meaning, are also paradigms found in Catholic Social Teaching, another conceptual frame that is foundational to Homeboy Industries.

Homeboy Industries and Catholic Social Teaching: A Theoretical Frame

Though not formally aligned with Homeboy Industries, the precepts of Catholic Social Teaching are inherent in the philosophy of the founder and the initiatives of Homeboy Industries itself. Later in this chapter, we will see how the words of the former gang members themselves speak to this alignment, and affirm the strong relationship between Catholic Social Teaching and the work of Homeboy Industries.

Several of the precepts of Catholic Social Teaching are most relevant in this context and are addressed separately here.

Dignity and Human Rights

While other cultures and religions may assert that all persons have dignity, the Catholic perspective is distinctive for two key reasons. First, Catholic Social Teaching places God as the cause of our dignity and at the center of our human rights. And thus, humans, made in the image of God, deserve to be treated with dignity and are of immeasurable value. Second, the Catholic tradition separates itself from other secular versions of human rights because it situates itself within human communities (Massaro, 2016). Dignity is achieved only within a community of persons, in one human's relationship to another. Human rights cannot be extended in isolation; we need one another to provide for and protect the rights of every individual. Homeboy Industries affirms this precept in its care of individuals who have been demonized by society, embracing them and welcoming them into a new community of life and hope for the future.

Solidarity

Those who have rights must also have obligations to others. This is the basis of solidarity. As humans living in community, we must be givers as well as receivers and acknowledge our mutual interdependence. Recognizing the fabric that constitutes our social relationships, and the attendant rights and obligations, begins as an individual attitude and is fully formed when it is expressed through a commitment to the caring of others (Massaro, 2016). Similarly, at Homeboy Industries, clients are taken in, taken care of, and then begin the slow but important process of learning how to take care of others—by holding down a job, refraining from destructive behavior, and building and sustaining the community of Homeboy Industries for those who will follow. Father Greg believes that Homeboy has never used a strategy to succeed; it has relied on the strength of solidarity (Boyle, 2010b).

Family

Catholic Social Teaching asserts that the well-being of society depends upon the family. Family should be a place of safe harbor, where the unconditional love of God can be understood and experienced (Massaro, 2016).

However, in today's changing society, the traditional nuclear family is rare. In particular, former gang members are often absent a family and have experienced a life devoid of unconditional love. This does not mean that we abandon the sacred nature of family, but rather that we embrace a broader notion of what that concept entails. For the former gang members, Homeboy Industries becomes their family, and the safe place to land. The union they share with their coworkers and former gang enemies at Homeboy Industries is deeper than anything they have ever known in their family of origin, or their gang (Boyle, 2010b). It is the place where they learn how to be part of a family and how to create loving, connected, whole families of their own.

The Dignity of Work

There is grace in work, but only if it honors and respects the right of the human person. Catholic Social Teaching portrays work as something intrinsically good for all people. Massaro (2016) characterized it this way: "Through work, ordinary people regularly discover rich sources of meaning, a renewed sense of purpose, and the opportunity to develop to their full potential" (p. 101). This is the essence of Homeboy Industries, as developed by Father Greg. His belief in the significance of a job to the worth and quality of an individual's life has undergirded the work of Homeboy Industries for the last 30 years. From doing small tasks in the church to baking bread and printing t-shirts, work gives Homeboy clients purpose, a sense of pride, and the knowledge that they can live a life outside of the gang culture.

The Poor and Vulnerable

Of all of the tenets of Catholic Social Teaching, the tenet which requires a preferential option for the poor and vulnerable is perhaps the one that most deeply answers the call of the Catholic faith. While identifying with the concerns of the poor is not new to the Christian tradition, and noting Jesus's advocacy for the marginalized described earlier in this chapter, this precept suggests that "the Church interprets its entire mission as one of service to those in dire need" (Massaro, 2016, p. 118). In response, Homeboy Industries (n.d., "Frequently Asked Questions") serves primarily formerly incarcerated and gang-involved youth: 100% are low income, 99.9% are people of color, and all need a second chance in life and someone to believe in them. And, whether newly introduced to the facility, or veteran community members, "the homies" will tell you that Homeboy Industries provides the trusting relationships and a secure base of support to help them discover their best selves and find the second chance they deserve (Arocha, 2015).

Homeboy Industries: Listening to the Voices of the Homies

The voices of the Homeboys tell us more about this urban Catholic-led education initiative than any of the previous facts, figures, or theories can provide. Recent scholarship focusing on Homeboy Industries (Arocha, 2015) used qualitative inquiry, and posed the question: How does the situated learning experience of Latino male gang members at Homeboy Industries affect their perspective about and affiliation with gang life?

Soaking in Homeboys: Collecting Stories

Father Greg talks about "soaking in the love" of Homeboy (Boyle, 2010b). From the first moment a homie arrives at Homeboy Industries, he is shown love. This method of *soaking* in the experiences of Homeboys Industries parallels the method that Arocha (2015) used to collect the stories of the Homeboys. Through the triangulation of extended interviews, observations, and a comprehensive review of online videos referred to as "Thought of the Day" at Homeboy Industries, Arocha gained an insider's perspective on the daily lives and hopes for this vulnerable population.

The themes that emerged from the data revolved around the former gang members' daily lives and the kinds of *learning* that takes place in the daily situated experiences in which they participate. While some of the knowledge they acquired focused on practical aspects of living outside of the gang, most of what they shared focused on a kind of intangible knowledge acquisition that they embraced. The themes in the following discussion reflect this deeper, more profound kind of learning, and align with the previous theoretical frame of Catholic Social Teaching (Arocha, 2015).

Learning to be Family

Though many of the former gang members had never experienced a close-knit family, the concept of family was important to them. The negative experiences of their past stirred in them a desire to have a "perfect family." One former gang member talked about "raising himself," and said that he had always wanted a father. Another homie said, "I never had a father. I never had a mother. I never had anybody to love me" (Arocha, 2015, p. 49). And another young man without a family talked about his childhood: "Growing up I was never taken to the park. I never was pushed on swing. I was never told I love you … it was something I never had" (Arocha, 2015, p. 49). The community members at Homeboy speak of great longing of the family unit, and have particular disdain for foster care. One homie who did not have parents, and had been in foster care all of his youth, lamented, "I never had anybody to love. Only foster parents, and they do it for the money" (Arocha, 2015, p. 51).

According to Arocha's (2015) research at Homeboy, former gang members learned two important things about family. First, they learned the "hard skills" of parenting—how to be fathers who controlled their temper, how to sustain employment, and how to maintain a healthy lifestyle. These skills were acquired in classes that homies attended in their rehabilitation efforts at Homeboy Industries. The second value they learned about family from Homeboy came from the community of practice consciously created by Father Greg. The community modeled family every day, starting with a "Thought for the Day" reflection. Father Greg showed them how to create a family, be the head of a family, and care for their own selves and others. He was the unspoken head of the family at Homeboy Industries, and he practiced unconditional love and offered forgiveness to every homie on a daily basis (Arocha, 2015).

The notion of a "perfect family" for the homies was an aspiration but also a curse. The perfect family does not exist, and for homies who have difficult and fractured pasts, the perfect family is especially out of reach. However, having the aspirational ideal that they might, one day, have a family that had not experienced the trauma of their own past, created a hope in them for their future. Thus, for most, the first family that a former gang member from Homeboy experiences is Homeboy Industries itself. The program fashions itself as a community and, within that community, there is kinship (Arocha, 2015).

Learning About Community, Kinship, and Solidarity

The former gang members defined community as a sense of belonging and family that they had not experienced before. Father Greg, in his "Thought of the Day," asked: "Does your belonging end in becoming? That's the whole measure. If it ends in becoming, then you're part of something that's real, genuine, and authentic" (Arocha, 2015, p. 63). Homeboy Industries is an authentic community because the member's belonging ends in becoming, becoming the truth of who they are. Homies talked about inhabiting that truth, which is, as Father Greg says, exactly what God had in mind when he made them. One homie told this story:

> I would walk into Homeboy Industries—when I was in the streets, I would walk in like a madman … I was disrespecting everybody, causing chaos like a tornado … and as soon as I walked in the door, Father Greg would get up out of a meeting, and just walk me back, and calm me down, and redirect me back to the streets and tell me he loves me. (Arocha, 2015, p. 64)

This feeling of being loved unconditionally was foreign to the homies. But, as one member said, "You've got to be ready for it. If you're not ready for it … it's always here" (Arocha, 2015, p. 65). It takes many tries for some former gang members to permanently engage in the rehabilitation work at Homeboy Industries. Many researchers and funders want to see immediate successful outcomes from Homeboy, but those data are not as easy to deliver when dealing with a place like Homeboy. Father Greg believes that this type of outcome-oriented perspective caters to a preference for the most well behaved, and the most likely to succeed. But he has said that if "success is our engine, then we sidestep the difficult and belligerent and eventually abandon the slow work of God" (Boyle, 2010b, p. 179). Father Greg quotes de Chardin's words when he affirms that Homeboy is about the "slow work of God" and drawing the difficult and belligerent into that kinship.

Father Greg has used Mother Teresa's words to explain the meaning of kinship. She said that the world's ills are because "we have forgotten that we belong to each other" (Boyle, 2010b, p. 101). This solidarity, understanding that we are all one and are responsible for one another, is particularly difficult in a gang environment that feeds on conflict and violence. However, at Homeboy, former gang members see the humanity in each other. One former gang member said:

> I don't see the person as an enemy any more…. Now I get the chance to talk to him—face to face—and find out who he really is, and him find out who I really am, and we share that bond as we grow together. And it's not an enemy thing any more. (Arocha, 2015, p. 53)

This drawing together of conflicting parties is the slow work of God. It is not easily measured or charted, but it creates a community of practice in which the primary practice is loving, and taking care of one's self and the other. This *inner attitude* that Massaro (2016) has spoken of must take root and demonstrate a person's commitment to the well-being of others. Former gang members who stop gang banging, who become contributing members of society and successful fathers and husbands, demonstrate this inner attitude in the most powerful way.

Learning About the Dignity of Self and the Dignity of Work

Kinship calls us to understand the dignity of the person, both ourselves and others. Father Greg (Boyle, 2010b) asserted, "We must stand with those whose dignity has been denied. We locate ourselves with the poor and the powerless and the voiceless. At the edges we join the easily despised and the readily left out" (p. 190). This sentiment beautifully aligns with the Catholic Social Teaching that exhorts us to claim a preferential option for the poor and the marginalized; however, dignity must also come from an understanding of one's self. As Father Greg has said:

> The more we can connect to our own mess and brokenness and need for healing, the more we can remind ourselves that we're all a cry for help. When you see that in another person, you won't recoil, but you will reach out because you see yourself there. (Arocha, 2015, p. 69)

One of the mottos of Homeboy, as noted earlier, is "Jobs not Jail." Inherent in this message is that there is something valuable in working, producing, and serving. When gang members walk into the doors at Homeboy Industries, they are asked whether they are on probation or parole. This question might scare anyone, knowing that revealing this detail might mean denial of employment. However, at Homeboy Industries, homies who answered this question with a "yes" were immediately told that they were qualified, and were offered an application (Arocha, 2015). Their past, no matter how dark, is their entrance to a job at Homeboy Industries. Many of their first jobs were janitorial in nature, but nonetheless, the homies spoke about how proud they were to have these jobs. One homie exclaimed, "I told myself I was going to be the best toilet cleaner that Homeboy has ever had!" (Arocha, 2015, p. 88). This remark illuminates Homeboy's belief in the individual, and the belief in the efficacy of work as a healing force that can reshape gang members' identities. Another homie said, "Every day I come to Homeboy and I see people that have worked here before, accomplishments they have seen. And every day I come here it gives me hope that the more I'm doing good, the better it will be (Arocha, 2015, p. 61). And, lastly, one homie spoke tenderly of his experience at Homeboy: "Because of Homeboy and the tools that they have given me ... I have meaning today ... I see myself living as a productive member of society. So hope is Homeboys, and [the belief] that I do have a future now" (Arocha, 2015, p. 61).

Learning About the Spirit: Miracles Everywhere

Father Greg's ministry, as a Catholic Jesuit priest, is informed by a world view influenced by the spirit of St. Ignatius. Thus, as indicated earlier, St.

Ignatius's work, including the Spiritual Exercises and the Daily Examen, are clearly in practice at Homeboy in various ways.

First, daily reflection is an important tool Father Greg uses to prompt the former gang members to think more deeply about their lives, both past and present. Each morning, the homeboys gather for inspiration to talk about God, to ask for guidance, and to celebrate the successes of their members. Many of these reflections are posted on Facebook (Arocha, 2015).

Second, Father Greg's introduction of the concept of "brokenness" leads former gang members to contemplate notions of sin and forgiveness, for themselves and for others. Homies come to understand that, though we are all sinners, forgiveness is always possible (Arocha, 2015). Father Greg joked that an unofficial motto of Homeboy is "You just can't disappoint us enough" (Boyle, 2010b, p. 179). Forgiveness is built into the DNA of Homeboy Industries, and the work is to allow this forgiveness to "soak in" to the lives of all the former gang members, and ourselves, so that they, and we—together—can be part of a peaceful resolution for these young men and women. Father Greg asserts that we cannot judge them from a higher moral plain, or mistakenly believe that some people matter more than others (Boyle, 2010a). Connecting with those who are perceived by society as broken is a tenet of Homeboy—and a human obligation.

Third, the community members of Homeboy Industries see themselves as miracles. In interview after interview, each homie talked about how he or she felt like a "miracle." For former gang members, this revelation is hard won as many of them have difficulties shedding the image of themselves as the "bad son." When they begin with this mindset, to hear them speak of themselves as miracles feels like a miracle in itself. They explained that they could not have imagined having a job, embraced the opportunities they currently had, or felt the freedom they experienced outside of jail without their participation in Homeboy Industries. The belief in miracles, and the ability to see their lives as miracles, is certainly part of a deep reflection and deep embrace of the deity within themselves. One homie spoke candidly when he said, "Coming through these doors … there's always a higher power. Every time I hear someone speak about something positive, there's always a reason behind it … and that reason is God" (Arocha, 2015, p. 62).

Last, St. Ignatius (1914) made clear the importance of having a guide for the examination of one's day or one's life journey. Father Greg leads with the disposition and philosophy of St. Ignatius, who modeled his life after Christ, advocating such practices as unconditional love and forgiveness. In his daily practice at Homeboys, Father Greg creates the culture that embraces this mentoring relationship, not only receiving mentoring from a guide, but also being a guide for others. Father Greg has led by example what it meant to be a Good Samaritan and to relate to and touch the untouchable gang member (Arocha, 2015). And Father Greg admitted that the homies have, at times, counseled him as well (Boyle, 2010a). Further, when enemies work together, as they do at Homeboy, it upsets the status quo on the streets, and gang members ask, "How can you work with that guy?" (Boyle, 2010b, p. 9). This circumstance itself is a valuable mentoring moment, where simply by practicing kinship, gang members outside of Homeboy can experience a different way of being in the world. In the 2016 annual report, Homeboy Industries describes how Homeboy has formalized the mentoring relationship by creating categories of mentors or guides, as former gang members grow in their confidence to be of service to others. For example, a trainee is one who is participating in the 18-month job training program, whereas a navigator is a Homeboy Industry graduate who has turned his life around and is officially able to mentor others.

Learning from others, learning with others, and seeing the worth in that guidance, knowing that we are all children of God, is part of the fabric of Homeboy Industries and the model of Catholic faith that sustains it.

Conclusion

And so, we ask, is Homeboy Industries successful in responding to the call for social justice as a Catholic-led initiative in urban education? Father Greg uses the wisdom of Mother Teresa to answer this question: "We are not called to be successful, but to be faithful" (Boyle, 2010b, p. 167). In this regard, the voices of the homies have affirmed that Homeboy Industries has been faithful to the call for social justice. Those who have benefitted from the situated learning experiences and the care provided by Father Greg and his Homeboy family have had their lives changed and are able to choose life outside of the gang culture. Homeboy's (2016) acceptance of gang members with a "no matter whatness" attitude (Boyle, 2010b, p. 60) models Christ's love for all God's creation, and his unconditional embrace of those created in God's image. Catholic Social Teaching affirms the mission of Homeboy Industries in each of its precepts and calls on each of us to walk with the broken, as Father Greg exhorts. There will be challenges ahead, but as long as we do not forget that we belong to each other, there will be sustenance enough to persevere in this important work.

REFERENCES

Arocha, M. (2015). *Situated learning and Latino male gang members at Homeboy Industries* (Doctoral dissertation). Retrieved from ProQuest Dissertations and Theses database. (3740850)

Boyle, G. (2010a). The challenge of serving a diverse church: Being Christ for others. *Journal of Catholic Education, 13*(3), 380–391. Retrieved from http://digitalcommons.lmu.edu/ce/vol13/iss3/7

Boyle, G. (2010b). *Tattoos on the heart*. New York, NY: Free Press.

Choi, D. Y., & Kiesner, F. (2007). Homeboy Industries: An incubator of hope and businesses. *Entrepreneurship Theory and Practice, 31*, 769–786. doi:10.1111/j.1540-6520.2007.00199.x

Desmond, M. (2012). *A Jesuit priest takes L.A. gang members and provides jobs and hope with Homeboy Industries*. On Being: Krista Tippet Podcast. Retrieved from https://onbeing.org/author/marydesmond/

Flores, E., & Hondagneu-Sotelo, P. (2012). Chicano gang members in recovery: The public talk of negotiating Chicano masculinities. *Social Problems, 60*, 476–490. doi:10.1525/sp.2013.60.4.476

Homeboy Industries. (n.d.). *Educational services*. Retrieved from http://www.homeboyindustries.org/what-we-do/curriculum-education/

Homeboy Industries. (n.d.). *Frequently asked questions*. Retrieved from http://www.homeboyindustries.org/what-we-do/faq

Homeboy Industries. (n.d.). *Homeboy Industries*. Retrieved from http://www.homeboyindustries.org/

Homeboy Industries. (n.d.). *Why we do it*. Retrieved from http://www.homeboyindustries.org/why-we-do-it/

Homeboy Industries. (2016). *Annual report: 2016*. Los Angeles, CA: Author. Retrieved from http://homeboyindustries.org/hb_adm/img/news-events/HB-2016-AnnualReport.pdf

Ignatius of Loyola, St. (1914). *The fourth day: Meditation on two standards*. Retrieved from http://www.sacred-texts.com/chr/seil/seil22.htm

Klein, M. (1995). *The American street gang: Its nature, prevalence and control*. New York, NY: Oxford University Press.

Lave, J., & Wenger, E. (1991). *Situated learning: Legitimate peripheral participation*. Cambridge, MA: Cambridge University Press.

Massaro, T. (2016). *Living justice: Catholic social teaching in action* (3rd ed.). Lanham, MD: Rowan and Littlefield.

Morrow, C. (1999). *Jesuit Greg Boyle, gang priest*. Franciscan Media: St. Anthony Messenger. Retrieved from https://www.franciscanmedia.org/jesuit-greg-boyle-gang-priest/

Rios, V. (2011). *Punished: Policing the lives of black and Latino boys*. New York, NY: New York University Press.

Rodriguez, L. (2005). *Always running, la vida loca: Gang days in L.A.* New York, NY: Simon and Schuster.

Tita, G., Riley, J., Ridgeway, G., Grammich, C., Abrahamse, A., & Greenwood, P. (2003). *Reducing gun violence: Results from an intervention in East Los Angeles*. Santa Monica, CA: RAND Corporation.

Wenger, E. (1998). *Communities of practice: Learning, meaning, and identity*. Cambridge, England: Cambridge University Press.

ABOUT THE AUTHORS

Ursula S. Aldana is an Assistant Professor in the Catholic Educational Leadership Program in the School of Education at the University of San Francisco. Her research examines K–12 school culture with regard to issues of equity and access for racially/ethnically and linguistically diverse students. A former middle and high school teacher, she draws on her teaching experience in urban contexts as well as her personal experience with Catholic education to call on schools to better serve the whole child as a matter of social justice.

Mauricio Alberto Arocha is a History teacher at Hollywood High School, Los Angeles Unified School District and the Aviation Operations Officer at Los Alamitos Joint Forces Training Base, California. His qualitative dissertation research study aimed to provide insight as to the perceived impact of a Gang Intervention Program, Homeboy Industries, on Latino males. His study also provided insight as to the methods, behaviors, strategies, and situated learning perceived to positively affect former gang members at Homeboy Industries.

Jill Bickett is Director of the Doctoral Program in Educational Leadership for Social Justice at Loyola Marymount University. She is a lifelong educational leader, serving as teacher and primary administrator in the Catholic secondary school context. Her research interests include Catholic education, single sex education, gender, service, and leadership.

Ryan Clark serves as Coordinator of Partnerships and Team Development with Notre Dame ACE Academies. He executes ongoing best practices in school leadership coaching, university-school partnership, high-performing urban school models, school turnaround, team development and other areas critical to the successful growth and evolution of the Notre Dame Ace Academy model. Clark served as faculty of supervision and instruction for the ACE Teaching Fellows program from 2006–2010 where he taught courses and supervised teacher formation. He has been teaching and working in K–12 and higher education for over 20 years as a classroom teacher, administrator, and researcher.

Michael Fehrenbach is a De La Salle Christian Brother who has served a variety of functions in service to the Church and the De LaSalle Christian Brothers. He was instrumental in giving birth to the San Miguel Schools in the Midwest District and served on the first Board of Directors for San Miguel Schools, Chicago. In 2002, Michael joined the staff of San Miguel Schools, Chicago as COO. While serving in that capacity he was instrumental in the design and implementation of Catalyst Schools (Chicago Public Schools Charter Schools established in the Lasallian Tradition). He currently serves as Coordinator of Faculty and Staff formation for the Christian Brothers of the Midwest.

L. Mickey Fenzel is Professor and Chair of the Pastoral Counseling Department at Loyola University Maryland and former Associate Dean and Interim Dean of Loyola's School of Education, where he helped to prepare teachers for urban public and parochial schools. His book, *Improving Urban Middle Schools: Lessons from the Nativity Schools,* was awarded a best book prize in 2010 by Alpha Sigma Nu and the Association of Jesuit Colleges and Universities. Dr. Fenzel has published in a number of journals including the Journal of Catholic Education, the *Journal of Education for Students Placed at Risk,* and the *Journal of Early Adolescence,* for which he serves on the editorial board.

Rob Helfenbein is Associate Dean of the School of Education at Loyola University Maryland and has published numerous pieces about contemporary education theory in journals such as *Curriculum Inquiry, the Journal of Curriculum Theorizing, Educational Studies,* and *The Urban Review,* in addition to coediting three books. He is currently serving as Editor of the Journal of Curriculum Theorizing and current research interests include curriculum theorizing in urban contexts, cultural studies of education, and the impact of globalization on the lived experience of schools.

Sajit U. Kabadi is currently the Chair of the Theology Department at Regis Jesuit High School in Colorado and an affiliate faculty member at Metropolitian State University in their Secondary Education Department where he teaches Multicultural Education courses. His research includes exploring issues of diversity, equity, and inclusion in Catholic, Jesuit education, particularly looking at ways to interweave these aspects more intentionally within Catholic, Jesuit social justice pedagogy. He brings over three decades of experience in Catholic, Jesuit education as a student, volunteer, teacher, administrator, diversity officer, and board member.

Peter Litchka is Professor of Education at Loyola University Maryland, where he also serves as the Director of the Graduate Program for Educational Leadership. He has been a professional educator for more than 46 years, including teacher, school leader, and superintendent. He has authored or coauthored numerous books and articles in the field of educational leadership, and has worked with school leaders and educational organizations in the United States as well as Israel, Poland, and Turkey.

Elizabeth Riveros Serrato is the Executive Coordinator of the Quality Improvement Program for Popular Education at the International Federation of Fe y Alegría. She has broad experience in the education field, including participation and development of processes and systems to promote quality education and education evaluation, involvement in the definition of public policies that defend quality education, and dedication to teacher training through ongoing seminars and workshops. Based out of Bogotá, Colombia, Elizabeth accompanies the improvement of quality and innovation in 418 centers in 15 of the countries where Fe y Alegría operates.

Terry Shields, over the last 20 years, has focused on improving equity in our educational system for students from economically-poor families in urban areas. In that time he has studied high-performing public charter and private faith-based schools and supported the school leaders committed to their success. He established and served as the Executive Director of the NativityMiguel Coalition and launched The Network for Building Excellent Schools and coordinated leadership development and strategic growth initiatives for eligible schools.

Ed Siderewicz, a former Christian Brother, is Cofounder and Director of Mission & External Relations for Catalyst Schools, faith-inspired charter schools in the centuries-old Lasallian model of education and pedagogy. Previously, Ed cofounded two San Miguel Schools in Chicago and, in 2010, Ed and the San Miguel team were invited to replicate the San Miguel model in the public system. Today, Catalyst Schools has two elementary schools and one high school that serve over 1,600 students in two of Chicago's most impoverished neighborhoods.

Paul E. Thornton went from St. Benedict's to Harvard, graduating in 1967. He has worked with St. Benedict's Headmaster, Fr. Edwin Leahy, OSB, a 1963 St. Benedict's classmate, since 1973. He is Associate Headmaster and Director of Planned Giving.

Melodie Wyttenbach is the Academic Director of the Mary Ann Remick Leadership Program for the Alliance for Catholic Education at the University of Notre Dame. Wyttenbach's professional leadership experiences in the Catholic sector include serving as president and principal of Nativity Jesuit Academy, a high-performing urban Catholic school serving the Latino community in a school choice environment and at the national level as Director of Mission Effectiveness for the NativityMiguel Network of Schools. Her research interests include: project, team, and organizational management, educational leadership for culturally and linguistically diverse students, and social justice leadership.